Essays in Old Testament Ethics

Essays in Old Testament Ethics

(J. PHILIP HYATT, *In Memoriam*)

Edited by
James L. Crenshaw and John T. Willis

KTAV PUBLISHING HOUSE, INC.
NEW YORK

© COPYRIGHT 1974
KTAV PUBLISHING HOUSE, INC.

Library of Congress Cataloging in Publication Data

Main entry under title:
Essays in Old Testament ethics.
   Chronological list of James Philip Hyatt's works: p.
   Includes bibliographical references.
   CONTENTS: Fohrer, G. The righteous man in Job 31.—Crenshaw, J. L. The eternal gospel (Eccl. 3:11).—May, H. G. Aspects of the imagery of world dominion and world state in the Old Testament. [etc.]
   1. Bible. O.T.—Ethics. 2. Hyatt, James Philip, 1909-1972. 3. Hyatt, James Philip, 1909-1972—Bibliography. I. Crenshaw, James L., ed. II. Willis, John T., 1933— ed. III. Hyatt, James Philip.

MANUFACTURED IN THE UNITED STATES OF AMERICA

TABLE OF CONTENTS

Preface vii

Curriculum Vitae x

Bibliography xi

Transliteration of Hebrew xxxii

Abbreviations xxxii

Georg Fohrer—The Righteous Man in Job 31 1

James L. Crenshaw—The Eternal Gospel (Eccl. 3:11) 23

Herbert G. May—Aspects of the Imagery of World Dominion and World State in the Old Testament 57

Hans Walter Wolff—Problems between the Generations in the Old Testament 77

Dennis J. McCarthy, S. J.—The Wrath of Yahweh and the Structural Unity of the Deuteronomistic History 97

Sheldon H. Blank—The Prophet As Paradigm 111

William F. Stinespring—A Problem of Theological Ethics in Hosea .. 131

John T. Willis—Ethics in a Cultic Setting 145

Brian W. Kovacs—Is There A Class-Ethic in Proverbs? 171

Lou H. Silberman—The Human Deed in a Time of Despair: The Ethics of Apocalyptic 191

Walter Harrelson—The Significance of "Last Words" for Intertestamental Ethics ... 203

Samuel Sandmel—Virtue and Reward in Philo ... 215

Millar Burrows—Old Testament Ethics and the Ethics of Jesus ... 225

J. A. Sanders—The Ethic of Election in Luke's Great Banquet Parable ... 245

PREFACE

On November 6, 1972 Death marched boldly into Phil Hyatt's office and overpowered him while he sat at his desk and labored to understand the enigmas of life as clarified by the Old Testament. This demanding activity, from which he was taken so abruptly by divine summons, had been his chief objective for the greater part of his life. The impact of those many years in which he brought to life once more the Israelite encounter with her God in ancient times has been felt by countless students, both at Wellesley College where he taught for a short time, and at Vanderbilt Divinity School, at which he served with distinction for thirty-two years. During this time he wrote many books and numerous articles, justly earning respect among his colleagues and shaping the views of students of the Old Testament both far and near. The esteem in which he was held led to his election as President of the Society of Biblical Literature, and to a brief tenure as editor of the *Journal of Biblical Literature*.

It is fitting, therefore, that we honor the memory of J. Philip Hyatt in a volume that seeks to understand a long neglected area of Old Testament research. Inasmuch as the central focus of his work has always been related in one way or another to the divine imperative, even when that demand was only dimly grasped by the prophetic spokesman and even less clearly understood by his hearers and readers, the choice of ethics as the theme of this volume is particularly appropriate. Phil's desire to discern the correct response to God's manifest love for humanity found expression in the local church. The Reverend Frank Drowota, long time minister of Woodmont Christian

Church, and close friend of the Hyatts for over twenty-five years, sums up the impact Phil made upon his church as follows:

> In this Athens of the south [he] wanted to see a strong interdenominational seminary that would permeate the Bible Belt with a religion capable of changing the whole of life . . . It naturally follows that here in the local church, where the going was toughest, where ultra-conservatism was the dominant spirit, he chose to cast his lot. Others might retreat from the institutional church but Phil was ever at its center. So he became a source of strength to his minister—and more, he became the voice of a prophet . . . The ancient shepherd of the flock seeking to comfort and heal was in a real sense incarnate in Phil's life . . . Few of us were aware of the physical suffering that was his . . . For those of us who knew, that made his smile the warmer . . . Recently he received honorary degrees from T.C.U. and from his old school, Baylor. He liked to say that the Campbellites and Baptists came closer together in that event . . . In him I sensed a remarkable balance between Ivory Tower and Earthy Garden, between Town and Gown, between an understanding of prophetic religion and the modern ministry in suburban churches. It is entirely fitting that the last 30 hours of his life should have been spent in Church, at home, and at the Divinity School. . . .

It is symbolic of Phil's attempt to apply the findings of scholarly research to the everyday religious situation that the cost of publishing this volume has been underwritten by the Vanderbilt Divinity School and by friends from Woodmont Christian Church. A special word of gratitude is due two of Phil's colleagues, Dean Walter Harrelson, whose enthusiastic support of the project from the very beginning has been a constant source of strength, and Herman Norton, Phil's longtime colleague and friend, as well as the above mentioned donors.

We, the editors, have learned much from Phil Hyatt, with whom we studied for several years. His persistent reminder that the Hebrew text rather than secondary literature was the starting point for all exegesis, his insistence upon an understanding of the ancient Near Eastern setting as the *sine qua non* of biblical interpretation, his utter disdain for all pretense and "assured results" of scholarship, his genuine concern for the welfare of his students, his openness to people from all confessions, his stern demand for excellence, his authentic humanity amid the turmoil that characterizes modern man—these and much more have planted themselves indelibly in our memory.

That memory would, nevertheless, be incomplete without a word about his faithful companion, Betty. For over thirty years she shared his life, and enriched it one hundred fold, confirming for him the truth of the ancient biblical proverb that a good wife is a gift of the Lord. To her we present this token of our esteem for Phil, in the hope that it may be a worthy tribute to a life well lived.

JAMES L. CRENSHAW
JOHN T. WILLIS

J. PHILIP HYATT: CURRICULUM VITAE

HYATT, James Philip, university prof., clergyman; b. Monticello, Ark., Feb. 16, 1909; s. Robert Lee and Mamie (Stanley) H.; d. Nov. 6, 1972; A.B., Baylor Univ., Waco, Tex., 1929; A.M., Brown Univ., 1930; B.D., Yale 1933, Ph.D., 1938; student Am. Sch. of Oriental Research, Jerusalem (Two Brothers fellow of Yale), 1931-32; U. Marburg, Germany (summer), 1932; D.D. (hon.) Christian Theol. Seminary, 1967; m. Elizabeth Bard, Sept. 12, 1932; children—James Lee, (dec.), Charles Sidney, David Philip. Ordained to ministry, Baptist Ch., 1929; pastor Hull Meml. Bapt. Ch., Cheshire, Conn., 1932-35; instr. Biblical Hist., Wellesley Coll., 1935-38; asst. prof., 1938-41; associate professor of Old Testament, Vanderbilt University, Nashville, Tenn., 1941-44, professor, 1944-72, chmn. graduate department of religion, 1944-64, acting dean Divinity Sch., 1956-57; visiting prof. Univ. of Chicago, winter 1944; Garret Biblical Inst., summer 1945, Union Theol. Seminary (New York), summer 1950, Iliff School of Theology, summer 1958, also Perkins School of Theology, Summer, 1961. Ford faculty fellow, Hebrew Union College, 1952. Fellow Society for Religion in Higher Edn.; member of the Old Testament sect., Standard Bible Committee; Mem. Am. Oriental Soc. (vice pres., middle west br., 1943-44); American Academy Religion (v.p. 1941); Soc. Bibl. Lit. (pres. Southern sect., 1949-50, pres. 1956); British Society of Old Testament Study (asso.), Phi Beta Kappa; Democrat; Mem. Disciples of Christ (minister, 1946—). Archaeological editor Journal of Bible and Religion, 1939-48. Editor, Journal Biblical Lit. 1948-49; The Bible in Modern Scholarship 1965. Who's Who in America (1968-1969).

BIBLIOGRAPHY

I. BOOKS

Hyatt, J. Philip, Beatty, R. C. and Spears, M. K., eds. *Vanderbilt Studies in the Humanities* I. Nashville: Vanderbilt University Press, 1951.

———, ed. *The Bible in Modern Scholarship: Papers Read at the 100th Meeting of the Society of Biblical Literature*. Nashville: Abingdon Press, 1965.

———. *The Book of Jeremiah: Introduction and Exegesis* in *The Interpreter's Bible* V. New York: Abingdon Press, 1956.

———. *The Heritage of Biblical Faith: An Aid to Reading the Bible*. St. Louis: Bethany Press, 1964.

———. *Jeremiah: Prophet of Courage and Hope*. Nashville: Abingdon Press, 1958.

———. *The Prophetic Criticism of Israelite Worship* (Goldenson Lecture for 1963). Cincinnati: Hebrew Union College Press, 1963.

———. *Prophetic Religion*. Nashville: Abingdon Press, 1947.

———. *The Treatment of Final Vowels in Early Neo-Babylonian*. New Haven: Yale University Press, 1941.

———. *Exodus* (New Century Bible). London: Oliphants, 1971.

II. ARTICLES

1934

Boecklin, R. and Hyatt, J. P. "A New Inscription of Jerash," *American Journal of Archaeology* XXXVIII (1934), 511-522.

1937

Hyatt, J. Philip. "The Contribution of Archaeology to the Understanding of the Bible," *The Baylor Bulletin* XL (August, 1937), 183-190.

———. "A New-Babylonian Parallel to *Bethel-Sar-eser,* Zech 7_2," *Journal of Biblical Literature* LVI (December, 1937), 387-394.

1938

———. "A Bibliography of Important Books and Articles on Biblical Archaeology," *Journal of Bible and Religion* VI (Summer, 1938), 144-145, 172-174.

1939

———. "Canaanite Ugarit—Modern Ras Shamra," *The Biblical Archaeologist* II (February, 1939), 1-8.

———. "The Deity Bethel and the Old Testament," *Journal of the American Oriental Society* LIX (March, 1939), 81-98.

———. "Biblical Archaeology in The College," *Journal of Bible and Religion* VII (May, 1939), 79-83, 112.

1940

———. "Solomon in All His Glory," *Journal of Bible and Religion* VIII (February, 1940), 27-30.

———. "Freud on Moses and the Genesis of Monotheism," *Journal of Bible and Religion* VIII (May, 1940), 85-88.

———. "The Peril from the North in Jeremiah," *Journal of Biblical Literature* LIX (December, 1940), 499-513.

1941

———. "A Note on Yiwwada in Ps. 74:5," *American Journal of Semitic Languages* LVIII (January, 1941), 99-100.

———. "The Original Text of Jeremiah 11:15-16," *Journal of Biblical Literature* LX (March, 1941), 57-60.

———. "Torah in the Book of Jeremiah," *Journal of Biblical Literature* LX (December, 1941), 381-396.

1942

———. "Jeremiah and Deuteronomy," *Journal of Near Eastern Studies* I (April, 1942), 156-173.

———. "The Ras Shamra Discoveries and the Interpretation of the Old Testament," *Journal of Bible and Religion* X (May, 1942), 67-75.

———. "The Old Testament Idea of God and Its Modern Relevance," *Religion in Life* XI (Summer, 1942), 350-358.

———. "Abraham, the Friend of God," *The Teacher* (August, 1942), 3-4.

1943

———. "Jeremiah and War," *The Crozer Quarterly* XX (January, 1943), 52-58.

———. "The Message of the Seventh-Century Prophets for Today," *Journal of Bible and Religion* XI (May, 1943), 93-97.

———. "The Writing of an Old Testament Book," *The Biblical Archaeologist* VI (December, 1943), 71-80.

1944

———. "The Sources of the Suffering Servant Idea," *Journal of Near Eastern Studies* III (April, 1944), 79-86.
———. " 'Adam' in Palestine," *Journal of Bible and Religion* XII (November, 1944), 232-236.

1945

———. "The Old Testament View of Man," *Religion in Life* XIV (Autumn, 1945), 526-534.
———. "Genesis," *An Encyclopedia of Religion* ed. by Vergilius Ferm (1945), 296.
———. "Exodus," *An Encyclopedia of Religion* ed. by Vergilius Ferm (1945), 267.
———. "Leviticus," *An Encyclopedia of Religion* ed. by Vergilius Ferm (1945), 442.
———. "Numbers," *An Encyclopedia of Religion* ed. by Vergilius Ferm (1945), 537-538.
———. "Deuteronomy," *An Encyclopedia of Religion* ed. by Vergilius Ferm (1945), 225.
———. "Joshua," *An Encyclopedia of Religion* ed. by Vergilius Ferm (1945), 400-401.
———. "Judges," *An Encyclopedia of Religion* ed. by Vergilius Ferm (1945), 407.
———. "Ruth," *An Encyclopedia of Religion* ed. by Vergilius Ferm (1945), 674.
———. "Samuel, I and II," *An Encyclopedia of Religion* ed. by Vergilius Ferm (1945), 686-687.
———. "Kings, I and II," *An Encyclopedia of Religion* ed. by Vergilius Ferm (1945), 419.
———. "Chronicles, I and II," *An Encyclopedia of Religion* ed. by Vergilius Ferm (1945), 167.
———. "Ezra," *An Encyclopedia of Religion* ed. by Vergilius Ferm (1945), 269.
———. "Nehemiah," *An Encyclopedia of Religion* ed. by Vergilius Ferm (1945), 523.
———. "Esther," *An Encyclopedia of Religion* ed. by Vergilius Ferm (1945), 256.

———. "D," *An Encyclopedia of Religion* ed. by Vergilius Ferm (1945), 215.

———. "E," *An Encyclopedia of Religion* ed. by Vergilius Ferm (1945), 239.

———. "J," *An Encyclopedia of Religion* ed. by Vergilius Ferm (1945), 384.

———. "S," *An Encyclopedia of Religion* ed. by Vergilius Ferm (1945), 675.

———. "Cole Lectureship," *An Encyclopedia of Religion* ed. by Vergilius Ferm (1945), 181.

———. "Gesenius, Friedrich Heinrich Wilhelm," *An Encyclopedia of Religion* ed. by Vergilius Ferm (1945), 298.

———. "Gilgamesh Epic," *An Encyclopedia of Religion* ed. by Vergilius Ferm (1945), 299.

———. "Moloch or Molech," *An Encyclopedia of Religion* ed. by Vergilius Ferm (1945), 502.

———. "Pre-Adamite," *An Encyclopedia of Religion* ed. by Vergilius Ferm (1945), 603.

———. "Smith, William Robertson," *An Encyclopedia of Religion* ed. by Vergilius Ferm (1945), 715-716.

———. "Tribal God," *An Encyclopedia of Religion* ed. by Vergilius Ferm (1945), 794.

1948

———. "The Date and Background of Zephaniah," *Journal of Near Eastern Studies* VII (January, 1948), 25-29.

1949

———. "The Book of Amos," *Interpretation* III (July, 1949), 338-348.

1951

———. "The Ministry of Scholarship," *Crozer Quarterly* XXVIII (July, 1951), 212-216.

———, Beatty, R. C. and Spears, M. K., eds. "The Deuteronomic Edition of Jeremiah," *Vanderbilt Studies in the Humanities* I. Nashville: Vanderbilt University Press, 1951, 71-95.

1952

———. "The Revised Standard Version of the Bible," *The Christian-Evangelist* XC (September, 1952), 944-945, 950.

———. "The Revised Standard Version," *Adult Teacher* V (September, 1952), 1-6.

———. "On the Meaning and Origin of Micah 6:8," *Anglican Theological Review* XXXIV (October, 1952), 233-240.

———. "Archaeology and the Translation of the Old Testament," *An Introduction to the Revised Standard Version of the Old Testament* by Members of the Revision Committee. New York: Thomas Nelson & Sons, 1952, 49-56.

1953

———. "Are the Criticisms Justified?" *The Christian-Evangelist* XCI (April, 1953), 398-400.

———. "Answering Criticism of the Revised Standard Version," *The Pastor* XVI (July, 1953), 1-2, 39.

———. "The God of Love in the Old Testament," *To Do & To Teach* ed. by Roscoe M. Pierson. Lexington: The College of the Bible, 1953, 15-26.

1955

———. "Babylonia," *The Twentieth Century Encyclopedia of Religious Knowledge* II (1955), 102-103.

———. "Yahweh as 'The God of My Father,'" *Vetus Testamentum* V (1955), 130-136.

1956

———. "The View of Man in the Qumran 'Hodayot,'" *New Testament Studies* II (May, 1956), 276-284.

———. "The Meaning of the Scrolls," *The Pastor* XIX (June, 1956), 10.

———. "The Translation and Meaning of Amos 5:23-24," *Zeitschrift für die Alttestamentliche Wissenschaft* LXVIII (1956), 17-24.

———. "New Light on Nebuchadrezzer and Judean History," *Journal of Biblical Literature* LXXV (1956), 277-284.

1957

———. "The Dead Sea Discoveries: Retrospect and Challenge," *Journal of Biblical Literature* LXXVI (1957), 1-12.

1958

———. "Art," *Hastings' Dictionary of the Bible* 2nd. ed., revised by F. C. Grant and H. H. Rowley. Edinburgh: T. & T. Clark, 1958-1959, 57.

———. "Arts and Crafts," *Hastings' Dictionary of the Bible* 2nd. ed., revised by F. C. Grant and H. H. Rowley. Edinburgh: T. & T. Clark, 1958-1959, 58-59.

———. "Dress," *Hastings' Dictionary of the Bible* 2nd. ed., revised by F. C. Grant and H. H. Rowley. Edinburgh: T. & T. Clark, 1958-1959, 222-225.

———. "Hezekiah," *Hastings Dictionary of the Bible* 2nd. ed., revised by F. C. Grant and H. H. Rowley. Edinburgh: T. & T. Clark, 1958-1959, 381-382.

———. "Hunting," *Hastings' Dictionary of the Bible* 2nd. ed., revised by F. C. Grant and H. H. Rowley. Edinburgh: T. & T. Clark, 1958-1959, 407.

———. "Magic, Divination, and Sorcery," *Hastings' Dictionary of the Bible* 2nd. ed., revised by F. C. Grant and H. H. Rowley. Edinburgh: T. & T. Clark, 1958-1959, 607-611.

———. "Nahum," *Hastings' Dictionary of the Bible* 2nd. ed., revised by F. C. Grant and H. H. Rowley. Edinburgh: T. & T. Clark, 1958-1959, 685-686.

———. "Ruth," *Hastings' Dictionary of the Bible* 2nd, ed., revised by F. C. Grant and H. H. Rowley. Edinburgh: T. & T. Clark, 1958-1959, 865.

———. "Slave, Slavery," *Hastings' Dictionary of the Bible* 2nd. ed., revised by F. C. Grant and H. H. Rowley. Edinburgh: T. & T. Clark, 1958-1959, 924-926.

———. "Bethel (Deity)," *Interpreter's Dictionary of the Bible* I. New York: Abingdon Press, 1958, 390-391.

———. "Circumcision," *Interpreters' Dictionary of the Bible* I. New York: Abingdon Press, 1958, 629-631.

1959

———. "A Bibliography of Millar Burrows' Works," *Vetus Testamentum* IX (1959), 423-432.

1960

———. "The Dead Sea Discoveries," *The Baylor Line* XXII (January-February, 1960), 4-8.

———. "The Place of the Old Testament in the Christian Faith," *Encounter* XXI (Spring, 1960), 181-193.

———. "The Origin and Meaning of Christian Baptism," *Encounter* XXI (Summer, 1960), 255-268.

———. "Eleazar," *Encyclopedia Americana* X (1960), 60.

———. "Jeremiah," *Encyclopedia Americana* XVI (1960), 18-20.

———. "Jeremiah, Book of," *Encyclopedia Americana* XVI (1960), 20-23.

———. "Textual Criticism of the Old Testament," *Encyclopedia Americana* III (1960), 658-662.

———. "Amalekites," *Encyclopedia Britannica* I (1960), 702-703.

———. "Ammonites," *Encyclopedia Britannica* I (1960), 799.

———. "Caleb," *Encyclopedia Britannica* IV (1960), 610-611.

———. "Deuteronomy," *Encyclopedia Britannica* VII (1960), 321-323.

———. "Hoshea," *Encyclopedia Britannica* XI (1960), 740.

———. "Jeremiah, Book of," *Encyclopedia Britannica* XII (1960), 1000-1002.

1961

———. "Yehezkel Kaufmann's View of the Religion of Israel," *Journal of Bible and Religion* XXIX (January, 1961), 52-57.

———. "The Writing of an Old Testament Book," *The Biblical Archaeologist Reader* ed. by D. N. Freedman and G. E. Wright. New York: Anchor Books, 1961, 22-31.

1962

———. "Amos," *Peake's Commentary on the Bible,* New and Revised Edition ed. by Matthew Black and H. H. Rowley. London: Thomas Nelson & Sons, 1962, 617-625.

———. "Habakkuk," *Peake's Commentary on the Bible,* New and Revised Edition ed. by Matthew Black and H. H. Rowley. London: Thomas Nelson & Sons, 1962, 637-639.

———. "Nahum," *Peake's Commentary on the Bible,* New and Revised Edition ed. by Matthew Black and H. H. Rowley. London: Thomas Nelson & Sons, 1962, 635-636.

———. "Zephaniah," *Peake's Commentary on the Bible,* New and Revised Edition ed. by Matthew Black and H. H. Rowley. London: Thomas Nelson & Sons, 1962, 640-642.

1963

———. "The Place of the Old Testament in the Christian Faith," *The Reconstruction of Theology* ed. by Ralph G. Wilburn. St. Louis: Bethany Press, 1963, 47-64. (refer to identical article in *Encounter*, 1960).

———. "The Origin and Meaning of Christian Baptism," *The Reconstruction of Theology* ed. by Ralph G. Wilburn. St. Louis: Bethany Press, 1963, 267-286. (refer to identical article in *Encounter*, 1960).

1964

———. "The Origin of Mosaic Yahwism," *The Teacher's Yoke* ed. by Vardaman, Garrett, and Adair. Waco: Baylor University Press, 1964, 85-93.

1965

———. "Moses and the Ethical Decalogue," *Encounter* XXVI (1965), 199-206.

1966

———. "The Beginning of Jeremiah's Prophecy," *Zeitschrift für die Alttestamentliche Wissenschaft* LXXVIII (1966), 204-214.

1967

———. "Was Yahweh Originally a Creator Deity?" *Journal of Biblical Literature* LXXXVI (1967), 369-377.

1970

"Were There an Ancient Historical Credo in Israel and an Independent Sinai Tradition?" in Harry Thomas Frank and William L. Reed, eds., *Translating and Understanding the Old Testament: Essays in Honor of Herbert Gordon May* (Nashville: Abingdon Press), pp. 152-70.

III. BOOK REVIEWS IN SCHOLARLY JOURNALS

1938

Hyatt, J. Philip. Review of *Biblical Backgrounds* by J. McKee Adams, *Journal of Bible and Religion* VI (1938), 165.

1939

————. Review of *Ain Shems Excavations. Part IV* by Elihu Grant and G. Ernest Wright, *Journal of Bible and Religion* VII (1939), 217.

————. Review of *Archaeology and the New Testament* by Stephen L. Caiger, *Journal of Bible and Religion* VII (1939), 214-215.

————. Review of *The Excavation of Tell Beit Mirsim. Vol. II: The Bronze Age* by W. F. Albright, *Journal of Bible and Religion* VII (May, 1939), 99-100.

————. Review of *Gerasa, City of the Decapolis* ed. by Carl H. Kraeling, *Journal of Bible and Religion* VII (1939), 97-99.

————. Review of *They Wrote on Clay* by Edward Chiera, *Journal of Bible and Religion* VII (1939), 150-51.

1940

————. Review of *Ain Shems Excavations. Part V* by Elihu Grant and G. Ernest Wright, *Journal of Bible and Religion* VIII (August, 1940), 164-165.

————. Review of *Nuzi* by Richard F. S. Starr, *Journal of Bible and Religion* VIII (August, 1940), 166-167, 176.

————. Review of *The Megiddo Ivories* by Gordon Loud, *Journal of Bible and Religion* VIII (November, 1940), 224-226.

————. Review of *The Other Side of the Jordan* by Nelson Glueck, *Journal of Bible and Religion* VIII (November, 1940), 226-227.

1941

————. Review of *The Bible in Its Ancient and English Versions* ed. by H. Wheeler Robinson, *Journal of Bible and Religion* IX (August, 1941), 187-188.

————. Review of *Diggers for Facts: The Bible in the Light of Archaeology* by J. O. Kinnaman, *Journal of Bible and Religion* IX (August, 1941), 197.

————. Review of *The Prophets and Their Times* by J. M. Powis Smith, *The Review of Religion* VI (November, 1941), 53-56.

1942

————. Review of *What Mean These Stones? The Significance of Archaeology for Biblical Studies* by Millar Burrows, *Journal of Bible and Religion* X (February, 1942), 59-61.

———. Review of *An Indexed Bibliography of the Writings of William Foxwell Albright* by Harry M. Orlinsky, *Journal of Bible and Religion* X (August, 1942), 181-182.

———. Review of *The Living Past* by Cyrus H. Gordon, *Journal of Bible and Religion* X (August, 1942), 172-173.

———. Review of *When Egypt Ruled the East* by George Steindorff and Keith C. Seele, *Journal of Bible and Religion* X (August, 1942), 174.

———. Review of *Archaeology and the Religion of Israel* by William F. Albright, *Journal of Bible and Religion* X (November, 1942), 240-242.

———. Review of *The Bearing of Archaeology on the Old Testament* by George L. Robinson, *Journal of Bible and Religion* X (November, 1942), 239-240.

———. Review of *Biblical Hebrew for Beginners* by Ovid R. Sellers and Edwin Voigt, *Journal of Bible and Religion* X (November, 1942), 250.

———. Review of *The Social Background of the Old Testament* by David Jacobson, *Journal of Biblical Literature* LXI (December, 1942), 289-294.

1943

———. Review of *Berytus,* Vol. VII, Fasc, 1, 2, *Journal of Bible and Religion* XI (November, 1943), 256.

1944

———. Review of *The Ladder of Progress in Palestine: A Story of Archaeological Adventure* by Chester Charlton McCown, *Journal of Bible and Religion* XII (February, 1944), 63-64.

———. Review of *Palestinian Figurines in Relation to Certain Goddesses Known Through Literature* by James F. Pritchard, *Journal of Bible and Religion* XII (February, 1944), 62-63.

———. Review of *The Excavation of Tell Beit Mirsim* by W. F. Albright, *Journal of Bible and Religion* XII (May, 1944), 134-135.

———. Review of *The Loves and Wars of Baal and Anat and Other Poems from Ugarit* trans. and ed. by Cyrus H. Gordon, *Journal of Bible and Religion* XII (August, 1944), 207-208.

———. Review of *The Westminster Dictionary of the Bible* by John D. Davis, *The Pastor* VIII (December, 1944), 39.

1945

———. Review of *Canaanite Parallels in the Book of Psalms* by John Hastings Patton, *Journal of Bible and Religion* XIII (May, 1945), 113-114.

———. Review of *Palestine, Land of Promise* by Walter Clay Lowdermilk, *Journal of Bible and Religion* XIII (May, 1945), 111-112.

———. Review of *The Westminster Historical Atlas to the Bible* ed. by G. Ernest Wright and Floyd V. Filson, *Journal of Bible and Religion* XIII (May, 1945), 106-108.

———. Review of *Sumerian Literary Texts from Nippur in the Museum of the Ancient Orient at Istanbul* by S. N. Kramer, *Journal of Bible and Religion* XIII (August, 1945), 175.

1946

———. Review of *Elementary Hebrew* by E. Leslie Carlson, *Journal of Bible and Religion* XIV (February, 1946), 51.

———. Review of *The River Jordan* by Nelson Glueck, *Journal of Religious Thought* III (Spring-Summer, 1946), 200-201.

———. Review of *Enki and Ninhursag: A Sumerian "Paradise" Myth* by Samuel N. Kramer, *Journal of Bible and Religion* XIV (August, 1946), 172.

———. Review of *Light from the Ancient Past: The Archeological Background of the Hebrew-Christian Religion* by Jack Finegan, *Journal of Bible and Religion* XIV (November, 1946), 248-249.

———. Review of *The Old Testament: Its Form and Purpose* by Lindsay B. Longacre, *Journal of Biblical Literature* LXV (December, 1946), 411-412.

———. Review of *The Wisdom of Ecclesiastes* by Robert Gordis, *Journal of Biblical Literature* LXV (December, 1946), 415-418.

1947

———. Review of *The Distinctive Ideas of the Old Testament* by Norman H. Snaith, *Journal of Bible and Religion* XV (April, 1947), 112-113.

———. Review of *Zephanja: Textkritisch und Literarisch Untersucht* by Gillis Gerleman, *Journal of Biblical Literature* LXVI (June, 1947), 240-243.

1948

———. Review of *The Holy Spirit in the Life of Today* by F. W. Dillistone, *Interpretation* II (January, 1948), 104-106.

———. Review of *The Intellectual Adventure of Ancient Man* by H. and H. A. Frankfort, et. al., *Journal of Bible and Religion* XVI (April, 1948), 117-118.

———. Review of *A Classified Bibliography of the Writings of George Aaron Barton* prepared by Beatrice Allard Brooks, *Journal of Biblical Literature* LXVII (June, 1948), 189.

———. Review of *The Study of the Bible Today and Tomorrow* ed. by Harold R. Willoughby, *Journal of Biblical Literature* LXVII (June, 1948), 177-180.

———. Review of *Their Faith and Ours. Part I: The Old Testament* by Muriel Streibert Curtis, *Journal of Biblical Literature* LXVII (June, 1948), 188.

———. Review of *Foundations in the Dust: A Story of Mesopotamian Exploration* by Seton Lloyd, *Journal of Biblical Literature* LXVII (December, 1948), 411.

———. Review of *The Journal of Jewish Studies,* Vol. I, Nos. 1-2, *Journal of Biblical Literature* LXVII (December, 1948), 411-412.

———. Review of *The Society for Old Testament Study: Book List 1948* ed. by H. H. Rowley, *Journal of Biblical Literature* LXVII (December, 1948), 412.

———. Review of *The Witness of the Prophets* by Gordon Pratt Baker, *Journal of Biblical Literature* LXVII (December, 1948), 411.

1949

———. Review of *A Bibliography of Bible Study for Theological Students, Journal of Biblical Literature* LXVIII (March, 1949), 81.

———. Review of *The Westminster Study Edition of the Holy Bible, Journal of Biblical Literature* LXVIII (March, 1949), 80-81.

———. Review of *The Book of the Twelve Prophets. Vol. I* by Julius A. Bewer, *Journal of Biblical Literature* LXVIII (June, 1949), 193.

———. Review of *Old Testament Commentary* ed. by Herbert C. Alleman and Elmer E. Flack, *Journal of Biblical Literature* LXVIII (June, 1949), 179-180.

———. Review of *Studia Theologica,* Vol. I, Fasc. I-II, *Journal of Biblical Literature* LXVIII (June, 1949), 193.

———. Review of *The Goodly Fellowship of the Prophets* by John Paterson, *The Review of Religion* XIV (November, 1949), 96-97.

1950

———. Review of *The Psalms Translated and Interpreted in the Light of Hebrew Life and Worship* by Elmer A. Leslie, *Journal of Biblical Literature* LXIX (June, 1950), 184-186.

———. Review of *Jesus* by Martin Dibelius, *Journal of Biblical Literature* LXIX (September, 1950), 299.

1951

———. Review of *The Praises of Israel* by John Paterson, *Crozer Quarterly* XXVIII (October, 1951), 352-353.

———. Review of *The Old Testament Against Its Environment* by G. Ernest Wright, *The Pastor* XV (December, 1951), 38.

1952

———. Review of *Moses* by Sholem Asch, *The Pastor* XV (January, 1952), 46.

———. Review of *The Ancestry of Our English Bible* by Ira Maurice Price, *Journal of Biblical Literature* LXXI (March, 1952), 65.

———. Review of *The Psalms and Their Meaning for Today* by Samuel Terrien, *The Pastor* XV (May, 1952), 37-38.

———. Review of *The Babylonian Genesis: The Story of the Creation* by Alexander Heidel, *Journal of Biblical Literature* LXXI (June, 1952), 130.

———. Review of *A Foreword to the Old Testament* by H. St. J. Hart, *The Pastor* XVI (September, 1952), 46.

———. Review of *The Interpreter's Bible, Vol. I, The Pastor* XVI (December, 1952), 34-35.

1953

———. Review of *The Dead Sea Scrolls: A Preliminary Survey* by A. Dupont-Sommer, *The Pastor* XVI (January, 1953), 39.

———. Review of *The Zadokite Fragments and the Dead Sea Scrolls* by H. H. Rowley, *The Pastor* XVII (December, 1953), 39-40.

1954

———. Review of *Everyday Life in Babylon and Assyria* by Georges Contenau, *The Pastor* XVIII (October, 1954), 45.

1955

———. Review of *The Old Testament: Keystone of Human Culture* by William A. Irwin, *Adult Bible Course* I (January-March, 1955), Cover III.

———. Review of *The Ancient Near East in Pictures Relating to the Old Testament* by James B. Pritchard, *Journal of American Oriental Society* LXXV (April-June, 1955), 126-127.

———. Review of *The Psalms Translated and Interpreted in the Light of Hebrew Life and Worship* by Elmer A. Leslie, *Adult Bible Course* I (April-June, 1955), Cover III.

1956

———. Review of *The Scrolls from the Dead Sea* by Edmund Wilson, *The Jewish Sect of Qumran and the Essenes* by A. Dupont-Sommer, *Discoveries in the Judaean Desert: Qumran Cave I* by Barthélemy and Milik, *The Pastor* XIX (February, 1956), 36-38.

———. Review of *Jeremiah—Chronologically Arranged, Translated, and Interpreted* by Elmer A. Leslie, *Journal of Biblical Literature* LXXV (March, 1956), 82-83.

———. Review of *The Dead Sea Scrolls* by Millar Burrows, *Encounter* XVII (Summer, 1956), 292-294.

———. Review of *From Faith to Faith: Essays on Old Testament Literature* by B. Davie Napier, *Religion in Life* XXV (Summer, 1956), 465-466.

———. Review of *The Dead Sea Scrolls and the Originality of Christ* by Geoffrey Graystone, *The Pastor* XIX (August, 1956), 28-29.

1957

———. Review of *The Bible as History* by Werner Keller, *The New Christian Advocate* I (March, 1957), 72-73.

———. Review of. *The Prophets: Pioneers to Christianity* by Walter G. Williams, *Journal of Biblical Literature* LXXVI (1957), 161-162.

———. Review of *The Scrolls from the Dead Sea* by Edmund Wilson, *The Dead Sea Scrolls and the Originality of Christ* by Geoffrey Graystone, *The Meaning of the Dead Sea Scrolls* by A. Powell Davies, *The Dead Sea Scriptures* by Theodor Gaster, *Encounter* XVIII (Winter, 1957), 81-82.

1958

———. Review of *The Book of the Acts of God: Christian Scholarship Interprets the Bible* by G. Ernest Wright and Reginald H. Fuller, *Religion in Life* XXVIII (Winter, 1958-1959), 150-152.

———. Review of *Prophetic Faith in Isaiah* by Sheldon H. Blank, *Studies in Bibliography and Booklore* (December, 1958), 140-141.

1959

———. Review of *More Light on the Dead Sea Scrolls* by Millar Burrows, *New Christian Advocate* III (February, 1959), 86.

———. Review of *Les Manuscrits de la Mer Morte, Journal of Biblical Literature* LXXVIII (March, 1959), 80-83.

———. Review of *Sermons on Genesis* by Harold A. Bosley, *The Christian Evangelist-Front Rank* (March, 1959), 28.

———. Review of *The Root Subh in the Old Testament* by W. L. Holladay, *Vetus Testamentum* IX (April, 1959), 218-221.

———. Review of *The Book of Nahum: A Commentary* by Walter A. Maier, *The Christian Century* LXXVI (July, 1959), 852.

———. Review of *The Psalms as Christian Praise* by R. B. Y. Scott, *The Christian Evangelist-Front Rank* XCVII (August, 1959), 30.

1960

———. Review of *The Dead Sea Community: Its Origin and Teachings* by K. Schubert, *The Christian* XCVIII (September, 1960), 28.

———. Review of *Old Testament Theology* by Ludwig Kohler and *A Companion to the Bible,* by J. -J. Von Allmen, *Encounter* XXI (Winter, 1960), 121-123.

1961

———. Review of *God and History in the Old Testament* by Harvey H. Guthrie, Jr., *The Christian Century* LXXVIII (January, 1961), 16-17.

———. Review of *Bible in Bold Translation, Southern Observer* VIII (May, 1961), 67-68.

1962

———. Review of *The Scrolls and Christian Origins* by Matthew Black, *Christian Advocate* VI (January, 1962), 17-18.

———. Review of *Religion in the Old Testament* by Robert H. Pfeiffer, *The Christian Century* LXXIX (February, 1962), 202-203.

———. Review of *The New Testament Octapla* ed. by Luther A. Weigle, *Southern Observer* IX (June, 1962), 83-84.

———. Review of *The Way of Israel* by James Muilenburg, *Pulpit Digest* XLII (July-August, 1962), 50-52.

———. Review of *The New Testament Octapla* ed. by Luther A. Weigle, *The Christian* C (September, 1962), 28.

———. Review of *Israel's Prophetic Heritage: Essays in Honor of James Muilenburg* ed. by B. W. Anderson and W. Harrelson, *Union Seminary Quarterly Review* XVIII (November, 1962), 53-55.

———. Review of *The Latter Prophets* by T. Henshaw, *Journal of Semitic Studies* (1962), 163-166.

1963

———. Review of *Old Testament Theology, Vol. I* by Gerhard von Rad, *Christian Advocate* VII (January, 1963), 20.

———. Review of *The New Bible Dictionary* ed. by J. D. Douglas, *Religion in Life* XXXII (Autumn, 1963), 645-646.

1964

———. Review of *The Faith of Qumran: Theology of the Dead Sea Scrolls* by Helmer Ringgren, *The Christian* CII (August, 1964), 28.

———. Review of *I & II Kings: A Commentary* by John Gray, *Religion in Life* XXXIV (Winter, 1964-1965), 134-135.

1965

———. Review of *The Legends of Genesis: The Biblical Saga and History* by Hermann Gunkel, *The Christian* CIII (August, 1965), 28.

———. Review of *I & II Samuel: A Commentary* by Hans Wilhelm Hertzberg, *The Christian* CIII (October, 1965), 28.

———. Review of *Jeremiah: Introduction, Translation, and Notes* by John Bright, *Religion in Life* XXXV (Winter, 1965-1966), 147-148.

1966

———. Review of *The Theology of the Samaritans* by John Macdonald, *The Christian* CIV (April, 1966), 28.

———. Review of *Irony in the Old Testament* by Edwin M. Good, *Religion in Life* XXV (Spring, 1966), 307-308.

———. Review of *Job: Introduction, Translation, and Notes* by Marvin H. Pope, *Religion in Life* XXV (Autumn, 1966), 652-654.

1967

———. Review of *The Rule of Qumran and Its Meaning: Introduction, Translation, and Commentary* by A. R. C. Leaney, *The Christian* CV (January, 1967), 28.

———. Review of *The Meaning of the Old Testament: An Essay in Hermeneutics* by Daniel Lys, *The Christian* CV (July, 1967), 28.

———. Review of *Proverbs, Ecclesiastes* by R. B. Y. Scott, *Religion in Life* XXXVI (Summer, 1967), 292-294.

1968

———. Review of *Hebrew Syntax: An Outline* by Ronald J. Williams, *Journal of the American Academy of Religion* XXXVI (June, 1968), 180-181.

———. Review of *"Hesed" in the Bible* by Nelson Glueck, *Journal of the American Academy of Religion* XXXVI (June, 1968), 136.

1970

———. Review of *The New English Bible in Virginia Quarterly Review,* XLVI (Summer, 1970), 514-20.

———. Review of Robert H. Bryant, *The Bible's Authority Today* in *Journal of the American Academy of Religion,* XXXVIII (Sept. 1970), 334-36.

———. Review of Robert North, *Archeo-Biblical Egypt,* in *ibid.,* XXXVIII (March, 1970), 92-3.

———. Review of Rolf Rendtorff, *God's History: A Way Through the Old Testament,* in *Encounter,* XXXI (Summer, 1970), 289-90.

IV. DEVOTIONAL WORKS

1939

Hyatt, J. Philip. "A Baylor Exile in New England," *The Baylor Century* I (May, 1939), 5, 13.

1942

———. "The Hebrew Shepherd Boy Who Became Prime Minister of Egypt," *The Teacher* (September, 1942), 4-6.

1943

———. "Freedom from Fear," *The Baptist Training Union Magazine* (July, 1943), 11-12.

———. "God's Decrees for Moral Living," *The Teacher* (October, 1943), 4-5.

1944

———. "Support Bill S. 1161," *Baptist and Reflector* CX (December, 1944), 4.

1946

———. "A Prophet Speaks to Our Day," *The Pastor* IX (June, 1946), 13-15.
———. "The God Who Is Above All," *The Pastor* IX (July, 1946), 2-3.
———. "God In History," *The Pastor* X (September, 1946), 14-15.
———. "The Meaning of Suffering," *The Pastor* X (October, 1946), 19-20.

1947

———. "Scientist with a Shovel," *Girls Today* VI (May, 1947), 3, 7.
———. "Gaining Wisdom from Ancient Writings," *The Bethany Bible Teacher* XXXIII (July-September, 1947), 1-3.

1948

———. "How to Interpret the Prophets," *The Bethany Church School Guide* XXII (September, 1948), 559-560.
———. "Religion in the Old Testament," *Highroad* VII (April), 2-10; (May), 2-11; and (June), 2-8.
———. "Religion in the Old Testament," *Workers With Youth* I (April), 28-40; (May), 26-39; and (June), 28-38.

1949

———. "The Rise and Fall of a Nation," *Adult Student* VIII (January), 45-64; (February), 49-64; and (March), 49-64.

1950

———. "Studies in Psalms," *Christian Action* V (April-June, 1950), 21-48.

1951

———. "The Birth of a Nation," *The Bethany Guide* XXVI (October, 1951), 32-34.
———. "Discovery of the Oldest Biblical Manuscript," *Classmate* LVIII (October, 1951), 13-14.
———. "Old Testament Teaching About God's Discipline," *Adult Teacher* IV (November, 1951), 4-6.

1952

———. "The Bible in a Living Language," *Workers With Youth* V (September, 1952), 2-4.

———. "The Bible is for You," *Motive* XIII (October, 1952), 6-8.

———. "The Religion of the Old Testament," *Studies in Christian Living* I (Autumn, 1952), 28-64.

———. "Resources for Use With Studies in Christian Living," (with Alma and Harold Sheridan), *Workers With Youth* V (November, 1952), 38-50; (December, 1952), 40-50.

———. "Reading the Bible Today," *The Upper Room Pulpit* X (December, 1952), 3-7.

1954

———. "The Story of the English Bible: The Leader in Action," *Adult Teacher* VII (August), 39-46; (September), 34-47.

———. "Road Map for the Book of Job," *Adult Student* XIII (October, 1954), 6-8.

1955

———. "Growing Up to Salvation," *The Upper Room Pulpit* XII (January, 1955), 11-17.

———. "Prophets of the Southern Kingdom," *The Bethany Guide* XXIX (April, 1955), 30-31, 33.

———. "The Contribution of the Hebrew Prophets," *Workers With Youth* VIII (June, 1955), 2-5.

———. "Explaining the Text," *Adult Student* VII (July, 1955), 16, 20-1, 25-6, 30-1; IX (September, 1955), 26, 30-1, 35-6, 40-1; VIII (August), 25-6, 30-1, 35-6.

———. "The Impatience of Job," *The Pastor* XIX (September, 1955), 8-10.

———. "Why Do the Innocent Suffer?" *The Pastor* XIX (October, 1955), 9-10.

———. "Values in Reading Job," *The Pastor* XIX (November, 1955), 6-7.

1957

———. "Light from the Dead Sea," *Workers With Youth* X (June, 1957), 16-18.

———. "What Are the Dead Sea Scrolls," *Workers With Youth* X (June, 1957), 6-9.

1958

———. *Meeting God Through Isaiah.* Nashville: The Upper Room, 1958.

1959

———. "A New Look at the Dead Sea Scrolls," *Adult Student* XVIII (April, 1959), 2-5.

———. "A Look at 12 Books," *The Bethany Guide* XXXIII (July, 1959), 28-29.

———. "Archaeology and the Bible," *Christian Action* XIV (September, 1959), 55-63.

1960

———. "Exploring the Bible Text," *The International Lesson Annual* ed. by Charles M. Laymon. New York: Abingdon Press, 1960, 250-2; 257-8; 265-6; 272-3; 279-80; 287-8; 296-7; 306-7; 313-5; 321-3; 330-2.

———. "Exploring the Bible Text," *The International Lesson Annual* ed. by Charles M. Laymon. New York: Abingdon Press, 1960, 235-237, 243-245.

1961

———. "Jeremiah's Message for Today," *Christian Action* XVI (September), 20-38; (August), 21-39.

1962

———. "Crumbling Walls," *Adult Teacher* XV (February, 1962), 12-14.

———. "From Hebrew to English," *Twelve Fifteen* XI (May, 1962), 5, 11.

———. "The Face of Temptation," *Sermons from the Upper Room Chapel* compiled by James H. Overton, Jr. Nashville: The Upper Room, 1962, 68-74.

1966

———. "Exploring the Bible Text," *The International Lesson Annual* ed. by Horace R. Weaver. New York: Abingdon Press, 1965, 338-40; 345-7; 353-4; 362-4; 371-3; 378-79; 386-7; 393-5; 401-3; 409-10; 417-9.

1967

———. "Are the Prophets Relevant Today?" *The Bethany Guide* XLII (October, 1967), 7-10.

1970

"Growing Up to Salvation," in Charles L. Wallis, ed., *The Minister's Manual (Doren's) 1971 Edition* (New York, Evanston, and London: Harper & Row, 1970), pp. 275-77.

TRANSLITERATION OF HEBREW

א	—'	שׂ	—s
ב	—b, bh	שׁ	—sh
ג	—g, gh	ת	—t, th
ד	—d, dh	־	—a
ה	—h	־ֲ	—ᵃ
ו	—v	ָ	—ā
ז	—z	ְ	—ᵉ
ח	—ḥ	ֱ or ֱ	—ᵉ
ט	—ṭ	ֳ	—ᵃᵉ
י	—y	ֵ	—ē
כ	—k, kh	ֵ	—ê
ל	—l	ִ	—i
מ	—m	ִי	—î
נ	—n	ָ	—ᵒ
ס	—s	ֹ	—ō
ע	—'	וֹ	—ô
פ	—p, ph	ֻ	—u
צ	—ts	וּ	—û
ק	—q		
ר	—r		

ABBREVIATIONS FOR BIBLICAL BOOKS (1)

Gen.—Genesis
Ex.—Exodus
Lev.—Levitcus
Nu.—Numbers
Dt.—Deuteronomy
Josh.—Joshua
Jgs.—Judges
Ruth—Ruth
1 Sam.—1 Samuel
2 Sam.—2 Samuel
1 Kgs.—1 Kings
2 Kgs.—2 Kings
1 Ch.—1 Chronicles
2 Ch.—2 Chronicles
Ezr.—Ezra
Neh.—Nehemiah
Est.—Esther
Job—Job
Ps(s).—Psalm(s)
Prov.—Proverbs
Eccl.—Ecclesiastes
Cant.—Song of Solomon
      (Canticles)
Isa.—Isaiah
Jer.—Jeremiah
Lam.—Lamentations

ABBREVIATIONS FOR BIBLICAL BOOKS (2)

Ezk.—Ezekiel
Dan.—Daniel
Hos.—Hosea
Joel—Joel
Am.—Amos
Ob.—Obadiah
Jonah—Jonah
Mic.—Micah
Nah.—Nahum
Hab.—Habakkuk
Zeph.—Zephaniah
Hag.—Haggai
Zec.—Zechariah
Mal.—Malachi
Mt.—Matthew
Mk.—Mark
Lk.—Luke
Jn.—John
Acts—Acts
Rom.—Romans
1 Cor.—1 Corinthians
2 Cor.—2 Corinthians
Gal.—Galatians
Eph.—Ephesians

ABBREVIATIONS FOR BIBLICAL BOOKS (3)

Phil.—Philippians
Col.—Colossians
1 Thess.—1 Thessalonians
2 Thess.—2 Thessalonians
1 Tim.—1 Timothy
2 Tim.—2 Timothy
Tit.—Titus
Philem.—Philemon
He.—Hebrews
Jas.—James
1 Pet.—1 Peter
2 Pet.—2 Peter
1 Jn.—1 John
2 Jn.—2 John
3 Jn.—3 John
Rev.—Revelation

GENERAL ABBREVIATIONS

Babyl.—Babylonian
ca.—circa = about, approximately
cf.—compare
ch.—chapter; chs.—chapters
col.—column; cols.—columns
ed(s).—editor(s), edited
e.g.—for example
f.—following verse or page; ff.—following verses or pages
l.—line; ll.—lines
LXX—Septuagint
MT—Massoretic Text
n.—note; nn.—notes
p.—page; pp.—pages
par.—parallels
tr.—translated
v.—verse; vv.—verses

INTERTESTAMENTAL MATERIAL

Bar.—Baruch
2 Esd.—2 Esdras
Ps. Sol.—Psalms of Solomon
Sir.—Ben Sira
Tob.—Tobit
Wisd.—Wisdom of Solomon

QUMRAN MATERIAL

1Q—Qumran Cave I
1QH—The Hodayot or Thanksgiving Psalms
1QM—The War Scroll
1QSa—Rule of the Congregation
4QD^b—The second (b) copy of the Damascus Document from Qumran Cave Four
4QFlor—Florilegium (or Eschatological Midrashim) of Qumran Cave Four
4QM^a—The first (a) copy of the War (Between) the Sons of Light and Sons of Darkness Scroll from Qumran Cave Four
11QMelch—Melchizedek text from Qumran Cave Eleven
11QPs^a—The large Psalms Scroll from Qumran Cave Eleven
CD—The Damascus Document from the Cairo Genizah

ABBREVIATIONS OF BOOKS AND JOURNALS

AB—Anchor Bible
AndNQ—Andover Newton Quarterly
ANET—Ancient Near Eastern Texts
AOT—Altorientalische Texte zum Alten Testament
ATD—Das Alte Testament Deutsch
ATR—Anglican Theological Review
Aug—Augustinianum
AzTh—Arbeiten zur Theologie
BAT—Die Botschaft des Alten Testaments
BBB—Bonner Biblische Beiträge
BeO—Bibbia e Oriente
Bibl—Biblica
BJRL—Bulletin of the Johns Rylands Library

BK—Biblischer Kommentar Altes Testament
BSAW—Berichte der Sächsischen Akademie der Wissenschaften zu Leipzig
BSTR—Breslauer Studien zur Theologie und Religionsgeschichte
BWANT—Beiträge zur Wissenschaft vom Alten und Neuen Testament
BZAW—Beihefte zur Zeitschrift für die alttestamentliche Wissenschaft
CBQ—Catholic Biblical Quarterly
CentB—Century Bible
DBS—Dictionnaire de la Bible, Supplément
DJD—Discoveries in the Judaean Desert
ETL—Ephemerides Theologicae Lovanienses
EvTh—Evangelische Theologie
FRLANT—Forschungen zur Religion und Literatur des Alten und Neuen Testaments
GHKAT—Göttinger Hand-Kommentar zum Alten Testament
HAT—Handbuch zum Alten Testament
HUCA—Hebrew Union College Annual
IB—The Interpreter's Bible
ICC—The International Critical Commentary
IDB—The Interpreter's Dictionary of the Bible
In—Interpretation
JB—Jerusalem Bible
JBL—Journal of Biblical Literature
JBR—Journal of Bible and Religion
JEA—Journal of Egyptian Archeology
JNES—Journal of Near Eastern Studies
JSJ—Journal for the Study of Judaism
JThC—Journal for Theology and the Church
JTS—Journal of Theological Studies
KAT—Kommentar zum Alten Testament
KHAT—Kurzer Hand-Kommentar zum Alten Testament
KlSchr—Kleine Schriften
LBS—The Library of Biblical Studies
NT—Novum Testamentum
NorTT—Norsk Teologisk Tidsskrift
OTL—The Old Testament Library
OTS—Oudtestamentische Studiën
POS—Pretoria Oriental Studies
RB—Revue Biblique
RHPR—Revue d'Histoire et de Philosophie Religieuses
RevQ—Revue de Qumran
SBL—The Society of Biblical Literature

SBT—Studies in Biblical Theology
SPOA—Les Sagesses du Proché-Orient Ancien
SVT—Supplements to Vetus Testamentum
TBC—Torch Bible Commentary
TDNT—Theological Dictionary of the New Testament
TGUOS—Transactions of the Glasgow University Oriental Society
ThB—Theologische Bücherei
ThHAT—Theologisches Handwörterbuch zum Alten Testament
ThR—Theologische Rundschau
ThSt—Theologische Studien
ThZ—Theologische Zeitschrift
UF—Ugarit-Forschungen
USQR—Union Seminary Quarterly Review
VT—Vetus Testamentum
WMANT—Wissenschaftliche Monographien zum Alten und Neuen Testament
WuD—Wort und Dienst
WZ—Wissenschaftliche Zeitschrift
ZAW—Zeitschrift für die alttestamentliche Wissenschaft
ZNW—Zeitschrift für die neutestamentliche Wissenschaft
ZKTh—Zeitschrift für katholische Theologie
ZThK—Zeitschrift für Theologie und Kirche

THE RIGHTEOUS MAN IN JOB 31

GEORG FOHRER

Professor of Old
Testament at Erlangen
and editor of *Zeitschrift
für die alttestamentliche
Wissenschaft*

I

The question concerning the presuppositions, bases, and consequences of ethics which is raised in Job's oath of purity in Job 31 cannot be determined by studying this chapter in isolation or answered from this chapter alone. Rather, it is necessary to keep the whole of the original poem of Job in view. Job 31 is a part of the structure of this poem, and the oath of purity has a specific function within its over-all purpose. This is clear not only from an analysis of the poem of Job, but also from the text of Job 31 and 29-30, which together form a larger unity.

1. The original text of Job 31 ended with Job's challenge to God (vv. 35-37)[1]:

"Oh, that I had one to hear me!
    Here is my signature! Let the Almighty answer me!
. . . .[2]
    The indictment written by my adversary!
Surely I would carry it on my shoulder;
    I would bind it on me as a crown;
I would give him an account of all my steps;
    like a prince I would approach him."

This challenge begins with a twofold wish. To be sure, the verbs used here, viz., "to hear" and "to answer," occur in prayers (Pss. 4:2 [Eng. 1]; 86:1; 102:3 [2]; 119:145,149; 143:1), but in this passage they are not derived from prayer terminology, but from legal terminology. Job's wishes are confirmed by his reference to the inscription under the proof of innocence, the "signature." Thus, the accused wants to disprove the accusation. That this accusation was written corresponds to Egyptian legal custom, where all legal proceedings were introduced by a written accusation.[3] Job expresses his certainty about the proof of his innocence by describing what he had done when the indictment was actually made: he would carry the written accusation which was levelled against him on his shoulder and bind it on his head, so that he could counteract its imprecatory power. In a kind of ordeal he could demonstrate in this way that this imprecatory power cannot find anything against him and consequently that he is innocent. This constitutes the test of his oath of purity. As a further proof of his innocence, Job wanted to spread out his life before God with his head exalted like a prince.

In addition to all this, Job also longs for an immediate discussion with God, for the restoration of his former prosperity, and for the certainty that he will be victorious and the feeling that he will triumph over the divine accusation which he believes to be responsible for his suffering. For him at this stage, the right behavior in his suffering is to receive the accusation without fear and anxiety, but in stubbornness and pride—in the secure knowledge of his own righteousness and purity, which makes each accusation appear so absurd that it emphasizes his innocence.

This raises two questions: Will God accept Job's challenge, prepare himself for the encounter with him, and engage in such a discussion? And will he sanction, acknowledge, and accept as right Job's behavior in his suffering? In the original poem of Job, God's speech in reply to these questions came immediately after Job's challenge. It is provoked by Job 29-31, especially 31:35-37, and therefore must be kept in view along with Job's answer following it in interpreting Job 31.

However, Job's oath of purity consists not only in his challenge to God, but also is closely connected with the wish in Job 29:2, which introduces Job 29-31:

> "Oh, that I were as in the months of old,
>   as in the days when God watched over me!"

Not only can Job demand an encounter with God, confident that he will be victorious because he knows that he is blameless and righteous, but for the same reasons he can and must also desire the restoration of his former happiness and prosperity, which he thinks God has taken away from him. Thus, the desire for restoration (29:2) and the challenge to God (31:35-37) are the framework for Job 29-31. Moreover, 29:2 points back to Job's earlier life and loss of prosperity and happiness as described in the Prologue, as well as to Job's discussions with his friends, which are given in detail and which increase in severity through three series of speeches.

If the introductory wish and the concluding challenge to God unite the speeches of Job in Job 29-31 into a large unit, and if these speeches in turn are connected with the entire poem of Job, then Job's speeches in chaps. 29-31 represent a certain stage in the discussion: the desire for a life full of the former prosperity and happiness will be fulfilled by the encounter with the God whom Job challenged. Also, the behavior of the suffering Job is characterized by the fact that he wants to regain his former prosperity and happiness, and that he is certain that he will succeed as soon as he has demonstrated his blamelessness and righteousness to God.

Thus the context of Job 31 is clear. Building on his earlier complaints, Job describes the change that had taken place in his life from prosperity and happiness to misfortune, and in doing so he yearns for his former prosperity and happiness (Job 29) and complains about his present misfortune (Job 30). He utters his oath as a proof of his innocence (Job 31:1-34, 38-40a), the oath for which he had set the stage three times earlier in his speeches against his friends (cf. the indirect evidence in Job 21:6-34; the assertion of innocence in 23:10-12; and the vow in 27:2-6), and resumes once again the earlier desires and attempts to persuade God to intervene on his behalf or to induce him into an encounter with him (Job 31:35-37); cf. his demand that God meet him in a lawsuit in 13:13ff.; his appeal to God as the avenger of blood and injustice in 16:18ff.; and his challenge to God as a defence witness and attorney in 19:25ff.). Then also, Job's oath of purity with its challenge to God actually evokes God's appearance and speech (Job 38ff.).

2. In view of this, it is difficult to understand why Job 29-31 are usually considered to be "Job's Concluding Speech," and are said to compose the final stage in the discussion between Job and his friends. These speeches do not point backward, but intend to bring about something new after demonstrating that the theology of Job's friends is false. The last speeches between Job and his friends revert back to the

first, and the discussion goes around in a circle. Therefore, further reflections of this type cannot be expected to solve Job's problem. God alone can solve Job's problem, as Job so often had wished. The speeches in Job 29-31 move toward the realization of this wish, which finally becomes reality in the speech of God, although in a way different from that which Job expected. Thus, Job 29-31 serve to prepare the way for God's appearance and, on the basis of Job 31:35-37, can best be characterized as "Job's Speech of Challenge to God."

A form-critical analysis leads to the same result. The structure of Job's speeches in chs. 29-31 is similar to that of the lament, in which the worshipper often relates the "narrative" of his distress and the sworn assertion of his innocence.[4] The narrative is based on the motif of "Then and Now," which comes from the funeral song.[5] The purpose of the proof of innocence is either to secure a favorable hearing or a promise of salvation through a cult prophetic oracle, or to perform the ritual of a divine judgment in the legal process. Of course, the Joban poet has not simply subordinated himself to this scheme, because obviously the cultus was not very important to him and he did not intend to carry out a lament ritual in his poem, and because he did not have Job aspire to a real legal procedure, but to a personal encounter with God and to his intervention. Job does not expect an oracle of Yahweh to come to or upon him as he waits passively, but in Job 31:35-37 he addresses a legal challenge to God. Of course, he is not requesting a real divine judgment in a legal process, but is using legal language figuratively in requesting a divine intervention. Notwithstanding this, the description of Job's misfortune against the background of his former prosperity and happiness and his oath of purity correspond to the events which lie behind the lament or the legal procedure. Likewise, the following speeches of Yahweh formally correspond to the Yahweh oracle or divine judgment, and the concluding repentance of Job to man's appropriation of this judgment. Once again, this makes clear the close connection between Job 29-31 on the one hand and the divine oracle and Job's reply on the other.

II

The formal analysis of Job 31 already provides some thoughts regarding the question of ethics in this chapter. This analysis may be limited to vv. 1-34, 38-40a, since we have already dealt with vv. 35-37 in Section I.

1. Job 31:1-34, 38-40a is composed of nine strophes, most of which have four verses. The exceptions are the fourth strophe with three verses, and the seventh and ninth strophes with five verses each. Moreover, the alleged transgressions which Job denies that he had committed do not always correspond to the length of the strophes. But sometimes two transgressions are mentioned in one strophe, and sometimes one transgression is mentioned in two strophes. This produces the following summary:

First strophe (vv. 1-4):	1. Lasciviousness
Second strophe (vv. 5-8):	2. Falsehood
	3. Covetousness
Third strophe (vv. 9-12):	4. Adultery
Fourth strophe (vv. 13-15):	5. Disregard for the right of servants
Fifth and sixth strophes (vv. 16-23):	6. Hard-heartedness against the poor
Seventh strophe (vv. 24-28):	7. Trust in riches
	8. Superstition
Eighth strophe (vv. 29-32):	9. Hatred of enemies
	10. Inhospitality
Ninth strophe (vv. 33-34, 38-40a):	11. Hypocrisy
	12. Exploitation of land

This analysis reveals two different formal elements, which, however, have not simply been taken over and reproduced. Rather, they have been combined into a new whole with a specific function. They have to do with the number of transgressions which Job is supposed to have committed, and with the manner in which Job denies that he has committed them.

2. The number of transgressions which Job is supposed to have committed has parallels and prototypes as far as form is concerned. According to the present text, if one includes vv. 38-40a, Job is accused of twelve different transgressions, so that it seems logical to think that a series consisting of the number twelve lies behind Job 31 as a prototype or model. However, the situation does not seem to be so simple, because the first transgression in vv. 1-4 is treated in a different way from those in the following strophes, viz., Job does not use the oath formula, but speaks of a b^{e}rîth which has obliged him to avoid this transgression. Moreover, since these verses are missing in the LXX, one could be inclined to deny them to the Joban poet. Vv. 38-40a are also disruptive. The treatment of the last transgression is out of place in its present position; there can be no question but that it belongs before vv. 35-37. The form of vv. 38-40a suggests that they should be connected with the strophes in vv. 5-23 which have the same form; therefore, it has been suggested that they should be transposed after vv. 8, 12, or 15. However, the individual sections in vv. 5-23 are connected with each other so well that their inner coherence would be broken by inserting vv. 38-40a. Thus the only place that vv. 38-40a can be transferred is after vv. 33-34, although they fit awkwardly there. In any case, vv. 1-4 and 38-40a represent two expansions of an earlier body of material which dealt with ten transgressions. In these ten, the first and the last (falsehood in vv. 5-6, and hypocrisy in vv. 33-34) are almost identical, so that it is best to think of these ten transgressions as a coherent unit complete within itself.

Certainly there is no reason to demand that vv. 1-4 come from the Joban poet, especially since these verses refer entirely to the condition of Job. In the same way, vv. 38-40a presuppose his possessions mentioned earlier in the Prologue. Accordingly it must be assumed that the Joban poet found and used a series of ten transgressions, but has expanded it into a series of twelve transgressions by making additions at the beginning and at the end.

Such series involving groups of ten or twelve occur first of all in the collections of precepts and ordinances (wrongly designated "apodictic law")[6] which have been combined in such an impressive way.[7] Groups of ten appear in the Decalog (Ex. 20:1-17), in the original text of the so-called Cultic Decalog (Ex. 34:10-26), in the original form of the *'ervah-* series (Lev. 18:6-18),[8] in the plural Decalog (Lev. 19:3-12), in the singular Decalog (Lev. 19:13-18,[9] and perhaps in the series used in Ezk. 18:5-9[10] and affecting the summary in Neh. 10:31-40 (30-39). Groups of twelve are found in the series of commands in Ex. 23:10-19, in the present form of the so-called cultic Decalog, in the present expanded form of the *'ervah-* series, in the *'arûr-* series in Dt. 27:15-26, in the scattered *môth yûmath-* series, and perhaps in Ezk. 18:5-9. Later similar groups were used for cultic forms which played a role in the admission to the cult, and which have been labelled "confession mirrors."[11] Ps. 15 contains such a confession mirror with ten statements of an ethical, non-cultic nature, and shorter series of this type occur in Isa. 33:14-16; Ps. 24:3-6; and 34:13-15 (12-14).

Also since the Wisdom teaching expanded different kinds of series and lists, and since Job 31 contains numerous parallels to Wisdom literature, it would be rash to maintain that Job's speech here is based on a series of apodictically formulated precepts and ordinances or even on a confession mirror. Rather, the Joban poet would seem to have used a group of precepts from the Wisdom teaching which had been expanded on the basis of these prototypes. He expanded such a group composed of ten parts into one composed of twelve. Consequently, the very first element of structure indicates that Wisdom teaching was the place of origin for the ethics found in Job 31.

3. Beyond the number of transgressions enumerated, the manner in which Job denies that he has committed these transgressions has parallels and prototypes as far as the form is concerned. Some scholars have pointed out similarities between Job 31 and the negative confessions in the Egyptian religion[12]: Before the dead person enters the "hall of truth" where Osiris and the 42 judges of the dead are enthroned and his heart is weighed on a balance, he must affirm

that he knows himself to be free from the sins which are enumerated in a long list. Many things in Job 31 are similar to these confessions, and it seems likely that they are mediated to the Joban poet through the Wisdom teaching. And yet, the stylistic structure of the Egyptian confessions is different from the conditional clauses of the Israelite oath; they seek to put cultic purity on the same level as ethical purity and differ from Israelite thought in the way they understand various individual concepts. Therefore, they cannot be regarded as the immediate prototype of Job 31.

Also, some scholars have compared Job 31 with the Babylonian Incantation Texts of the Surpu Series.[13] However, it should be noted "that all these texts are intended to liberate the individual man from the power of demons, but not from a conviction that ethical behavior alone is the way to the deity."[14] Because of this completely different situation, the Incantation Texts are excluded.

In place of this, the oath of purity should be mentioned as a prototype to Job 31. After the accused took the legal oath of purity, he was acquitted. Apparently this oath of purity is found in Hammurabi's Law Code[15] and is prescribed in Ex. 22:7, 9f. (6, 8f.) (cf. also 1 Kgs. 8:31ff.; 2 Ch. 6:22f.); The Elephantine Papyri contain a late example of it from the fifth century B.C.[16] If there is an insufficient number of witnesses and it cannot be proved that the accused is innocent in some other way, the lot oracle or the ordeal is used to determine whether he is guilty (cf. Job 9:30f.; Ex. 22:8 [9]; Nu. 5:5ff.). In this case, the lot oracle and the ordeal are regarded as evidence in the legal process. Usually the accused who has or wants to prove his innocence before the legal community pronounces a conditional self-imprecation; the affirmation of innocence appears less frequently.[17] The course of events can be reconstructed with some degree of probability: "In general the oath seems to have consisted of the accuser pronouncing a curse and the accused taking this curse upon himself as a conditional self-imprecation in the holy place either by repeating the curse or by making the curse his own by saying Amen. But when the person under suspicion expressed the oath, he believed that Yahweh would hear it in heaven and in case of perjury would carry out the punishment associated with the curse." [18]

Not only was it possible for the oath of purity to be connected with the legal process, but it could also be connected directly with the cult. It belongs to the cultic affirmations of innocence or "declarations of perfection," [19] to the negative confessions,[20] or to the assertions of innocence in the prayers of the accused (cf. Pss. 5; 7; 17; 26). It may be intended to bring about a divine judgment[21] or to induce God to intervene.[22] However, it is not very likely that one of these prototypes lies behind Job's oath of purity, because the statements which lead up to it in Job 23:10-12 and 27:2-6 have no cultic reference, and because elsewhere in the book of Job the legal terminology in Job's discussion with God is quite perceptible.

In view of this, it is most natural to think that Job's oath had its origin in the legal community. This appears in Job 31 in three forms:

(a) as an affirmation of innocence, in which reference is made to a *b^erîth* of the one making the oath, i.e., to an unconditional responsibility (vv. 1-4);

(b) as a conditional self-imprecation in the rare complete form with an imprecatory final clause (vv. 5-23, 38-40a), the intention of which is to express the complete confidence of the one taking the oath in his own righteousness (with modified forms in vv. 5-6, 13-14), and in which the desired punishment often corresponds to the ancient legal maxims containing the *jus talionis;*

(c) as a conditional self-imprecation in shortened form without a final clause, i.e., as a real oath (vv. 24-34).

4. The Joban poet has combined two formal elements—the instruction in the form of a series, and the oath of purity. He uses them as Job's reason for wanting to meet with God and for challenging him to a discussion (Job 31:35-37), and therefore they are intended to bring about the realization of Job's desire expressed initially in Job 29:2. This function fits the freedom of this form in general.

The first strophe (v. 1-4) begins with the affirmation of innocence by the one taking the oath, who accepts the obligation which it involves. In the form of two questions, he alludes to the punishment which had been threatened in case this obligation was violated, and confirms this with a further question.

The second strophe begins with conditional self-imprecations and has an imprecatory final clause (vv. 5-8). Twice a condition is cited, which sometimes follows the imprecation.

In the third strophe (vv. 9-12), condition and imprecation follow each other. These are connected by a comment on the seriousness of the transgression and on the punishment which it deserves. These three elements (act, punishment, and qualification of the transgression or the reason why it deserves punishment) appear to have been derived from the legal sphere (cf. Lev. 20:9, 11, 12, 14).

After giving the condition, the fourth strophe (vv. 13-15) states the punishment to be expected in the form of a question, but only by way of suggestion. Perhaps the real imprecation has been omitted, because this strophe is shorter than the others and contains only three verses. It contains only a concluding explanation and reason as to why the transgression which is named must be avoided.

The fifth and sixth strophes (vv. 16-23) refer to a larger group of similar conditions, which are interrupted by a didactic parenthesis. A brief imprecation with a reason follows them.

The real oath, i.e., the conditional self-imprecation without an imprecatory final clause, is found from the seventh strophe (vv. 24-28) on. In the seventh strophe, an allusion to the seriousness of the transgression follows three statements composing the oath.

The eighth strophe (vv. 29-32) contains two statements constituting the oath, a positive denial of transgression, and a positive affirmation of a good deed.

Finally, the ninth strophe (vv. 33-34, 38-40a) begins with one statement composing the oath together with a possible reason for committing the transgression which is named. Then once again we encounter the conditional self-imprecation with an imprecatory final clause in the order "condition—imprecation."

III.

What is there that is relevant for a man in Job, who thinks he can demonstrate his righteousness by means of the ingenious formal structure found in Job 31? What are the principles which determine his ethical behavior, and what is their origin?

1. It is easy to establish that the transgressions which Job denies that he had committed in his oath of purity play a substantial role in the Old Testament only in the Wisdom teaching. The references to the belief in retribution are also closely connected with these in Job 31. Thus, although the Joban poet has used the form of the judicial oath of purity of the accused which originated in the legal realm, and although Job 31:35-37 have been shaped in form and in motifs and expressions by the legal realm, the situation is completely different when it comes to the transgressions which are mentioned. They are neither actual and public crimes nor legal variable acts in general. Rather, Job is concerned about attitudes in man which cannot be controlled legally, attitudes which can only lead to sinful acts, or about secret sins among the suspected crimes which had not been exposed. This concern is based on the Wisdom teaching, and not on the Law.

Further, it is evident that only religious and ethical (primarily social) transgressions are mentioned in Job's oath of purity. The worship of the sun and the moon is to be viewed in this way, and, as an indication of apostasy from God, is to be regarded as a religious transgression. On the other hand, cultic wrongs in the real sense, i.e., transgressions against cultic regulations, are not included. This also corresponds with the fundamental attitude of the Wisdom teaching.

However, this general characterization is not yet adequate; in many respects the ethical viewpoint of Job 31 goes beyond those of the Wisdom teaching. Frequently scholars have called attention to the fact that Job 31 has refined and deepened the Wisdom teaching, and have even supposed that it "attains to the ethical loftiness of the Sermon on the Mount in certain places."[23] Moreover, there is an inclination toward that which is fundamental in Job 31, which is in contrast to the numerous individual demands of the law, and is to be observed for the first time in the prophets (cf. Isa. 1:16f.; Am. 5:14f.). Also, the ethical view of Job 31 refers not only to the external behavior of man like the law, but to his internal intention, the sincerity of which is tested with a precise and infallible standard for religio-ethical motives. Nevertheless, the oath of purity undoubtedly represents a high point of Old Testament ethics.

In general, the refining and deepening of ethics, its application to the internal attitude and intention, and its inclination toward that which is fundamental become clear over and over again.

Therefore, Job had made it a rule never to let his eyes look where the temptation might lead to a sinful act (vv. 1-4). Thus, the perceptible sinful deeds, which ordinarily came to an Israelite's mind, are absent in Job's oath of purity from the very beginning. From the start (and certainly not without reason immediately in the introductory expansion of the instruction of the Wisdom teaching used by the Joban poet), the emphasis lies on attitude and intention, and on the proof of a conscience strengthened in godliness. Admittedly, the obligation of the eyes in Job 31 is different from that in Mt. 5:28 in that looking in and of itself is not sinful, but when one yields to it, it leads to actions which are sinful and thus result in divine punishment.

In the denial of falsehood (vv. 5-6), the uniqueness of Job 31 appears in comparison with the Egyptian first negative confession of the dead before Osiris: "I have not acted falsely."[24] In Job, one observes an inclination toward that which is fundamental, which emphasizes truth and honesty in general.

In his denial of adultery (vv. 9-12), Job wants to show (as in the preceding cases) that not only had he committed no sinful acts, but also that he previously restrained the drives which led to them. That he had not committed adultery is due to the fact that he had abstained from every inducement to do so.

In the case of slaves (vv. 13-15), Job begins with the possibility of a lawsuit pending between himself as the master and a manservant or a maidservant. Frequently in such cases the slave was considered to be outside the pale of the law for all practical purposes irrespective of whether he had violated the law or not, the arbitrary action of his master was permitted, and he was treated unfairly by the legal community which was composed of free citizens. However, Job can say that he acted in a different way from this in a matter of dispute, and that the claims of his slaves were not shoved aside. Here he has gone far beyond the mere legal point of view. Job establishes his human behavior by his responsibility before God: "The criterion for one's responsibility toward his fellowman grows out of his responsibility before God."[25] Both of these (Job's behavior toward his slaves and his responsibility before God) have their religious basis in creation faith. The equality of having been created by the same God demands equality before the law, which has its origin in the divine will, and thus has ethical and legal consesequences. This is a revolutionary idea in a period when slaves, like cattle, were regarded as part of the property.

Job's behavior toward the poor (vv. 16-23) was governed by the fact that he felt a close relationship to them as a father or a brother. From his youth he had felt responsible for them, as a father feels responsible for his children or a brother for his sister. Perhaps it can be said that this is almost a paraphrase of the commandment, "Thou shalt love thy neighbor as thyself."[26]

On the question of wealth (vv. 24f.), again Job goes into the deeper motives which induce a man to commit sinful acts, because he knows the danger which wealth presents for faith and godliness. He has not relied on that which is perverse and vain like an ungodly person (cf. Job. 8:14), and has not let himself be led away from God by riches.

In his denial that he hated his enemies (vv. 29f.), first of all Job refers to gloating over an enemy who had suffered misfortune, and again mentions the inner attitude and intention as crucial. He assumes that it is evident that he has abstained from every hostile and hateful act. To be sure, not rejoicing over the ruin of an enemy is different from loving an enemy (Mt. 5:43-48; Lk. 6:27-36). However, the idea of a man refusing to take revenge himself and leaving vengeance to God occurs in place of this in the Old Testament (Dt. 32:35), and the vengeance of God is the dominant motif in the so-called Psalms of Vengeance (cf. Pss. 58; 109; 137). But when

God executes vengeance on the enemy, it is still conceivable that a man might gloat over the ruin of his enemy. This would be a real expression of hatred. Thus, one's refusal to retaliate and to gloat over the ruin of his enemy imply a refusal to hate his enemy. They represent a negative counterpart to loving one's enemy, or at least give the limits beyond which an active love for one's enemy begins.

Job had never even concealed his sins from men for fear of shame, and thus bought his authority as judge for the price of hypocrisy (vv. 33f.). This does not assume that he actually had sinned and then had made known his transgression publicly. Indeed, he had not transgressed. Rather he means that he did not conceal his sins when he committed them. Since he knew none, he committed none. However, Job's willingness to confess his guilt, which is truly rare, shows that any hypocrisy was far from his thoughts.

Job had not even committed trespasses against the land. This has reference to plundering and exploiting the land for the owner's own interests, which is not included in the law. Apparently the figurative expressions in vv. 38-40a intend to convey this idea. As it was ordinarily customary to make payment for the yield of the land and not to take it without payment, so Job restored to his land the yield of its harvest by cultivating it carefully. The statement that he had not harmed the vitality of its owners is to be understood in a similar way. This is based on the old idea of local minor gods which ruled as guardian spirits of the land. Job uses them figuratively in order to depict the peculiar creative power of the land, which languishes under an exploiting farmer. By way of contrast Job wants to say that he had not allowed his land to degenerate and be ruined, but had taken care of it and cultivated it.

There are only two cases in which the peculiarity of the ethical view in Job 31 is not stated. In reality, Job's affirmation that he had shunned superstitious customs (vv. 26-28) has a legal foundation, for according to Dt. 17:2-7 the practice of such customs is a transgression punishable by law since it means apostasy from God. And the custom of generous and liberal hospitality (vv. 31f.) was a sacred duty to the Oriental. To refuse or violate hospitality was regarded as a disgrace, so that no special merit was attached to the practice of hospitality. However, in these two cases the Joban poet was bound by the Wisdom instruction which he used, and was unable to extract deeper ethical qualities in stating Job's claim that he had shunned these transgressions.

3. In spite of the special peculiarities of the ethical view of Job 31 set forth in general above, which assures it of a high rank, one can also see its close connection with the Wisdom teaching.

Thus indeed, the obligation which Job laid upon his eyes (v. 1) emanates from the general Old Testament view that sin is rooted in "seeing" (cf. Gen. 3:6; 2 Sam. 11:2; Isa. 33:15). But the "eye" is of special significance to Wisdom teaching as the seat of evil impulses (Prov. 6:17; 10:10; 30:17; Sir. 14:9; 27:22), pride (Prov. 30:13), and sexual desire (Sir. 9:8; 26:9). Also Job's claim that he had determined not to look upon and turn his thoughts toward an unmarried girl corresponds completely with Sir. 9:5. Further, the question concerning the punishment which would be brought upon him for this transgression (v. 2) shows that at the time that he laid the obligation upon his eyes Job still considered the belief in retribution to be correct, although in the meantime, in the course of his discussion with his friends, he came to the conclusion that it was false. Finally, the idea that God sees man's ways (v. 4) is characteristic of Wisdom teaching, where its function is to motivate man to obey the will of God and to shun sin (cf. Pss. 33:13-15; 69:6 [5]; 94:11; 119:168; 139; Prov. 5:21; Sir. 17:15; 23:19).

Similar observations may be made with regard to vv. 5-8. We encounter the figure of the foot frequently in ethical contexts in Wisdom teaching (Ps. 119:59, 101; Prov. 1:15f.; 4:26; 6:18). It also warns frequently and emphatically against an offence against the truth (Prov. 12:22; 17:7; 19:22; 29:12). Moreover, Wisdom teaching has taken over from Egypt the idea that God weighs a man or his heart, but in doing so it has deleted the connection between this concept and the judgment of the dead in Egyptian literature, so that the Old Testament uses this idea only in a figurative sense (cf. Prov. 16:2; 21:2; 24:12). This figure means that God examines man scrupulously, and assumes the background of the belief in retribution. The terminology which Job uses when he states that he had followed the right way, the way of God, and had not "turned aside" from it also comes from Wisdom teaching (cf. Ps. 119:51; Prov. 4:5, 27).

With regard to vv. 9-12, it should be pointed out that Wisdom teaching frequently warns in detail and emphatically against illegitimate love, adultery and fornication (cf. Prov. 5; 6:24-35; 7:5-23; Sir. 23:18-27). As is the case throughout the Old Testament, this passage has reference to adultery as a violation of someone else's marriage. Consequently, legally it has to do with a transgression against someone else's possession. Religious and ethical motifs come into the picture in later Wisdom teaching (cf. Prov. 5:21-23; Sir. 9:8f.; 23:16, 23, 27). Job's statement that adultery is a "heinous crime" (v. 11) belongs to this later teaching. In v. 10, the idea of retribution also plays a role alongside the old principle of corporate liability.

That which Job says about his relationship to the poor (vv. 16-23) is based on the admonitions which frequently occur in prophecy and Wisdom teaching. The belief in retribution is clearly expressed in vv. 20-22: Because Job helped him who had no clothing, he blessed Job and brought down new prosperity and happiness to him through his prayers. Conversely, if Job had not helped the needy, he asks that punishment come upon the arm which refused to help and which mistreated the needy, so that retribution is brought on the very member of the body which sinned.

When Job affirms that he had not put his trust in wealth (vv. 24f.), this corresponds to the ideal figure of the godly man of the Old Testament, who puts his confidence (Ps. 78:7; Prov. 3:26) and his trust (cf. Jer. 17:7; Pss. 40:5 [4]; 71:5) in God. The Wisdom teaching specifically demands this (cf. Pss. 49:7 [6]; 52:9 [7]; 62:11 [10]; Prov. 11:28; Sir. 5:1, 3, 8; 11:24f.; 14:3; 31:5-8; 40:25f.).

When Job states that, as is obvious, he has refrained from every hostile and hateful deed against another (vv. 29-30), this corresponds both to the precept that one is to love his neighbor and a stranger

(Lev. 19:18, 34), and to similar positive and negative Sapiential admonitions (cf. Prov. 25:21f.; 20:22; 24:19; Sir. 27:30-28:7). Likewise, the view that one should not rejoice over the ruin of his enemy also appears in the Wisdom teaching (Prov. 17:5, 24:17f.), and thus there is also a connection between Job 31 and the Wisdom teaching at this point.

IV.

It cannot be disputed that the Job who utters the oath of purity in chapter 31 stands almost alone upon an ethical summit[27] (and we make this point not merely with the view of determining the time of origin of the poem of Job). The poet has attained this summit by making use of the form of a Wisdom instruction and by deriving his content from the ethical principles of the Wisdom teaching. But he has transcended these concepts by refining and deepening them, by generally transforming them into basic principles, and by relating outer behavior more strongly to inner intention. In this way, Wisdom ethics is raised to a higher level. However, Job 31 gives the impression of containing an internal conflict, since elements of the belief in retribution have been preserved side by side with the high ethical ideal in this chapter. It seems best to assume that the Joban poet intended the reader to see this conflict.

This seems likely because there is also another conflict in Job 31, and if we may judge from the structure of the poem of Job it is undoubtedly intentional. On the one hand, Job is the righteous, pure, and perfect man who can maintain that he is without sin. On the other hand, he appears as a Promethean and Titanic man from whom God had torn away prosperity and happiness, who confronts God boldly with the conviction that he is perfect in order to triumph over Him, and who wants to force Him to acknowledge his innocence by means of his undisputed righteousness. The fact that he undertakes this with the appearance of and under the cloak of the law only increases the impression of a conflict in this chapter. In this way the formal element of the legal oath of purity in the main part of Job 31 and the legal statements in Job 31:35-37 take effect. They make it possible for Job to act like a conquering hero who is certain that he will win a legally plain and indisputable victory over God, while in reality he adopts a heretical position and on the basis of his subjective good conscience contrasts the false teaching of his friends with a view that is just as false.

The conclusion of God's Speech (Job 40:2, 8-14) also makes this clear, as indeed certain statements show:

> Shall a faultfinder contend with the Almighty?
>   He who argues with God, let him answer it.
> Will you even put me in the wrong?
>   Will you condemn me that you may be justified?
> Have you an arm like God,
>   and can you thunder with a voice like his?

Ultimately, then, the issue at stake is not the righteousness of Job, but whether God or man is right. Can man set himself above God as the highest court of justice in order to carry through his demands? Indeed, the proof of innocence with which Job thought he could support his challenge to God with a good conscience means nothing else but that God's law is abolished by an opponent of his law. It is an attack on God's own demands, the purpose of which is to show that God is guilty and that in the end man is right. But this would be possible only if men were "like God". Accordingly, the question is whether Job in the most advanced stage of his earlier attitude is willing to take upon himself man's original sin (as he wanted to be God) or shrinks back from this. In order to take this step, he would have to take over sovereign authority and assume responsibility for carrying on a just world order (Job 40:11ff.), he would have to judge himself immediately as the one who wants to be God. The very elevation of the absolutely righteous man to the position of world ruler would mark him as a criminal worthy of death. His ethically perfect behavior would lead him into the worst kind of sin.

God's speech, then, gives an entirely different evaluation of Job's oath of purity and of the righteous man which it describes as they are viewed in isolation—an evaluation which also explains the intentional conflict in Job 31. By means of the structure of the oath of purity and of the role which is played in Job's appearance before God, the Joban poet calls in question the "pure" righteous conduct and the ethically perfect man, since not without further ado he must also be the trusting man, but he can also be Promethean, Titanic, and heretical. Taken as a whole, Job 31 describes the man who considers himself to be righteous before God because of his ethically perfect conduct and therefore must be rebuked by God, who can endure only when he subjects himself to the sovereign authority of this God and lives in communion with him (Job 40:2-5; 42:2-3, 5-6).

NOTES

1. In no case can Job 31:38-40a (v. 40b is a late caption) follow vv. 35-37, because they contain further assertions of innocence by Job and vv. 35-37 are clearly a conclusion. In this essay, vv. 38-40a will be placed after v. 34, although the correctness of this is uncertain, because this makes the allusion to the land somewhat late in the series. Furthermore, the complete oath formula with imprecatory final clause appears here as in vv. 5-23. Yet, this does not offer a better solution to the problem, since it proves to be impossible to insert something else into or to attach anything to the end of vv. 5-23.

2. A half verse has fallen out, so that the second half verse forms an independent clause and is left hanging in the air. The clause which has fallen out must have contained an additional demand, something like: "Oh that he would show me his written complaint!" G. Hölscher, *Das Buch Hiob* ²1952, 77.

3. E. Seidl, *Einführung in die ägyptische Rechtsgeschichte*, 1939, 20, 25, 27, 34ff.

4. Cf. in general H. Gunkel-J. Begrich, *Einleitung in die Psalmen*, 1933, 215f., 238, 251.

5. Cf. H. Jahnow, *Das hebräische Leichenlied*, 1923, 99, 179.

6. A. Alt, "Die Ursprünge des israelitischen Rechts," *Klein Schriften zur Geschichte des Volkes Israel*, I, 1953, 278-332.

7. G. Fohrer, "Das sogenannte apodiktisch formulierte Recht und der Dekalog," *Studien zur alttestamentlichen Theologie und Geschichte (1949-1966)*, 1969, 120-148.

8. K. Elliger, "Das Gesetz Leviticus 18," *ZAW*, 67 (1955), 1-25.

9. S. Mowinckel, "Zur Geschichte der Dekaloge," *ZAW*, 55 (1937), 218-235.

10. G. Fohrer, *Ezechiel*, 1953, 98-100.

11. K. Galling, "Der Beichtspiegel," *ZAW*, 47 (1929), 125-130.

12. Especially P. Humbert, *Recherches sur les sources égyptiennes de la littérature sapientiale d'Israël*, 1929, 91-96.

13. Cf. H. Zimmern, *Die Beschwörungstafeln Surpu*, 1896.

14. A. Jirku, *Altorientalischer Kommentar zum Alten Testament*, 1923, 87.

15. Code of Hammurabi § 103, 106, 107, 249, 266; cf. *AOT*, 380ff., and *ANET*, 170ff.

16. Cf. in general P. Volz, *ZAW*, 32 (1912), 126f.

17. Cf. J. Schneider, *TWNT*, V, 461.

18. R. Press, "Das Ordal im alten Israel," *ZAW*, 51 (1933), 138.

19. Cf. G. von Rad, "Die Vorgeschichte der Gattung von I Kor. 13, 4-7," *Alt Festschrift*, 1953, 153-168.

20. Cf. also F. Horst, "Der Eid im Alten Testament," *Gottes Recht*, 1961, 292-314.

21. On this cf. H. Richter, *Studien zu Hiob*, 1959.

22. Cf. C. Westermann, *Der Aufbau des Buches Hiob*, 1956.

23. A. Weiser, *Das Buch Hiob*, ²1956, 212.

24. Book of the Dead, chap. 125; cf. *AOT*, 10.

25. A. Weiser, *Das Buch Hiob*, 214.

26. *Ibid.*

27. Cf. also E. Osswald, "Hiob 31 im Rahmen der alttestamentlichen Ethik," *Theologische Versuche*, 2(1970), 9-26.

THE ETERNAL GOSPEL (ECCL. 3:11)

JAMES L. CRENSHAW

Associate Professor
of Old Testament
at Vanderbilt Divinity School

"That is the eternal, as distinct from the temporal gospel: one can love God but one must fear him."[1] With these words Carl Jung gives voice to a universal human experience in the presence of the holy. Such terror before God is a common element in Israelite religion, of course; but the experienced grace of Yahweh, who stood in a covenant relationship with his chosen people, tempered the fear. There is one book in the Old Testament where the fear of God seems to stand alone without any hint of divine compassion. That book is Eccl.[2] The focal passage for a study of its thought is 3:1-15, for it is here that the *Angst* awakened in the human breast before the hidden God manifests itself with unforgettable poignancy and raises the burning question: "Is man the object of divine compassion or caprice?"

I.

Both style and content suggest that 3:1-15 is a separate unit. The refrain[3] in 2:26 functions as a concluding summation, after which one expects a new departure. While there is no similar refrain or stylistic device at the end of 3:1-15, the content changes noticeably in 3:16. The argument for the unity of 3:1-15 based on subject matter is twofold. First, there is remarkable coherence (for Qoheleth!)[4] in 3:1-15, where the "riddle of time" and its consequences for human conduct are treated. Second, 3:16-4:3 is a thematic unit; it treats the so-called problem of retribution, namely the prosperity of the wicked and oppression of the righteous individual. The pivotal role of 3:1-15 is noteworthy; again and again the author returns to the themes introduced in this section (see especially 3:17; 8:5-6, 9; 9:11-12).[5]

The relationship between 3:1-15 and the rest of the book is an intimate one, suggesting that the author himself recognized the centrality of the unit. The initial section (3:1-9) recalls 1:3-11, a didactic poem describing the divorce between history and nature. In 3:10 the verbal similarity with 1:13b is striking, while 3:12-13 takes up Qoheleth's advice to enjoy life as expressed in 2:24. The emphasis upon the durability of divine creativity recalls the observation in

1:4, which differs sharply from Deutero-Isaiah's proclamation that the word of God stands forever (Isa. 40:8). Again 3:15 returns to and expands the statement found in 1:9, although the meaning of the elaboration is unclear despite the close parallel in Sir. 5:3.[6] The affinity between 3:1-15 and the rest of the book is not limited to what precedes the unit; on the contrary, many of its ideas recur at later junctures. The observation that everything has its appropriate time is repeated in 3:17, but here in a judgmental context. The tragic pessimism of 3:11 is permitted to surface again in 7:13-14 and 8:17 (perhaps also in 7:29 and 11:5), just as the conclusion to eat, drink and enjoy life (3:13) crops up at crucial stages of the argument (3:22; 5:17 [Eng. 18]; 8:15; cf. 9:7-10).

Both in syntax and vocabulary the peculiar stylistic features of the author are well represented in this small unit. Fourteen antithetic pairs expressive of totality[7] are juxtaposed in serial fashion (cf. 7:1-10), a stylistic trait particularly appropriate for an author who wishes to emphasize the relative value of all things under the sun (that is, on earth). The rhetorical question that functions as a negative assertion, a favorite device of the author,[8] stands in 3:9. The broken sentence,[9] still another special feature of Eccl. appears in 3:11, perhaps twice (*gam* and *mibbᵉlî*). The preference for participles also finds expression here (3:9), even with a pronoun, as do words otherwise found only in relatively late Old Testament texts (*zᵉman; sôph; she*). Attention should also be called to the extraordinary calm mood[10] despite the churning beneath the surface; the impersonal style employed in some sections does little to conceal the burning genuineness of Qoheleth's teachings. The favorite expressions of the author make their appearance in this small unit; here one encounters "under heaven", "toil", "gain", "gift of God", *"the* God", "I saw", "I knew", "time", and "end". Noteworthy omissions are "vanity of vanities" and "striving after wind".[11]

Inasmuch as the structure of the book is still a mystery, it is impossible to place 3:1-15 within the total argument. The attempts at structural analysis on the basis of logical coherence and stylistic characteristics have failed to create a consensus,[12] due chiefly to their subjective nature. Perhaps this failure bears witness to the aphoristic quality of the book, and suggests that the author may not have arranged his "collection of sentences" in any logical fashion, but permitted random observations to intrude at will.

Literary analysis of 3:1-15 is relatively certain. It consists of two sub-sections:[13] I. Inexorable Law (vv. 1-9) and II. Human Response (vv. 10-15). The first is composed of an introduction (3:1), fourteen contrasting pairs (3:2-8), and a rhetorical question (3:9), providing the transition to the second sub-section. The latter is made up of reflections on the nature of reality (3:10-11), observations about the proper human response to the way things are (3:12-13), and further reflection on the grounds for the conclusions about human conduct (3:14-15). Within the first sub-section the author has made use of chiasmus[14] to isolate the antitheses; the fourteen pairs of contrasts are introduced by the chief *Grenzsituationen* over which man has no control (birth and death) and are concluded by the great historical contingencies that effect life or death, namely war and peace. Between these two, birth and death, take place all that characterizes human existence: planting and uprooting (weeds?), killing and healing, tearing down and rebuilding, weeping and laughing, mourning and exulting, buying and selling,[15] making love and remaining continent, seeking and losing, retaining and discarding, tearing and mending, keeping silence and speaking, loving and hating.

The form of the didactic poem in 3:2-8 is closest to onomastica, or lists; it has its nearest biblical parallel in Job 38-41, but resembles encyclopedic lists from Egyptian and Mesopotamian wisdom literature.[16] A pedagogic device, such lists seem originally to have been a means of ordering the world so that one could make sense of his environment, but served admirably to teach the young scribe what could be known about a particular topic. The subject matter of onomastica is generally related to nature, hence the descriptive term "Naturweisheit".[17] The emphasis in Eccl. 3:2-8 is upon human activity. The form of 3:10-15 is that of the so-called royal testament or confession; a more appropriate term is autobiographical narrative.[18] The genre is typical of the Egyptian instructions, in which the Pharaoh or his vizier (counselor) advises his son as to the correct behavior before gods and men. But it is also found in Proverbs (7:6-27; 24:30-34). This counsel represents the lifetime achievement of the scribe, the vast accumulation of rich experience. Hence the "I have seen" and "I know" carry the authority of office and experience, and consequently are not to be taken lightly.[19] Qoheleth has juxtaposed onomastica, the cumulative information about human experience, and autobiographical narrative, the fruit of a lifetime of study. The latter makes the point that all human striving is futile, yes, even the desire to know, since God has concealed vital knowledge from man. The mood, then, is one of tragic pessimism.[20] This scepticism as to man's ability to know is heightened by the partial knowledge permitted him, namely that God does not act to insure the principle of retribution. The old idea of *ts^edhaqah* has given way to cold fear as the central stance. No longer can man know that he is *tsaddîq;* now salvation (life), if it comes, is a gift.[21]

The reason for Qoheleth's scepticism is expressed in 3:11, which has been a *Walpurgisnachts-Traum* for all commentators.[22] This nightmare of interpretation does not derive simply from the presence of the much-discussed *ha'olam,* but from the total sentiment of the verse. On the face of it 3:11 appears to be an elaboration of the pessimistic observation in 3:10, which is milder by far than 1:13b. The business (*ha'inyan*) is the frustrating search for *ha'olam,* to be discussed later. Just as 3:11 is integrally related to 3:10, it is also closely joined to 3:12-15, which gives the conclusions arising from the reflection on the nature of things, as well as the reasons for those deductions. Analysis of 3:11, then, should provide the key to the entire unit. Anticipating the discussion to follow, 3:11 raises the basic issues under discussion in wisdom literature today: (1) creation, (2) order, (3) enigma, (4) sovereignty, and (5) totality.

II.

The verse opens with an affirmation of the goodness of creation undoubtedly reminiscent of Gen.1, where the creative work is repeatedly described as *ṭôbh*. However, the key terms in the Priestly narrative of creation are passed over in favor of a vocabulary that is less theological in tone: *'eth hakkol 'asah yapheh*. Instead of the comprehensive "heavens and earth," Qoheleth employs an abstract *hakkol,* a favorite antithesis of *ḥeleq*. The reversal of word order serves to emphasize the object of *'asah:* everything he has made beautiful. The use of *'asah* instead of *bara'* accords with the author's revolutionary stance, and suggests that the strange form in 12:1 (*bor$^{e'}$-ekha*) is more correctly understood as a derivative of the root *bara',* "to dig cut".[23] The word would then be a double entendre for grave and cistern (wife; cf. Prov. 5:15-19), hence a fitting climax to Qoheleth's positive counsel set over against the warning of approaching death. The use of *yapheh* rather than *ṭôbh* is occasioned by the context, which allows a descriptive adjective of beauty but which renders one of goodness either contradictory or banal. Perhaps the use of *v^{e}la'^{a}sôth ṭôbh* in 3:12 is a conscious attempt at the transformation of theological vocabulary, for here the *ṭôbh* in 3:12 is completely neutral, has been emptied of all ethical content. In this regard it is noteworthy that 5:18(17) uses both *ṭôbh* and *yapheh* in a neutral sense of fitting or appropriate.

The statement that God has made everything beautiful is the fruit of experience; its truth no wise man would deny. Only the "fool" totally devoid of aesthetic appreciation could fail to perceive the grandeur of the created order, a beauty so moving that it elicited from the lips of the *"rationalistic"* sages hymns of praise to the Creator. This much even Qoheleth could affirm: God has made everything beautiful. Nevertheless, the affirmation stands under a cloud of qualifications. The introductory verse within the second section of the unit under discussion gives little hint of the negative tenor of what follows, but merely registers the experiential nature of the conclusion (3:10). Perhaps the verse should be read in the light of 1:13, where the adjective *ra'* modifies the "business" that God has given man. If this is correct, 3:10 already suggests that what follows is far from an ecstatic hymnic declaration. In any case, the rest of the verse, together with 3:12-15, qualify the affirmation to such an extent that one cannot claim that it provided any solace to Qoheleth's tragic pessimistic spirit. Historical existence is for him a living *in tormentis*.[24]

One of the reasons for the scepticism is Qoheleth's recognition that *hakkol* is denied him. Only a *ḥeleq* is *granted him,* and even that is a direct *gift* of God.[25] But Qoheleth could abide this reality if there were proof that the dispenser of the portion were graciously disposed toward his creatures. However, the evidence of experience suggested to Qoheleth that God was neither favorably nor unfavorably disposed toward man, but rather completely indifferent (9:1). "God is in heaven and you are on earth": here we see the key to Qoheleth's pathos as well as to his life style. Inasmuch as God is the distant unknowable ruler and guarantor of the universe, man should strive to remain outside his focus of attention. But such existence is devoid of ultimate meaning, since it is concerned with transitory things, hence the descriptive adjective *ra'*. Once again Qoheleth has used a word fraught with theological content, but in a thoroughly neutral manner. Indeed, the same "neutralization" is evident in *ḥeleq,* so important in Israelite thought as the portion of divine blessing.

How different Qoheleth's affirmation that "God has made all things beautiful" is from Sir. 39:16! In a hymnic setting Sir. proclaims that "the works of God, *all of them,* are good" (*ma'ªsê 'el kolam ṭôbhîm*). Indeed Sir. admonishes his hearers to sing a hymn of praise to bless the Lord for all his works (39:14b), and suggests the appropriateness of affirming that all the works of God are good. Verse 17 implies, however, that a substantial number of doubters existed in Sir.'s day too, a theme to which we shall return. This intrusion of polemics into hymnic literature must not blind us to the significance of such praise to the sages, a point "marvelously" overdone by G. von Rad in his recent *Weisheit in Israel*.[26] The study of the wonders of creation generated a feeling of awe as well as of appreciation, most appropriately expressed in hymnody. Hence the sage frequently gave voice to songs of praise once he reached the frontiers of human knowledge. The impact of such praises lies behind Qoheleth's grudging (?) admission that God has made everything beautiful. For Qoheleth, though, this was nothing about which to sing.

The use of *hakkol* means that adversity as well as prosperity are adjudged beautiful. To this theme Qoheleth returns in 7:13-14, here in a clearly negative mood. The rhetorical question, "Who can make straight what he has made crooked?", implies that something has gone awry with the work of God (as it is specifically stated in 7:29). At the same time it calls attention to man's inability to undo what God has established for eternity. Both prosperity and adversity are God's doing, and man cannot probe into the future (7:14), that is, he can not distinguish whether something is good or bad in prospect. Just as in 3:11, so also in 7:14, the knowledge of a good creation provides no comfort to one who finds himself in adversity. Once again comparison with Sir. is instructive. In 39:16-35, a majestic broken hymn on the way nature itself reinforces the principle of retribution,[27] the emphasis is placed on polarities that are apparently contradictory, but in reality are means of ensuring that morality is rewarded and wickedness punished. Sir. appears to be unaware of the contradiction to his affirmation that all God's works are good when he concedes that bad things were created *from the beginning* for sinners (cf. Prov. 16:4). He does, however, recognize that good and bad things are in the eye of the beholder ("To the holy his ways are straight, just as they are obstacles to the wicked", v. 24). The indifferent universe of Qoheleth is replaced by one that is passionately involved in human affairs, and this conviction, like Qoheleth's, is said to be the result of experience ("Therefore from the beginning I have been convinced, and have thought this out and left it in writing: The works of the Lord are all good, and he will supply every need in its hour", vv. 32-33). Here speaks a *preacher* indeed, with his admonition to sing praise and bless Yahweh's name (v. 35); but it is not from this platform that the *Prediger* (Qoheleth) utters his voice.

Man's inability to comprehend the mystery of creation, mentioned in Eccl. 7:14, is taken up again in 11:5, a passage of uncertain meaning. The protasis seems to refer to two mysteries, the workings of the wind and the growth of a foetus (cf. Jn. 3:8). The apodosis presents no difficulty; it denies that man knows the work of God who made *hakkol*. The usefulness of such mysteries in addressing the problem of theodicy was quickly perceived; the argument of 2 Esd. 4 is heavily fraught with rhetorical questions dealing with the limits of human cognition. The context of Qoheleth's observation results in no diminution of pathos, even though 11:5 is set within several observations about business ventures. For Qoheleth there was no separation beween theology and ethics.

This tendency of creation faith to appear in wholly unexpected places, as well as in hymns celebrating the wonders of nature, would appear to corroborate the conclusion of several scholars that wisdom literature is grounded in creation faith.[28] In light of these frequent assertions, one might expect to find numerous references to creation in wisdom literature. Such is not the case, except in Sir., who cannot stand as normative for wisdom. In Prov. the creation theme rarely appears save in the general allusion to man's Maker (14:31; 16:4, 11; 17:5; 20:12; 22:2). In reality one cannot speak of creation faith in Prov. Even the reference to the creation of wisdom at the beginning of Yahweh's work subordinates creation theology to *hokhmah* speculation. The picture is somewhat different in Job, although the near absence of creation phraseology in the hymnic chs. 5 and 9, which are transparently coined from the same traditions as the doxologies of Amos (4:13; 5:8-9; 9:5-6), is remarkable.[29] Other passages recall the general creaturehood of man as emphasized in Prov. (Job 4:17; 10:8-11; 31:15; 32:22; 35:10; 36:3). Still others stress the majesty of him who stretched out the heavens hard as molten mirror (9:8; 26:7; 37:18; cf. 38:4-11) and conquered chaos (26:7-14; 40:15-24). The subordination of creation to wisdom occurs in Sir. too (1:4, 9; 24:9), as do the general references to man's Maker (4:6; 7:30; 10:12; 15:14; 32:13; 33:13; 38:15; 39:5). But the praise of God for his creative works reaches a new height with Sir. (11:4; 16:26-30; 17:1-20; 18:1-7; 33:15; 39:21-35; 42:15-43:33). Even farm labor and medicines[30] are said to have been created by God (7:15, 38:4). In short, creation theology plays a minor role in early Prov., a slightly greater role in Job, and a significant one in Sir. In this regard Qoheleth is closer to Prov. than to his near contemporary Sir.

The real point of the statement that wisdom literature is grounded in creation theology does not have to do with frequency of occurrence, but rather with the nature of authority.[31] Whereas the rest of the Old Testament, particularly the legal and prophetic traditions, appeals to the authority of a spoken word, revelation, that is, wisdom literature grounds its counsel in the nature of reality, or more correctly, in the original decrees of creation. The sages did not understand history in the way the prophets, priests and historians interpreted it,[32] namely as the arena within which God worked to bring about his plans for a covenant people. Neither redemptive nor retributive historical events play a role in their thoughts, which was much more concerned with the individual than the nation. This does not mean that the sage was bereft of normative "words"; on the contrary, the original creative deed established an order that remained normative for all time.[33] But the existence of such an order, which some scholars have called horizontal revelation,[34] is a theological construct.[35] The primordial message of God for his creatures is available to man through the use of his reason. Furthermore, the universe itself is not silent but rings forth with praise of the Creator. Hence the importance of the hearing ear, the fruit of diligent study at the seat of learning. And should man be unable to grasp the message of the universe, God has provided him with another witness, Dame Wisdom. No latecomer she, Lady Wisdom existed in the beginning before creation. Since she was present when the original decrees were pronounced, her message carries the urgency of life or death, and her love of man explains the evangelistic fervor. Unfortunately Qoheleth did not share this view of the universe and Wisdom; for him the world had become silent, had lost its dialogical character. Hence not a word is spoken about Dame Wisdom; the cold, indifferent universe has no place for her.[36]

When the sage grounded his counsel on the way things are, he was doing more than providing a basis for conduct in authoritative fashion. He was proclaiming his faith in the fundamental order that sustains the universe, the principle that rewards virtue and punishes vice. Indeed one gets the impression that creation faith functions more within the context of "retribution" than ethical motivation per se. In order to affirm justice in the world despite appearances to the contrary, it was essential that the wise man believe in creation rather than chaos. Purpose, intention, goal were mandatory; the belief in creation assured *télos*. In essence then, creation faith undergirds the wise man's belief in order, to which we now turn.

III.

"He has made everything beautiful *in its time*" (*bhe'ittô*). Here is the first effort at qualifying the beauty of the created order. Such an observation arises from the existence of polarities in human experience, one of which is designated as good or beneficial, the other as evil or harmful. The first sub-section of the major unit under consideration is devoted to the naming of fourteen such antitheses (3:2-8). It is possible that Qoheleth makes use of a poem that was neutral in tone (as in 1:4-7), and by placing it in the present context has changed its import decisively. Its negative impact is enhanced by the concluding rhetorical question ("What gain has the worker from his toil?" v. 10). "For everything there is a season (*zeman*), and a time (*'eth*) for every matter under heaven" (3:1). The meaning of *'eth* is something like "occasion for" or "possibility for"; the verse observes that there is a right time and a wrong time for everything, a theme that frequently appears in wisdom literature. This idea dominates the book of Sir., the Greek text of which uses the pregnant *kairós* about sixty times.[37]

The form of 3:1-9 is that of didactic poetry, with the kernel of the poem drawing upon onomastica-like material. The poem is a work of art, especially in its use of chiasmus and paranomasia. Besides the example of chiasmus mentioned in the preceding discussion of structure, there is a fine specimen in 3:8 (love-hate, war-peace). The paranomasia appears in 3:4b (*sephôdh-reqôdh*), perhaps also in 3:3b and 3:4a (*libhnôth-libhkôth*).[38] The point of the poem in its present setting cannot be an affirmation that one should seek to act at the appropriate time, for Qoheleth observes that man cannot know that vital fact. Rather it laments the pre-determined monotony of all human affairs, the fact that the veil of secrecy hangs over everything that happens. Implicit in the poem is the recognition that man can do only one of these antitheses at a time, but he cannot know which to choose at any given *'eth*. In 3:17 the conviction that God has appointed a time for every matter is set within a context of the theodicy question, in a sense resolving the issue. The fact that Qoheleth relentlessly continues his attack on divine justice suggests a secondary origin for this verse, unless one is willing to assume that Qoheleth, like Sir. and some maxims in the book of Prov., was attempting to hold together antithetic viewpoints to achieve totality.[39] In 9:12 Qoheleth returns to the idea that man does not know his time, and concludes that his fate (*miqreh*) is one with that of the beasts (he will be snared at an evil time; cf. 3:18-21).

How does Qoheleth's use of the idea of an appropriate time for everything compare with that of other wisdom texts? It has been observed that "In essence the goal of wisdom instruction was the recognition of the right time, the right place and the right degree of human conduct."[40] Put another way, the distinctive feature of wisdom thinking is order. The sages believed that God had established "fixed decrees" comparable with natural law by which the universe was sustained. In addition God was the guarantor of this order, punishing or rewarding human conduct so as to assure the survival of the universe itself. This idea Israel borrowed from her neighbors; both in Egyptian and Mesopotamian literature order was essential to the sages.[41] Man's task, accordingly, was to discern the order of the world by means of examined experience. Once a hidden secret was opened to him, the sage coined it in a proverb, thus achieving a degree of mastery over the world. The accumulation of discoveries as to the nature of this order was transmitted from generation to generation, each time being tested by new experience. For no word was final; each proverb was subject to confirmation or disconfirmation. Cosmic and ethical order was explored, so that man might learn how to behave toward God and his fellowmen. This effort to discover hidden decrees, while utilitarian in character, was far more than the attempt to discern what is good for man.[42] In essence it was a discovery of and participation in the ordering of the world, that is, the prevention of a return to chaos. For this reason righteousness involved God, man, and creation itself. Thus an urgency in the proverbial literature is comprehensible; so too is the scornful attitude expressed toward the "fool". If a mastery of the appropriate time, place and degree of conduct is essential to the order of the universe, an impulse to dogma and systematization is built into wisdom thinking.[43]

This "dogma", usually referred to in German scholarship as the *Tun-Ergehen-Zusammenhang*,[44] and in English literature as Act-Consequence or Cause-Effect Principle, is likewise a constituent factor in wisdom literature, but by no means exclusively so.[45] A result of the belief in purpose and order, the retribution schema was not merely a grounding of ethical teaching; that is, it did not emerge simply to provide motivation for conduct. Although it has been argued that the principle of order became independent of God and constituted a "law" to which even Yahweh was subject,[46] this thesis is difficult, if not impossible, to support textually.[47] The existence of the book of Job indicates, neverthless, that some people were willing to entertain such notions. In a sense Job's defense stands or falls on the principle of retribution that he has rejected, and the author's point is that God is free to act in a way that is disconsonant with the "law" of individual retribution.[48]

The fact that a "dogma" about reward and punishment arose is illustrative of the optimism with which the sage viewed both the world and his ability to understand the divine mysteries. While the wise man readily conceded that there was a limit to his knowledge, this bit of humility does not negate the existence of the belief in individual retribution. Of course, the sages were aware of a breach in the wall, but succeeded remarkably well in plugging the hole even after the breach had widened to a chasm under the ruthless attacks of Job and Qoheleth. We are now in a position to answer the question about Qoheleth's use of the idea of the right time as compared with that of other wisdom texts. In a word, Qoheleth has theologized the ancient teaching:[49] by joining the idea of the appropriate time to a theological determinism, Qoheleth has limited man and in a sense God also. There is no individual retribution, and man cannot know what the appropriate deed is for any moment. Indeed, man is unable even to distinguish good and bad (or perhaps shades of good). "Say not, 'Why were the former days better than these?' For it is not from wisdom that you ask this" (7:10). If this verse is understood in light of Sir. 36:1-17, especially v.6 ("Show signs anew, and work further wonders; make thy hand and thy right arm glorious"), its relevance to the theodicy question is readily discernible. Even if one does not use Sir.'s text as a key to the postulating of an audience for whom this word of Qoheleth was intended, the observation is clearly an attack against the way things are, that is, against God who is responsible for the current state of affairs.

The simple formula, "Say not" is used pre-eminently in contexts dealing with the justice of God. Even where the denial of the principle of retribution is missing, as in Prov. 20:22 and 24:29, the problem under discussion is integrally related to divine justice. This ancient formula, in use as early as the Egyptian Instruction of Amen-em-ope, was taken up by Sir. with enthusiasm. Almost without exception the contexts are theodicial in character; in nearly every instance Sir. is fighting against those who deny the principle of rewards for the good man and are arrogantly boasting that they sin with impunity.

> "Do not say, 'Who will have power over me?' for the Lord will surely punish you. Do not say, 'I sinned, and what happened to me?' for the Lord is slow to anger. Do not be so confident of atonement that you add sin to sin. Do not say, 'His mercy is great, he will forgive the multitude of my sins', for both mercy and wrath are with him, and his anger rests on sinners" (5:3-6).

Similar warnings are given throughout the text of Sir. "Do not say, 'He will consider the multitude of my gifts, and when I make an offering to the Most High God he will accept it'" (7:9). "Do not say, 'Because of the Lord I left the right way'; for he will not do what he hates. Do not say, 'It was he who led me astray' for he has no need for a sinful man" (15:11-12). "Do not say, 'I shall be hidden from the Lord, and who from on high will remember me?' Among so many people I shall not be known, for what is my soul in the boundless creation? ... Like a tempest which no one can see, so most of his works are concealed. Who will announce his acts of justice? Or who will await them? For the covenant is far off'" (16:17, 21-22). To these may be added a variant, "No one can say." In all three instances the subject matter is like that under discussion. "No one can say, 'What is this?' 'Why is that?' for in God's time all things will be sought after" (cf. Eccl. 3:15). "No one can say, 'What is this?' 'Why is that?' for everything has been created for its use" (39:21). "And no one can say, 'This is worse than that', for all things will prove good in their season" (39:34).

These polemical texts throw considerable light upon the sociotheological situation in which Sir. functioned as a teacher in the beth-midrash. Such prohibitives indicate that the sceptic has always harassed the sage who hoped against hope that somewhere, somehow inequity would disappear so that justice would shine with the brilliance of midday. The numerous references to the justice of God, many of which are so stated as to reveal the challenge resting behind them, witness to the difficulty of affirming the principle of retribution. One way of maintaining it was to claim that God sees everything that takes place. Accordingly there is a wealth of literature that lays stress upon the clarity of God's vision. No victim of near-sightedness or inattention, he scans the entire horizon and keeps an accurate record of man's deeds, whether good or bad. By the time of Sir. and Bar., epithets had arisen to emphasize God's full knowledge (*ḥôzeh khol,* Sir. 15:18; *ho eidos ta pánta,* Bar. 3:32),[50] each reminding the Israelite that he sins at his own peril or that his virtue does not escape notice.

The principle of retribution was challenged from the other side too. Not only were there doubters who questioned the justice of God on the basis of their experience; there were also men who believed that the deity was capable of overlooking or forgiving misconduct. Whether any of the sages prior to Sir. belonged to the ranks of these who questioned the "dogma" of retribution in favor of a merciful God is a disputed question. The text from Prov. that is sometimes quoted in this connection is ambiguous; it may refer to human forgiveness (28:13). In Job 11:6 Zophar argues that God exacts of Job *less* than his guilt deserves, but this is still a long way from divine mercy as celebrated in Old Testament literature outside the wisdom corpus. Much closer are Job 10:12 and 12:4, which refer to God as the source of the steadfast love and the one who responded to Job's prayer at an earlier period of his life. Such recollection of a by-gone vital religious experience by one who has now discovered that God is his personal antagonist is all the more impressive, and points to an oversight of much critical scholarship.[51] Perhaps Sir. has preserved a genuine aspect of wisdom, for it was indeed a "tiny step"[52] from hymns about the divine mysteries concealed in nature to the uttering of fervent prayers. This close relationship of hymn and prayer is also evident in Wisd., where a distinction between the two is sometimes impossible (11:23-12:2). It is noteworthy that some intertestamental literature seeks to combine divine justice and mercy (Tob. 3:2). How, then, does Qoheleth fit into the picture that has evolved from this discussion? For him there is no divine compassion. But neither is there divine justice. Such absolutization of the limited experience of one man is in tension with Qoheleth's thesis that God has put *ha'olam* in man's heart . . . a discussion of this difficult text is our immediate task.

IV.

"Also he has put eternity(?) into man's mind" (*gam 'eth-ha-'olam nathan b^elibbam*). The beauty of everything in its own time is not the final word Qoheleth has to say. By nature man is endowed with a compulsive drive not only to appreciate the beauty of creation on the aesthetic level, but also to know its character and meaning so as to gain self-certainty, security and happiness. Whence comes this ceaseless tug to know what holds the world together and to use this knowledge for one's well being? Does Qoheleth view such restlessness of the soul as a gift or curse? The answer to this question depends upon the meaning of *ha'olam*. If we dare to enter this well known playground of fantasy, it is with full knowledge that the meaning of this obscure *ha'olam* "is far off, and deep, very deep, who can find it out?" (Eccl. 7:24).

In the history of Qoheleth research, four basic solutions to the meaning of this word have inevitably suggested themselves:[53] (1) eternity, (2) world, (3) course of the world, and (4) knowledge or ignorance. The first three attempt to understand the MT as a defective form of *'ôlam*, whereas the fourth substitutes different vowels. The LXX translator of Qoheleth renders the phrase as follows: *kai ge sun ton aiona édoken*. This reading is in accord with the meaning of *'olam* in rabbinic literature where a distinction is made between this world (*'olam hazzeh*) and the world to come (*'olam habba'*). The usual objection to this understanding of the term in Qoheleth carries little weight, specifically that *ha'olam* never bears such an abstract meaning in the rest of the Old Testament. It is well known that Qoheleth's vocabulary and syntax are unique within the Hebrew canon. Nevertheless, it is significant that Qoheleth uses *'olam* in its usual Old Testament sense in 1:4, 10; 2:16; 3:14; 9:6. More cogent is the argument against such an interpretation of *ha'olam* from context; if eternity is meant, why the remorseful 3:11bβ? The special endowment of eternity, whatever that means, would have been cause for jubilation, not sorrow. How far Qoheleth is from a belief in man's innate endowment of eternity can be seen in his almost flippant rhetorical question dismissing the new idea of resurrection ("Who knows whether the spirit [breath] of man goes upward and the spirit of the beast goes down to the earth?" 3:21). Others have suggested that *ha'olam* means a desire for eternity;[54] amid the restless changes of temporality man has a notion of eternity. Unlike the animals man is conscious of the passing of time; the meaning of *ha'olam* would thus approximate that of *tselem* in Gen. 1:26.[55] But Eccl. 3:18-22 makes the point that the fate of man and beast is the same, hence the sting in the heart must be something else. Incidentally, it is remarkable that the sages refused to make use of the idea of the image of God, which does not occur until Sir. The reason for this refusal to take up such a concept may lie in wisdom's experiential character, which prefers analogies that surface from human experience rather than from speculation about the unseen.

The Vulgate reads *mundum tradidit disputationi eorum* at Eccl. 3:11, and Jerome's commentary conveys the same idea: *saeculum didit in corda eorum*. Following this lead some scholars use such phrases as "love of the world", *"Weltsinn"*, or *"Welt"*.[56] Inasmuch as *'olam* in the Old Testament always has a temporal meaning, others argue that Qoheleth uses the term to refer to a period of time, particularly to the remotest age.[57] The emphasis would then be upon the knowledge that the world is running its course, passing away, and with it man too. The defective writing of *ha'olam* has led others to suggest that the root is *'lm,* to conceal.[58] A meaning such as ignorance is then given to the form. But the same consonants can be read in a different manner, namely "knowledge", although this meaning does not suit the context. Among the many emendations that have been offered one is worthy of consideration: *ha'amal* (toil).

The meaning of *ha'olam* is further complicated by the following *belibbam*. Despite the attractiveness of K. Galling's[59] emendation to *bô* or *lô,* the loss of which is credibly explained as the result of dittography and metathesis (*mibbeli* to *lbm*), we cannot go this route. The acknowledged logical coherence is no cogent argument, and the dismissal of 1 Kgs. 10:24 and Jer. 31:33 (cf. Ps. 119:11) as irrevelant for the understanding of Eccl. 3:11 on the grounds that nowhere else is *ha'olam* said to be placed in man's heart is unsatisfactory. The *belibbam* must refer to mankind in 3:10, also in the plural (*libhnê ha'adham*). But Galling is correct that the meaning of Eccl. 3:11 must be temporal; God has given man a life that is characterized by transitoriness, yet man tries to find out the future. The desire to calculate, to seek after what is yet to be in such manner as to secure oneself for whatever befalls him—this is God's gift. Yet man's tendency to strive for permanence, to assure the survival of his name, is destined to fail. So, too, is every inquiry about past and future events, even if man is so created that he must ask about his moment under the sun.

Whatever the meaning of *ha'olam* may be, the context emphasizes man's inability to discover it. With this judgment as to man's limitations of knowledge we have arrived at a significant theme in wisdom literature. The idea is expressed beautifully in Prov. 25:2 ("It is the glory of God to conceal things (*haster*), but the glory of kings is to search things out"). The unchecked optimism is strikingly different from Qoheleth's lament; perhaps the tradition that Solomon was a sage par excellence (or at least a patron of the wise men) stands behind this optimism. Here was a king who, according to the tradition, was granted special insight so that his wisdom surpassed that of non-Israelites. Similarly Hezekiah was a sponsor of the wise men, and may have sat for this portrait. The task facing both kings, and others whose connection with the sages is not known, was to search out the mysteries that God had concealed.

The limits of human wisdom are recalled in isolated proverbs (Prov. 16:1, 9; 19:21; 20:24; 21:30, 27:1), hymns (Job 5:9; 28:20-23), and "school questions" (catechisms; so Prov. 30:2-4; Job 11:7-12). Thus Qoheleth stands in a long tradition when recognizing that the divine mysteries hidden in the world cannot be grasped. This ignorance is not due to laziness, for Qoheleth has determined to be wise. Despite his efforts, however, he succeeds only in discovering the profundity of what is being sought ("But it was far from me. That which is, is far off, and deep, very deep; who can find it out?" Eccl. 7:23b-24).

One thing Qoheleth does discover is that the order of the world is in disarray (3:16-4:3), that there is no relationship between one's being and his welfare. The position of old wisdom, that a man's external affairs correctly mirror his inner character, is rejected. Qoheleth knows that the wicked reap the harvest of the innocent, and vice versa (9:11-12). Inasmuch as one cannot count on reward for virtue or punishment for vice, what is good for man is to enjoy himself, for even that ability is a gift of God. This is man's lot:

walking under a mysterious closed universe, never certain before any possibility, step by step dependent upon God's free gift, ever ready to bear the riddle and stress of life.⁶⁰ What this means is spelled out in 3:16-4:3.

This uncertainty about the future was difficult to accept. The result was an attempt to gain some means of making contact with the unknown. Divination was essential to the Babylonian sages.⁶¹ But what about the Israelite wise man? It has been argued that the Joseph narrative and Daniel are wisdom in orientation;⁶² if true, this would provide proof that divination played a decisive role in Israelite wisdom too. Particularly significant to this thesis is the interpretation of dreams, for it was assumed that a dream was one of the many legitimate means of revelation. Accordingly, Joseph was not only an important recipient of dreams, but also a valuable and skilled interpreter of royal dreams. Likewise Daniel was able to narrate and explain the meaning of King Nebuchadnezzar's dream that even the wisest Babylonian counselors could not do. There is little if any justification for seeing these texts as even remotely related to wisdom literature, for the differences are far too numerous to be ignored. In any case dream interpretation as recorded in the Old Testament did not threaten divine sovereignty, for it was Yahweh who enabled the wise man to read the contours of divine plans for the future. Divination as such was ruled out, chiefly because of God's freedom to act as he chose. In this regard Qoheleth is representative of Israelite wisdom: "For in many dreams . . . is also vanity" (5:7 [6]).

V.

We come now to "der Pfeil des Geistes zerbricht".⁶³ The desire to know the hidden mysteries of God is denied any fulfillment: "Yet so that he cannot find out what God has done . . ." (*mibbᵉlî ʾᵃsher loʾ -yimtsaʾ haʾadham ʾeth-hammaʿᵃseh ʾᵃsher-ʿasah haʾᵃᵉlohim*). Whatever it is that God has placed in man's mind will do him no good, for God (not Yahweh) has made him incapable of discovering it. Here we are approaching the demonic; this text is not far from others in the ancient Near East describing a god's jealousy lest human creatures achieve a status or power that threatens the deity, or from those accounts of a divine test with a stacked deck of cards. In both cases man is made aware of "possibilities" that are not really open to him, and all his striving is $h^abhel\ h^abhalîm$.

The way to this viewpoint was prepared in Israel by the book of Job, the framework of which depicts just such a test in complete disregard for the well-being of the servant who for the moment becomes a target for divine arrows. What is at stake in the poetry, however, is the vital issue of God's freedom over against the principle of retribution. While there is provided no solution to the problem of theodicy, at least the freedom of God is proclaimed powerfully. Even the divine speeches of sublime irrelevance may be expressive of God's freedom; so free is he that he does not feel compelled to answer Job's Promethean challenge. Rather God permits nature itself to speak in his behalf.[64] The frequent claim of Job that "God must" is totally ignored; no principle is allowed to rob God of his freedom to act. The result, as Job finally realized, is that man is completely at the mercy of God, and his only alternative is to put his hand to his mouth and repent in dust and ashes. But at least there is hope that the prior relationship will now be restored, and that the last word is not of mortal man cowering before his Maker in terror.

For Qoheleth there can be no talk about a vital prayer relationship with God.[65] On the contrary, the idea of the fear of God has reverted to the numinous of by-gone eras. For the other sages the fear of the Lord is the beginning of wisdom; it is the Israelite equivalent of our term "religion". For Qoheleth it signifies cold terror; the fear of the Lord means that one is in mortal danger when dealing with God, who interferes in human affairs only at the point of judgment. Such a sense of the word is evident in 3:14; 5:7(6); and 8:13, perhaps elsewhere. Thus "only fear of the invisible God remains, and every feeling of relationship and of trust in his character known to the devout is missing."[66] A great gulf separates man from God; "the knowledge of this distance is the key to the understanding of the book of Qoheleth."[67] Ancient Israel, too, had recognized a gulf between man and God, but had believed that the distance was spanned by a Lord who was active in the lives of his people. "Bei K. dagegen bleibt nur Furcht vor der Unbegreiflichkeit Gottes übrig und es fehlt jedes Gefühl der Verbundenheit und des Vetrauens";[68] this fear arises from the sense of "littleness and unworthiness over against the overpowering, invisible and holy, before whom one must quake and tremble."[69]

Now it is possible for the fear of God to provide the basis for a vital relationship with God and to form the foundation for ethical conduct. Can that be the case with Qoheleth? Unfortunately the answer is negative; nowhere does Qoheleth suggest that *yir'ath 'aelohîm* had a positive aspect. On the contrary, the fear of God does not control his life in any significant manner; it does, however, temper his conduct to a degree. Inasmuch as one cannot perceive the absolute difference between good and evil, it is dangerous to choose one life style to the exclusion of another. This is the source of the moderate "hedonism", which seeks to encompass the best of everything, that is, to embrace the totality (*hakkol*).

VI.

The secret with which God has endowed man in such a way as to render it useless save as a sting makes it impossible for mortal man to comprehend the entirety. From A to Z (birth to death), that is forbidden him (*mero'sh ve'adh sôph*). Still it is clear to him that *in its time* everything is beautiful, and that includes all polarities. Since all knowledge is partial, there can be no absolutes, no certainties. This also goes for traditional virtues; they have lost their power to compel and to sustain faith. All that remains is a cautious open-armed attempt to enjoy one's lot without grudging the whole, which is in God's hands.

Qoheleth has even coined a stylistic device to express his desire to hold in creative tension each half of a polarity. This device is comparable to our "both . . . and". Twice in 3:11 this so-called "Zwaraber-Aussage"[70] manifests itself. Both the *gam* and the *mibbeli* are devices that break the sentence; the author wishes to say that apparent contradictions are true. In most instances the positive assertion represents traditional wisdom, whereas the correction of the statement arises from Qoheleth's experience. In this manner Qoheleth remains true to the dialogical character of wisdom, for he refuses to accept something if it does not accord with his own experience.

The content of Qoheleth's thought is also ambiguous. In the interest of totality he combines an openness to the world and conservatism, faith and scepticism, denial of new ideas and receptivity to various streams of thought.[71] But his openness is different from that of the Israelite sage who felt remarkably at home in the world, and whose openness was to the benevolent God to whom the battle belonged (Prov. 21:31). Rather his is a willingness to listen to the unheard of, or the seldom voiced, viewpoints within Israel and from afar. On the other hand, he remains conservative, completely unwilling to take the step of nihilism to which his logic impels him. His retention of Yahwistic faith, while certainly on the outer fringe, is a remarkable inconsequence;[72] perhaps W. Zimmerli is right that the Old Testament religious man may rebel, may indeed rear himself up against suffering and injustice throughout the world, but it does not occur to him to deny his God.[73]

The faith that Qoheleth voices is a strange blend of caution and extreme rebellion. It has been said that wisdom literature has less as its intention the creating of luck than the avoidance of misfortune, hence that "in erster Linie will sie Vorsicht sein".[74] In this regard Qoheleth certainly advises against any action that would bring misfortune down upon one's head, and even concedes that the light is sweet. On the other hand, his teaching borders on heresy. While he may advise against following Job in struggling with one who is stronger than the challenger, at the same time he swims alone against the powerful stream of the whole "wisdom establishment". In so doing he calls the sages back to the limits of their knowledge, and thus remains true to ancient Yahwism—and ancient wisdom.[75] The nearly flippant "Who knows?" stands as a strong reminder of God's freedom and man's creatureliness, warns against any and all systems that seek to explain the whole of reality, and forces man to accept life as it is granted him without anxious thoughts about the future.

This grasping after comprehensiveness has led J. G. Herder to see in Qoheleth a Faust-like conflict between two souls;[76] perhaps the analogy from H. Hesse's *Steppenwolf* would be better, for the idea of a thousand souls within the breast more accurately portrays the desire for *hakkol* so important to Qoheleth. In this respect alone Sir. was an excellent disciple of Qoheleth,[77] for the principle of comprehensiveness plays a dominant role in his thought. Even the fundamental polarity, life and death, so significant to Qoheleth, has left an indelible mark upon Sir.'s thought, both in his frequent struggles with those who deny the concept of retribution and in his almost matter-of-fact observation that the ancient sentence is written, "You must die" (14:17; cf. 8:7; 38:22). Qoheleth, too, was sadly aware of that sentence, for the spectre of death looms large over all he writes (some have said, "the smell of the tomb!"). Inasmuch as no one has any word about when and how death takes him, man and beast are alike, and non-existence preferable to life in certain cases, since there are relative grades of life. Here alone do we hear a sage conclude, "So I hated life" (2:17a). The reason for this startling observation, it would appear, one can discover in Eccl. 3:11. "He has made everything beautiful in its time; also he has put eternity into man's mind, yet so that he cannot find out what God has done from the beginning to the end."

Before attempting to draw this discussion to a close, a few words about 3:12-15 are necessary, inasmuch as they draw the practical consequences of divine secrecy and provide further reflection upon the work of God. Since the mystery of life is hidden, man should enjoy life as much as possible, but (*gam* is adversative here as in 5:18[19]) ever mindful that even the "bit of healthy animal life which comes with the years of vigor"[78] is a gift of God. Just as in Gen. 1:7 there is a note of gloom in the background arising from the fact that man's breath is a gift and can be withdrawn at any moment, so here the negative aspect must not be overlooked. Again Qoheleth returns to the crucial term, this time clearly in a temporal sense; what God does endures forever (*lᵉʻôlam*), and *nothing can alter it* (cf. Sir. 18:6). Here Qoheleth uses an ancient formula[79] known to us from Egypt as well as Dt. 4:2; 13:1(12:32); and Jer. 26:2. As a final comment about divine determinism Qoheleth varies the disciplinary theory of suffering to suggest that the permanence of divine activity has as its purpose the instilling of fear in human beings. The monotony of such determinism strikes Qoheleth as ludicrous; this must be the explanation for the strange metaphor of God searching in circles (*vᵉha'ᵃᵉlohim yᵉbhaggesh 'eth-nirdaph*) for what he has already seen once (cf. Sir. 39:17).

VII.

There is a sense in which every generation is in conflict with the understanding of reality as proclaimed by a previous age; wisdom literature welcomed such validation or disconfirmation of its claims inasmuch as it refused to incapsulate the quintessence of moral conduct as the answer to every situation. This refusal bore witness to the sage's humility, for only God could speak the last word. The danger of the resulting moral relativism is illustrated by Qoheleth, who has lost the optimism of by-gone ages and whose view of man's incapacity is truly revolutionary. For him cruel reality has shattered the moral universe, leaving chaos. Unlike Job who waged a gigantic Jacob-like struggle for God's blessing, Qoheleth was so impressed with the inability of man to discover the true nature of reality that he shrugged his shoulders and became a lonely man, no longer in dialogue with the world.[80] Unable to draw strength and courage from a vital relationship with God, who seems not to have been a "You" to him, Qoheleth can only say: "whether it is love or hate man does not know" (9:1). Here stands secular man;[81] one is tempted also to say, "Here one confronts gallows humor".[82]

We hear Qoheleth admonish us to enjoy youth *for* we grow old; to enjoy toil *yet* it is sorry business; to enjoy the *woman* whom we love *but* there is not one in a thousand(!); to eat, drink and wear festive garments *yet* sorrow, fasting and mourning are better; to pursue knowledge *but* it only increases sorrow; to embrace life, *yet* like the sword of Damocles the ancient sentence, "You must die," hangs over us. We also know that all these observations stand under the shadow of Qoheleth's plaintive cry, "So I hated life," and haunting query, "Who knows what is good for man?" (6:12). How then can one derive from such "laughter" the necessary insight to justify the term "gallows humor"? Surely it is not to be found in Qoheleth's passive ethics,[83] the strict obedience and total submission to an indifferent God devoid of compassion, forgiveness, and redemption. If contact with Transcendence is made neither in the counsel nor in the despair of Qoheleth, where does he become a "lonely man of faith"?[84] The insight of K. Miskotte is on the right track: Qoheleth's grasping of *Life* is Yahweh's way of holding his own in expectation.[85] The key word for us is "way" which we understand in the sense of *path;* hence we conclude that Qoheleth stands as a haunting reminder to all humanity, believers and unbelievers, that there is no certainty except that of the ancient decree, "You must die".[86] Reflecting upon the consequent existence *in tormentis,* we, too, sooner or later find ourselves where Qoheleth was,[87] for who can really say whether we encounter divine caprice or compassion, or indeed nothing? This much we know (Qoheleth would have said *yadha'tî*): only he who has ever recognized the claims of the eternal gospel (dread, *Angst*) upon his life is open to the possibility of a temporal gospel (forgiveness, love). But if and when we cannot affirm the latter, yes, have even shrugged our shoulders ("who knows?") and become utterly lonely, Qoheleth beckons to us and we walk together in the sweet light (11:7) of companionship (4:10) on the way toward becoming lonely men of faith[88] in a silent universe.[89]

NOTES

1. C. G. Jung, *Answer to Job,* 1969, 169.
2. E. Pfeiffer, "Die Gottesfurcht im Buche Kohelet", *Gottes Wort und Gottes Land. Festschrift für H. W. Hertzberg,* 1965, 133-158 examines the textual basis for J. Fichtner's thesis that Qoheleth uses the fear of God in its original numinous sense; Pfeiffer's essay, replete with extensive quotations of pertinent literature, appears to confirm Fichtner's observations; see *Die altorientalische Weisheit in ihrer israelitisch-jüdischen Ausprägung, BZAW,* 62, 1933, 52-53.
3. "This also is vanity and a striving after wind." The refrain appears in various forms at 1:14; 2:11, 17, 26; 4:4, 16; 6:9; with which may be compared 2:15, 19, 21, 23; 3:19; 4:8; 5:9(10); 6:2; 8:10, 14; 11:7.
4. "Das Spruchgefüge ist eine Einheit, wie es auch einem Skopus hat, den von der Zeit als *Kairós* und *aion*"—K. Galling, *Der Prediger, HAT,* 1940, 59. G. von Rad, *Weisheit in Israel,* 1970, 293, thinks there is an inner unity of the entire book, one that is not of linear thought development but the unity of style, topic and theme.
5. H. Gese, "Die Krisis der Weisheit bei Koheleth", *SPOA,* 1963, 148.
6. Literally, "God is seeking the circle of things gone by." Does it mean that he has no interest in human affairs, R. Gordis, *Koheleth, the Man and His World,* 1951, 234? The verse in Qoheleth may be a gloss from 1:9 or 3:14, meaning "Er verwirklicht, was verwirklicht werden muss"—Galling, *Der Prediger,* 63.
7. J. Pedersen, "Scepticisme israélite", *RHPR,* 10 (1930), 352; P. Boccaccio, "I termini contrari come espressioni della totalità in ebraico", *Bibl,* 33 (1952), 173-190. However, the reduplication of *'eth* constitutes a problem for this view, as Galling, "Die Rätsel der Zeit im Urteil Kohelets (Koh. 3:1-15)", *ZThK,* 58, 1961), 5-6, has recognized.
8. R. Kroeber, *Der Prediger,* 1963, 37, counts 29 rhetorical questions, not one of which is a real question.
9. K. Galling, "Stand und Aufgabe der Kohelet-Forschung", *ThR,* 6 (1934), 369. Indicators of broken sentences are: v^egam (2:14; 3:13; 7:6), *gam zeh* (2:24), *ûbh^{e}khen* (8:10), *kî gam-yôdhe'a 'ānî* (8:12), and v^e (9:18).
10. Pedersen, "Scepticisme israélite", 341. W. Zimmerli, *Der Prediger,* ATD, 1962, thinks of incipient rebellion in three places (1:13; 3:10; 6:10). See the commentary on these verses.
11. Kroeber, *Der Prediger,* 30-42 (especially 37-42) perceives that the broken sentence is more than a pedagogical method, inasmuch as it denotes the inner breach of wisdom. Therefore he writes: "Die Widersprüche Qoheleths sind nicht Zeichen gedanklicher Unklarheit, sondern als Spiegelbilder der Wirklichkeit das Merkmal seiner realistischen Lebensbeziehung", p. 37. Kroeber understands the question as a form of statement, and calls attention to other stylistic devices of Qoheleth: sectional indicators (*rā'îthî, yadha'ti, v^{e}shabhti '^{a}ni va'er'eh, ûphantithi 'ani lir^e'ôth*), preference for participles, absence of vav consecutive, and so forth.
12. This applies to all attempts to explain the structure in terms of logical sequence: H. L. Ginsberg, "The Structure and Contents of the Book of Koheleth", *SVT,* 3 (1955), 138-149; and redaction, as well as structural analysis or new criticism: A. Wright, "The Riddle of the Sphinx: The Structure of the Book of Qoheleth", *CBQ,* XXX (1968), 313-334.
13. Galling, "Das Rätsel der Zeit im Urteil Kohelets (Koh. 3:1-15)", 2, thinks of four sections, vv. 1-8, 9-11, 12-13, 14-15.
14. Birth-death-war-peace (3:2a and 3:8b).

15. The meaning of 3:5a is disputed. On the basis of 1 Kgs. 3:25 and Isa. 5:2a, it has been argued that the allusions are to heaping up rocks during war to make a field uncultivable and to clearing away stones so as to plant something. But the contrasts so understood are not easily related. The Midrash Qoheleth Rabba interpreted the verse as a veiled reference to sexuality, hence in synonymous parallelism with 5:2b. This view rests on a pun between 'ᵃbhānîm and banîm, and necessitates an emendation. Neither the popular saying in Jer. 2:27 ("You are my father" (to a tree); "You have given me birth" (to a stone)) nor the statement by John the Baptist that God is able to raise up children of Abraham from these stones (Mt. 3:9) supports such an interpretation. It may be noted, however, that Ovid knew a tradition according to which the two survivors in the Mesopotamian flood narrative engendered offspring by throwing stones over their shoulders (see W. G. Lambert, *Babylonian Wisdom Literature*, 1960, 93). A third possibility has been suggested by Galling, who takes as his point of departure the insight of O. Eissfeldt ("Der Beutel der Lebendigen", *BSAW* (Phil. hist. Klasse, Bd. 105), (1960) that Yahweh was thought of as keeping a record of the devout in a bag. Since small stones in a bag have been found at Nuzi, constituting the means by which a shepherd kept an accurate account of his sheep and goats, Galling argues that the metaphor is an illusion to profits and losses, hence the business of buying and selling ("Das Rätsel der Zeit im Urteil Kohelets (Koh. 3:1-15)", 10-12). We follow Galling, although with reservation.

16. See G. von Rad, "Hiob 38 und die altägyptische Weisheit", *SVT*, 3 (1955), 293-301.

17. H. Richter, "Die Naturweisheit des Alten Testaments in Buche Hiob", *ZAW*, 70 (1958), 1-20.

18. R. N. Whybray, *The Succession Narrative* (*SBT*, 1968), 72-76. For a discussion of the literary genres in wisdom literature, see the author's contribution to *The Old Testament and Form Criticism*, ed. J. H. Hayes, 1974.

19. See the author's *Prophetic Conflict. BZAW*, 124, 1971, 116-123 (" 'esâ and dabar: The Problem of Authority/Certitude in Wisdom and Prophetic Literature").

20. H. W. Hertzberg, *Der Prediger. KAT*, 1963, 230, uses this phrase with reference to the mood of Gen. 1-4 which Qoheleth has in mind.

21. H. Gese, "Die Krisis der Weisheit bei Koheleth", 139-151.

22. This quotation is taken from Kroeber, *Der Prediger*, 31, who is citing H. Graetz, *Kohelet oder der Salomonische Prediger*, 1871, 3: The interpretation of Qoheleth in 2,000 years "ist ein förmlicher exegetischer Walpurgisnachts-Traum".

23. P. Humbert, "Emploi et portée du verbe bara' (créer) dans l'Ancien Testament", *ThZ*, 3 (1947), 402.

24. Galling, "Das Rätsel der Zeit im Urteil Kohelets (Koh. 3:1-15)", 1, writes that Qoheleth is the first in the Old Testament to discover the historicity of man as *in tormentis* and to treat it thematically, thus constituting a "crisis of enlightenment in Israel". Galling denies that 3:11 refers to the creation of the world (p. 2), taking it as an allusion to a favorable moment for action that brings it to culmination.

25. The root *ntn* occurs throughout the book of Qoheleth; it emphasizes the fact that salvation is no longer automatic, the result of standing in *tsᵉdhaqah*. "Für ihn muss das Heil ein direkt an den Menschen gerichtetes Geschenk Gottes sein"—Gese, "Die Krisis der Weisheit bei Koheleth", 151.

26. 1971, 211-216 and passim.

27. This theme is developed in "midrash form" by the author of Wisd.

28. W. Zimmerli, "Ort und Grenze der Weisheit im Rahmen der alttestamentlichen Theologie", *SPOA*, 121-136 (especially 135-136); C. Westermann, "Weisheit im

Sprichwort", *Schalom: Studien zur Glaube und Geschichte Israels. A. Jepsen Festschrift,* 1971, 82-83.

29. See the author's discussion of these similarities in "The Influence of the Wise upon Amos", *ZAW,* 79 (1967), 49-50.

30. J. Marböck, *Weisheit im Wandel,* 1971, 154-160, recognizes the great significance of Sir.'s discussion of the physician. See also von Rad, *Weisheit in Israel,* 325-329, for the impact of the collapse of the belief that sickness was indicative of rebellion against the Creator.

31. So Zimmerli, "Ort und Grenze der Weisheit im Rahmen der alttestamentlichen Theologie", 129-134. Westermann, "Weisheit im Sprichwort", 73-85 (especially 75-78), argues that *Mahnspruch* is secondary to *Aussagespruch,* indeed that the earliest proverbs had no need of imperatives and admonitions, since "to know was to act". The last observation is open to serious question: knowledge did not necessarily compel action, as the numerous disputations within the Old Testament and ancient Near Eastern literature prove.

32. See von Rad, *Weisheit in Israel,* 337-363 and H. J. Hermisson, "Weisheit und Geschichte", *Probleme biblischer Theologie. Festschrift G. von Rad,* ed. H. W. Wolff, 1971, 136-154. The latter article is a good example of the kind of reasoning the author criticized in "Method in Determining Wisdom Influence upon 'Historical' Literature", *JBL,* 88 (1969), 129-142. The mere labeling of opposing views does not render one's own position more cogent; the example from I Kgs. 13, which Hermisson criticizes as "superficial" (p. 148), was chosen precisely to *demonstrate* the superficiality of many claims of wisdom influence upon "historical" literature, and was written "tongue-in-cheek". Perhaps the warning was not entirely without fruit, for Hermisson frequently feels the necessity to add disclaimers (pp. 140, 141, 143, n. 11, 147-48, 151, 153, n. 21). Certainly one would agree with him that wisdom is not the only supposition of the succession narrative (p. 148). It is difficult for the present author to imagine Israelite culture as one in which only *one segment* (the wise) recognized and discussed: (1) the ill consequences of pride and value of humility, (2) the importance of the appropriate word for a given occasion, (3) the act-consequence schema, (4) the psychology of man (old age), and (5) great *individuals* (the king! and his family) through whom the deity worked to accomplish his purpose.

33. H. H. Schmid, *Gerechtigkeit als Weltordnung,* 1968, and *Wesen und Geschichte der Weisheit. BZAW,* 101, 1966.

34. Above all, J. C. Rylaarsdam, *Revelation in Jewish Wisdom Literature,* 1946.

35. For opposing views see H. D. Preuss, "Erwägungen zum theologischen Ort alttestamentlicher Weisheitsliteratur", *EvTh,* 30 (1970), 396-406 and von Rad, *Weisheit in Israel,* 102-131.

36. von Rad, *Weisheit in Israel,* 226, 300, contrasts the Israelite idea of Wisdom who "addresses man" and the Egyptian concept of Maat.

37. This number is taken from von Rad, *Weisheit in Israel,* 322.

38. D. G. Wildeboer, *Der Prediger. KHCAT,* 1898, 131.

39. Gordis, *Koheleth, the Man and His World,* passim, suggests another alternative, namely the use of quotations.

40. H. H. Schmid, *Wesen und Geschichte der Weisheit,* 190.

41. *Ibid.,* 33-36, 85-140.

42. Such an anthropocentric emphasis is central to the vastly important article by Zimmerli entitled "Zur Struktur der alttestamentlichen Weisheit", *ZAW,* 51 (1933), 177-204.

43. Preuss, "Erwägungen zum theologischen Ort alttestamentlicher Weisheitsliteratur", 397-98.
44. K. Koch, ed., *Um das Prinzip der Vergeltung in Religion und Recht des Alten Testament. Wege der Forschung,* 125, 1972. von Rad, *Weisheit in Israel,* 385, writes that it is more appropriate to speak of a dogmatic preoccupation of interpreters! One can only respond that the texts justify such preoccupation.
45. This point has been emphasized by the author in "Popular Questioning of the Justice of God in Ancient Israel", *ZAW,* 82 (1970), 382-384, and by von Rad, *Weisheit in Israel,* 252-253.
46. Preuss, "Erwägungen zum theologischen Ort alttestamentlicher Weisheitsliteratur", 398.
47. Gese, *Lehre und Wirklichkeit in der Alten Weisheit,* 1958, 45-50, and von Rad, *Weisheit in Israel,* 131-148.
48. For additional discussion see the author's "Popular Questioning of the Justice of God in Ancient Israel", 380-395.
49. von Rad, *Weisheit in Israel,* 188.
50. Fichtner, *Die altorientalische Weisheit in ihrer israelitisch-jüdischen Ausprägung,* 106-117.
51. See Fichtner's summary, *ibid.,* 110. The proverbs that demand love of one's enemy (Prov. 20:22; 24:17-18, 29; 25:21-22) may throw light on the problem under discussion. If God did not forgive even his devotees, how could he demand forgiveness of them, or at the very least, compassion? For extra-Israelite parallels see Merikare 112, 119; Anii 300; Amen-em-ope 22:1-8; and Babyl. Prov. 21-26.
52. von Rad, *Weisheit in Israel,* 389.
53. For a summary of current research see F. Ellermeier, *Qohelet,* 1967, 309-322 and O. Loretz, *Qohelet und der Alte Orient,* 1964, 281-285.
54. F. Delitzsch. The quotation is taken from Ellermeier, *Qohelet,* 311.
55. Zimmerli, *Der Prediger,* 172, writes that Qoheleth cannot accept the exaltation of man in Gen. 1:26 and Ps. 8, so he substitutes ha'olam. Wildeboer, *Der Prediger,* 133, also relates Gen. 1:26 to Eccl. 3:10, remarking that the influence of childhood education is manifest.
56. Gordis, *Koheleth, the Man and His World,* 231, and Kroeber, *Der Prediger,* 85, 116.
57. Loretz, *Qohelet und der Alte Orient,* 284-285.
58. M. Dahood, "Canaanite-Phoenician Influence in Qoheleth", *Bibl,* 33 (1952), 206 (darkness, ignorance, noting Ugaritic *glm*).
59. "Das Rätsel der Zeit im Urteil Kohelets (Koh. 3:1-15)", 4-5.
60. Zimmerli, *Der Prediger,* 174.
61. Lambert, *Babylonian Wisdom Literature,* 1.
62. For criticism of this view, see the author's essay, "Method in Determining Wisdom Influence upon 'Historical' Literature", 135-137.
63. Kroeber, *Der Prediger,* 135.
64. von Rad, *Weisheit in Israel,* 291, quoting K. Barth.
65. Hertzberg, *Der Prediger,* 226.
66. J. Hempel, *Gott und Mensch im Alten Testament. BWANT,* 38, 1936, 25.
67. Hertzberg, *Der Prediger,* 108.
68. Hempel, *Gott und Mensch im Alten Testament,* 25.
69. *Ibid.,* 4.
70. Zimmerli, *Der Prediger,* 220.
71. Kroeber, *Der Prediger,* 6.

72. von Rad, *Theologie des Alten Testament,* 1 (1957), 457.
73. *Die Weisheit des Predigers Salomo,* 1936, 29.
74. Kroeber, *Der Prediger,* 12.
75. Gese, "Die Krisis der Weisheit bei Koheleth", 139-151, especially 150-151.
76. See Kroeber, *Der Prediger,* 31. He refers to Herder, *Briefe, das Studium der Theologie betreffend,* ed. J. G. Müller, 1808, 135ff. Qoheleth's fondness for looking at both sides of an issue has been discussed recently by Ernest Horton, Jr., "Koheleth's Concept of Opposites", *Numen,* 19 (1972), 1-21. Horton isolates four principles employed by Qoheleth in dealing with opposites: (1) preference, (2) both-and, (3) cancellation, and (4) neither-nor. Unlike the Taoists who look for hidden meanings and attempt to connect opposites, Qoheleth is said to be content with mere description of polarities; he also differs from Taoists, according to Horton, in his preference for everyday concretizations over abstractions (p. 10), in his positive attitude to sex over against the Taoist's complementary view of the male-female polarities (p. 12), and in his negative assessment of man's ability to change things as opposed to the Taoist's optimism (pp. 12-13). Horton also notes the vast differences between Aristotle and Qoheleth, concluding that the latter is like Semitic literature in hedonism, but unlike it in the concept of opposites (pp. 15-19).
77. A discussion of the principle of comprehensiveness can be found in Marböck, *Weisheit im Wandel,* 152-154.
78. G. A. Barton, *Ecclesiastes. ICC,* 1908, 102.
79. W. Hermann, "Zu Kohelet 3, 14", *WZ Karl-Marx-Universität,* 3 (1953/54), 163-165.
80. von Rad, *Weisheit in Israel,* 300, notes the loss of dialogue with God and the world.
81. A. Lauha, "Die Krise des religiösen Glaubens bei Koheleth", *SVT,* 3 (1955), 183-191, particularly pp. 188-191.
82. Hertzberg, *Der Prediger,* 237.
83. Pedersen, "Scepticisme israélite", 322, 361, characterizes Qoheleth's ethics negatively as resignation and positively as prudence. Hertzberg, *Der Prediger,* 225, also writes of Qoheleth's ethics as passive. We follow Pedersen and Hertzberg, despite the recent defense of Qoheleth's ethics as positive, optimistic, possessing the nerve of life by G. von Rad, *Weisheit in Israel,* 298f., R. B. Y. Scott, *The Way of Wisdom,* 1971, 184-187. The following facts are decisive in our understanding of Qoheleth's ethics: (1) the positive counsel of Qoheleth hangs precariously between the initial blanket denial of any gain to pleasure and the final allegory of the approaching night that cancels all so-called profit; (2) the primary datum of religious experience, the freedom of God to draw near to man or to withdraw from him in silence, and its corollary, man's inability to hide from the Hidden God (see L. Perlitt, "Die Verborgenheit Gottes", *Probleme biblischer Theologie,* 367-382, especially pp. 367, 373) find expression in Qoheleth's lament that man cannot penetrate the darkness of mystery and his admonition that man should guard his lips lest he incur guilt, i.e., that he should fear God (see now M. Pálfy, "Allgemein-menschliche Beziehungen der Furcht im Alten Testament", *Schalom: Studien zu Glaube und Geschichte Israels,* 23-27, for a discussion of the redemptive aspect of the fear of God characteristic of the rest of the Old Testament; "So ist Gottesfurcht immer eine Gabe der Liebe Gottes: eine Heilsgabe als göttliche Forderung zum wahren Dienen Gottes, des Herrn", p. 26); (3) this Hidden God is clearly conceded to be Judge of all the living, even if one who is slack in carrying out his responsibilities, as evidenced by the sorry state of humanity (there is folly in high places, and none to comfort the

victims of such high handedness; man's lot is painful by day and vexatious by night; no women can be trusted and precious few men); (4) although this arbitrary Judge makes no effort to right the wrongs that have ripped open the social fabric and crushed the soul of a people, He is not a tyrant, for He gives to man the pleasures of youth (food, drink, sexuality), which are to be seized with gusto; (5) but even this nectar is bitter-sweet, since the Hidden God holds man accountable for these good things which last but a moment even for those fortunate enough to have sufficient power to enjoy them; and (6) Death, the final decree from the aching Void, comes to one and all, erasing in its wake the memory of former pleasures. In no case is the occasional polemical defense of divine justice, which would remove some of the sting from these conclusions, to be attributed to Qoheleth.

84. The phrase is taken from J. B. Solovietchek's article by that title in *Tradition*, 7 (1965), 5-67.

85. *When the Gods are Silent*, 1967, 453.

86. Scarcely enough time for the ink to dry passed between the composition of these words and the arrival of a telegram to Heidelberg, where I was on sabbatical, with the entirely unexpected news of Phil's death. Three years of working beside him have deepened the friendship of student days and enlarged its scope to dimensions other than the purely scholarly one. His death, then, is a great personal loss; it has been a privilege to know him, one for which I am truly thankful.

87. This alone provides an adequate explanation for the strange power of Qoheleth to attract believers and humanists and to evoke vastly different responses even among the former. To illustrate, Qoheleth has been called (1) the most shocking messianic prophecy in the Old Testament, Hertzberg, *Der Prediger,* 238; (2) the sage who taught Israel the proper fear of God and thus called her back to genuine monistic Yahwism, Gese, "Die Krisis der Weisheit bei Kohelet", 150-151; (3) the secular compromiser as opposed to Job, the *homo religiosus,* Lauha, "Die Krise des religiösen Glaubens bei Koheleth", 188-191; and (4) the crown of faith, Miskotte, *When the Gods are Silent,* 450.

88. Does Galling envision an openness to divine encounter when he asks if Qoheleth alludes to Job's silence, *which is an act of faith,* "Das Rätsel der Zeit im Urteil Kohelets (Koh. 3:1-15)", 15? We refer to something entirely different from traditional faith; rather it is a life under divine silence and indifference, but in faithful comradeship.

89. The poignant cry of Job in McLeish's *J.B.* that God "does not love. He is." would have been understood by Qoheleth. Would he also have comprehended Sarah's response: "But we do. That's the wonder."?

ASPECTS OF THE IMAGERY OF WORLD DOMINION AND WORLD STATE IN THE OLD TESTAMENT

Herbert G. May

Emeritus Professor,
Vanderbilt Divinity School
and Oberlin College

It is an honor to prepare an essay on behalf of my long-time fellow-member on the RSV Bible Committee, my frequent companion at national and international professional societies, and my colleague on the faculty at Vanderbilt Divinity School where I witnessed his remarkable qualities as a teacher. His death is a deeply felt personal loss.

The editors requested that I devote these pages to some aspects of particularity and universalism in the Old Testament. They may have recalled two related studies in *Translating and Understanding the Old Testament*,[1] a volume to which Phil himself contributed.[2] They are: "The Literary Category of the Book of Jonah," by Millar Burrows, and "Nationalism-Universalism and Internationalism in Ancient Israel," by Harry M. Orlinsky.[3] This study is a critique of neither, but a supplementary investigation of aspects of imagery and themes associated with world dominion and world state ideologies in the Old Testament.

The concept of world dominion in the Old Testament is related to the nation, its king, and its God, and may appear in both eschatological and noneschatological contexts. Its imagery may have symbolic, mythopoeic, and poetic aspects. The address to the contemporary king, claiming for him dominion to the ends of the earth, that all nations may serve and fall down before him and that he may live as long as the sun and moon (e.g., Pss. 72; 89) are hardly expressions of expected realities.[4] Interpretation of concepts of world dominion is complicated by the variety of views which Israel had of itself as a nation or people, such as that reflected in the Sinai covenant and the confederation of tribes on the one hand, and that represented by the royal Zion ideologies which accompanied the establishment of the monarchy and the building of the temple on the other.[5] Compare also the conception of Israel in the so-called theocratic and messianic eschatologies of the exilic and post-exilic periods, or in the P code and the Chronicler, or among the Hellenists and Hasidim of the later period. As G. W. Anderson points out, the student of the history of religion in ancient Israel cannot disregard what Israel was historically and empirically and the nature of Israel's self understanding.[6]

The terms "nationalism" and "universalism" do not represent necessarily mutually exclusive concepts. Professor Sandmel observes that before the exile a dominant motif was that God was bound up with the land, and that with the exile the relationship became more distinctly Deity and people, and outsiders could be received into the entity of God's elect people, and that yet there arose at this same time the view of an even more glorious return or second exodus of the exiled special people to their special homeland.[7] Here theological universalism and a form of nationalism appear together. The theological universalism of Second Isaiah is expressed in the confession of monotheism by the whole Gentile world ("every tongue" and "every knee"—Isa. 45:22-25), and yet we are informed that no more shall the uncircumcized and unclean enter the restored city of Jerusalem (52:1; cf. 52:11). Sandmel comments that the sentiment in 52:1 is not so pronounced as to be a counterbalance to the vision of streams of Gentiles coming to Jerusalem. A number of recent studies have had special interest in investigating nationalistic aspects of Second Isaiah's thought.[8]

We may initially profitably view our subject of the imagery of world dominion and world state from the perspective of the book of Jonah. The author and his hero take it for granted that the world is the dominion and creation of Yahweh. Jonah describes himself as a Hebrew that fears the God of heaven who made the sea and dry land. The author's purpose goes beyond this. It is to teach that the whole world, including Gentile peoples, symbolized by the people of Nineveh, even little children—and animals—are the object of God's compassion. Millar Burrows properly highlights Abraham Heschel's phrases, "the contingency of anger" and "the primacy of compassion", a compassion which has no geographical or national limitations.[9] Like the book of Ruth, but less directly, the book of Jonah is in part a protest against the particularistic views of the priestly establishment in power at the time of the author and illustrated in the books of Nehemiah and Ezra in the matter of mixed marriages, as Harry Orlinsky has shown.[10] There are obviously no specific references to mixed marriages in Jonah, and no indication, as there is in

Ruth, of Gentiles joining the people of Israel ("Your people shall be my people" in Ruth 1:16; cf. Isa. 56:6-8). Nor is there a monotheistic confession as in Isa. 45:22-25.[11] The book of Jonah takes for granted also the possibility of the worship of Yahweh by Gentiles. The sailors who cried in distress each to his god, after the storm feared Yahweh and made sacrifices and vows. We are not told where this took place.[12] The people of Nineveh feared God, and the king proclaimed a fast and prayed to God.[13]

Significantly, Nineveh is not condemned for its national crimes, such as its treatment of neighboring countries (contrast Am. 1 and 2; Nah. 2:12 [13]; 3:4,19b). Each one (*'īsh*) is exhorted to turn from his evil ways and the violence in his hands. The guilt of the city is due to the wickedness of its inhabitants rather than national behavior.[14] The author has Sodom and Gomorrah in mind, the cities which were "overthrown," for the same word (*hpk*) is used of these two cities in Gen. 19:21, 25, 29; Dt. 29:22 (23); Lam. 4:6; and Jer. 20:16. In Jer. 20:16 Sodom and Gomorrah are designated as "the cities which the Lord overthrew without mercy," a startling contrast with Jonah 4:11. There is in Jonah, in contrast with Nahum, no allusion to destruction at the hands of an enemy. See also the oracle against Assyria in Zeph. 2:13-15, where there is no compassion, and everyone who passes by hisses and shakes his fist.

These viewpoints in Jonah contrast with those expressed in the collections of oracles against the foreign nations, such as Isa. 13:1-23:18; Jer. 46:1-51:64; Ezk. 25:1-32:31 (see also Zeph. 2:1-15). As in Nahum's oracle, there is no suggestion that the gentile nations will relent and so escape destruction. The nations are hardly the object of the expression of divine compassion. The compassion of Yahweh for the infants of Nineveh seems to be in deliberate contrast with the oracle against Babylon in Isa. 13:16 from the exilic period: "Their infants will be dashed in pieces before their eyes" (see also Isa. 14:21 or the vengeful cry against Babylon in Ps. 137:8, 9). Nahum had reckoned it as Yahweh's judgment on Nineveh that "her little ones will be dashed in pieces at the head of every street" (3:10; see also Jer. 50:45; 51:20-23).[15]

A. Feuillet has suggested that the main object of the book of Jonah is to answer the question why the oracles against the heathen have not been fulfilled; the oracles are always conditional, even though they have been pronounced by God in an absolute manner and as unconditional (contrast Dt. 18:21-22; Jer. 28:5-9). The book of Jonah may well teach that even the most categorical of divine threats achieve their purpose when there is no longer need of their being fulfilled, although this is hardly the viewpoint of their authors.[16]

The author of Jonah may also be protesting against the particularity represented in the oracles against the foreign nations as they had become a part of the eschatology of the times of Jonah. They contain recognizable eschatologically oriented exilic and postexilic editing and additions; e.g., Isa. 13:1-22; 14:1-23; etc.; Jer. 46:25-28; 49:7-27; etc.[17] This is evident also in the context given to the oracles against the foreign nations in Jer. 46-51. In the LXX these oracles are placed after 25:13a, and they are followed by 25:15-38. The latter text was composed to form either the introduction or the conclusion of this collection of oracles,[18] and it places these oracles in a setting of "all the kingdoms of the world which are on the face of the earth," to whom disaster will come, for Yahweh is "summoning a sword against all the inhabitants of the earth," and Yahweh will enter into judgment "with all flesh." Compare the setting of Zephaniah's oracles against the nations (see 2:9-11; 3:8-10), and the often noted eschatological scheme of the positioning of the oracles against the nations in Ezekiel: (1) judgment against Judah and Jerusalem (chs. 1-24), (2) oracles against the nations (chs. 25-32), oracles of promise and restoration (chs. 33-48). A similar three-stage eschatological scheme has been suggested within Isaiah (chs. 1-12, 13-23, 34-35) and in the LXX of Jeremiah (1:1-25:14; 25:15-38; chs. 46-51).[19] An eschatological literary format may be involved in the seven oracles against Pharaoh and Egypt in Ezk. 29:1-32:32, and in the oracles against seven nations in Jer. 46:1-49:33, presented thus to be deliberately reminiscent of "the seven nations greater and mightier than yourselves: to be destroyed by Israel upon entrance to the promised land (Dt. 7:1), and therefore involving the eschatological theme of the Second Exodus.[20]

It is no accident that the oracles against the nations in Isaiah are followed by the "Isaiah Apocalypse" (chs. 24-27), which begins, "Behold Yahweh will lay waste the earth and make it desolate," preceded by the picture of the restoration of Tyre after seventy years and her merchandise dedicated to Yahweh and the priests (cf. Isa. 60:6-14, etc.). The oracles against the nations in Isaiah are associated with the general last great tumult of the nations in terms of the waters of chaos imagery (Isa. 7:12-14). The present writer has discussed in some detail this aspect of Old Testament symbolism, although not specifically as related to the oracles against the pagan nations or the concept of world dominion.[21] The downfall of the nations is followed by their subjection.[22]

With this in mind we may turn more directly to the imagery of the world dominion of Yahweh and the world state[23] in which the eschatological defeat and subjection of the nations is but one theme. Themes from many sources went into its formation.[24] Among them are the primordial conflict between chaos and cosmos, God as creator of heaven and earth, his enthronement and kingship, the celebration of the coronation of the king (David), the unconditional covenant with the house of David, the defeat and subjection of the nations, the holy mountain and the sacred city of Zion, etc.

There were also geographical, historical, and sociological factors in the development of the concept of the world dominion of Israel, and a discussion of these would perhaps be more directly pertinent to the theme of this volume. It has been suggested that salvation for Israel should be understood politically on the model of what David had accomplished, and the David celebrated in the royal cult was the David of the Israelite empire. The ideal limits of the Promised Land, from the River Euphrates to the Western Sea (see Dt. 11:24), etc., became a part of the imagery of world dominion. The political role of Persia in Palestine had influence particularly on temple-centered, theocratic eschatological viewpoints of the postexilic period—and of Second Isaiah.[25]

Among the more immediate influences in Israel's view of Yahweh as creator and king with a world-wide dominion was that of Canaan. El-Elyon, the God of Melchizedek, who in his name honored deity as King, was "creator (?) of heaven and earth" (Gen. 14:19), in whom the attributes of kingship and creation were probably combined, as at Ugarit.[26] Probable Canaanite sources of the imagery of the kingship of Yahweh are generally recognized.[27] At Ugarit, Baal is praised as "our king" and "Lord (*ba'al*) of Earth." After Baal had smitten Sea and River (a creation motif), he took his "eternal kingdom" (mlk 'lmk), his dominion "for generation after generation."[28] Baal's enthronement on his sacred mountain after his victory over Sea and River, as he sits on the sea, enthroned above the flood, is described in a recently published text. It is translated by Loren Fisher:

> Baal returns because of his throne to (his) mountain,
> Hadd, the Shepherd, because of the Flood to the midst of his mountain,
> (yea), the god of Sapan to the (midst of) the mountain of his victory.

It is because of his victory over Yamm (Sea) that Baal can return as creator king to his mountain. The Flood (*mdb*), the primordial waters, as the place of the enthronement of the deity recalls Pss. 29:10 and 104:3 and also Job 36:30b, where in a storm-god context, Marvin Pope would emend the text to read:

> "The roots of the sea are his throne."[29]

The imagery is apparent also in Ps. 89:6-19(5-18), which pictures the enthronement of Yahweh in the heavenly council, in the assembly of the holy ones, his rule over the raging of the sea, the crushing of the sea dragon Rahab, the defeat of God's enemies, and the creation of the heavens and earth, all frequently associated imagery, and it is natural that in this context the Holy One of Israel would be called "our King."[30] So also in Ps. 74, "God, my King" (vs. 12) is associated with the dividing of the sea, the crushing of the heads of Leviathan, the creation of the luminaries, the fixing of the bounds of the earth, and the establishment of the seasons, in a context of Yahweh's and Israel's foes and the Mt. Zion sanctuary. The world dominion of Yahweh gives the psalmist confidence. The Song of the Sea (Ex. 15) with its imagery of the wind of God and Yahweh's control of the sea (floods, deeps, waters) expectedly climaxes in Yahweh's mountain sanctuary where he will reign as king forever.[31] See also Isa. 51:9-16 for similar associated motifs. There is a mythopoeic identification of the primordial battle and the defeat of the enemies, in association with these other elements of the imagery.

In the royal psalms celebrating the coronation of the king appear themes which became characteristic of messianic (royal) eschatology and apocalypticism and were associated with the concept of world dominion of Israel. It is in part because of this that such psalms have often been regarded as messianic and eschatological, and an eschatological or at least proto-eschatological connotation is often difficult to deny.[32] Allowing for a mythopoeic view of kingship, as certainly one must for many aspects of Hebrew religious thought, a non-eschatological interpretation is plausible. A similar problem exists in the interpretation of certain prophetic oracles: Are Isa. 9:2-7 (1-6) and 11:1-9 truly eschatological, or were they composed to celebrate the accession of a contemporary king, such as Jehoahaz, Ahaz, or Hezekiah?[33] Any comments here will be limited largely to Pss. 2, 72, and 89, and to aspects of them relating to the preceding discussion.

Ps. 2 depicts a revolt of "nations and peoples," "the kings of the earth," "the rulers of the earth" against the king newly anointed on Yahweh's holy hill, Zion. A decree of the enthroned Yahweh has made the king his son, and contains the promise to make "the nations" his heritage, "the ends of the earth" his possession (see Dt. 7:1; 11:24, 25, for comparison and contrast). The king will defeat and subject the nations, breaking them with an iron rod and like a potter's vessel. Even if the psalmist had in mind rebellion of local

(Canaanite) kings, his imagery is that of a world-wide revolt against a world power. It is the gathering of the nations, as truly as in the eschatological scene in Joel 4:19-21 (3:9-21); etc., of which it is a prototype. The allusion is not to any specific historical situation, for the psalm belongs to a repetitive cultic occasion.[34] The kings and nations in royal psalms of this genre are something more than stock literary figures, and the address to the king more than borrowed court style.[35] The royal imagery reflects the nature of kingship in its relation to the cosmic scheme of things, and the conflict between the king or God and the opposing nations and kings is elemental, a manifestation of the primordial struggle between cosmos and chaos. The foes of the king are the enemy of God. In this kind of context the king's sonship of God and the world dominion of both are understandable.[36] The psalm closes with a warning to the pagan kings to fear God and be obeisant and with a blessing on those who trust God. The latter are the people of God, set over against the nations and peoples (cf. Ps. 72:9-11).

The consistent cosmic reference in the imagery of the psalm is reflected not only in the representation of Yahweh as King enthroned in the heavens, but also in the imagery of his royal son enthroned on Zion, Yahweh's "holy hill." Zion as Yahweh's "holy hill" is something more than a geographical entity. It is a theological reality, "the joy of the whole earth," "beautiful in elevation," and identified with the mythological Mt. Zaphon, presumably at the navel of the earth and reaching to the zenith, the cosmic mountain as depicted in Ps. 48:3 (2).[37]

Like Ps. 89, Ps. 72 discloses what is both a prophetic and a cultic concern for the character of the king's rule; the king's justice should be that of Yahweh (vss. 1-4; 12-14; cf. Ps. 101; Jer. 22:15-17).[38] In language which is not so much hyperbole as it is imagery expressing the mystique of the status of the king and of the kingship, blessings are invoked that the king may live as long as the sun and moon; cf. Pss. 21:5 (4); 61-7, 8 (6, 7); Ezk. 37:24, 25.[39] Only in an eschatological context could this possibly be taken literally as a reference to the eternal life of the king; mythopoeically it discloses something about the cosmic significance of the king and his relationship to the dynasty.

Consonant with this is the king's world-wide dominion (Ps. 72:8, 9). It is prayed that he may have dominion "from sea to sea, and from the River to the ends of the earth," and that from the ends of the earth (from Tarshish, the islands, Sheba, and Seba) tribute will be brought by kings, who will fall in obeisance at his feet (see Ps. 2:10; Zec. 9:10; Isa. 45:14; 49:23; 60:5-7, 14). However one may take "from sea to sea and from river to the ends of the earth" here in Ps. 72:8 or in Zec. 9:10, the context favors the general sense of a worldwide rule. It could at the same time be that the poet is not giving specific geographical limits so much as expressing extension.[40] Vv. 9-11 seem to imply subjection through conquest, and the theme may appear in the overtones of v. 17b. It is not coincidental that the king's dominion from sea to sea and from the river to the ends of the earth in v. 8 is coupled with the abject obeisance and implied defeat of the king's enemies in vv. 9-11.

This is not to ignore the larger context of the king who brings peace, deliverance, and justice to his people. But there are sentiments here which the author of the book of Jonah would not have found congenial. The psalmist's concern is not for the nations; it is for "thy people" and "thy poor," and it is their blood which is precious in his sight. The land in v. 14 is Israel. The translation of v. 17b must be consonant with this,[41] and may be taken as an illustration of the homage which the nations bring to the king, as they call the king blessed.[42]

We have called attention to Ugaritic analogies to certain themes in Ps. 89 integral to the theme of the world rule of Yahweh (p. 64 above). Yahweh enthroned in the assembly of El (cf. Ps. 82:1), as El in the assembly of the holy ones, the sons of the gods, is described as he who rules the primordial sea, who has crushed Rahab, who has scattered his enemies; these three are one activity, mythopoeically identified as victory in cosmic conflict, themes of the world rule of Yahweh. Yahweh is the Father of the king, and makes the king his first-born, his son (cf. Ps. 2), so the king also has a world dominion,[43] the enemies Yahweh crushes are the foes of the king. As Yahweh is incomparable with the members of the heavenly court, so David (= the king) is the highest (Elyon) of the kings of the earth. As the position of Yahweh in the heavenly courts symbolizes his dominion, so does the position of David (= the king) among the kings of the earth signify his dominion. This is probably also the import of v. 26 (25); Yahweh will set the hand of the king on the sea and his right hand on the rivers. Dahood suggests that these are mythical terms expressing world-wide dominion[44] (cf. Ps. 72:8-11). V. 26 (25) is reminiscent of Hab. 3:8, describing Yahweh's conflict with his (= Israel's) enemies, "the nations."

> Was thy wrath against the rivers, O LORD?
> Was thy anger against the rivers,
> or thy indignation against the sea,
> When thou didst ride upon thy horses,
> upon thy chariot of victory ($y^e sh\hat{u}'ah$)?
> So teach us to number our days
> that we may get a heart of wisdom.

So in Ps. 89:27 (26) Yahweh is the Rock of the king's victory ($y^e sh\hat{u}'ah$). Vv. 22-28 (21-27) may be related by a single theme, the victory of the king over his enemies. The victory over the king's enemies is his manifestation as the highest of the kings of the earth, and a part of his role as firstborn of Yahweh. The defeat and subjugation of the enemies of the king are to be interpreted here as in Pss. 2; 72; and 110, where world dominion is involved. This is something more than what is involved in 2 Sam. 7:11, where the cosmic cultic element is absent.

A careful comparison of Isa. 44:24-45:17 with the themes in the above-mentioned psalms discloses interesting and not coincidental analogies. Taking them in the order in which they occur in Isaiah, there are the following analogous themes: Yahweh as creator (44:24; 45:7, 11, 12); the status and the anointment of the king = Cyrus: (44:28; 45:1); Yahweh's defeat of the enemies before the king

(45:1-3; cf. 41:2-3); the obeisance of the nations (45:14);[45] the acknowledgment of Israel's God (45:14-15, 22-23; cf. also 45:8 with Pss. 72:3; 89:15 [14]; etc.). The recognition of the God of Israel is world-wide, from east to west (45:6), to the ends of the earth (45:22; 52:10; cf. 42:10-12).[46]

The analogies between Second Isaiah and Ps. 89 are striking, despite the differences which make Second Isaiah the shining light of Old Testament prophecy. The incomparable enthroned Yahweh in the heavenly courts in Ps. 89:6-9 (5-8) provides the background from which come the voices in Isa. 40, as many have recognized.[47] In 44:24 Yahweh sits enthroned above the firmament, and is extolled as creator. For the psalmist none among the heavenly beings, the sons of God, can be compared with him, and for the prophet the comparison is with an idol.[48] To both the Lord is the Holy One of Israel and King (Ps. 89:19 [18]; Isa. 41:14, 16, 20, 21; 43:15; 44:6; etc.). He controls the seas (Ps. 89:10 [9]; Isa. 50:2; 51:10, 15) and both refer to his conquest of the dragon Rahab (Ps. 89:11 [10]; Isa. 51:9).

As in Ps. 89:5, 30-38 (4, 29-37) the covenant with David and his dynasty is unalterable and unconditional, so with Second Isaiah the covenant with Israel is Davidic-like, an everlasting covenant, "a work of my faithful love for David" (Isa. 55:3; see J. L. McKenzie), and Noachic, a covenant of peace that is more sure than the mountains and hills, standing as firm as the heavens and the earth (Isa. 54:9-10; see Ps. 89:37 [36]). Like David, Israel will be a witness to the peoples, a leader and a commander for peoples, and nations that know not Israel will run to her because of her glorification by Yahweh. See also Isa. 42:6 and 49:8, where the servant Israel and the chosen one (cf. David in similar role in Ps. 89:4 [3]) is a witness given as people's covenant and nations' light. The meaning is to be deduced not only from the immediate context, but from the wider context of Second Isaiah. Baltzer properly calls attention to the absence of a *Heilszeit* ruler in Second Isaiah, and the *Demokratisierung* of the Davidic tradition, the transfer of the promise to David to the people of Israel.[49] Or as J. L. McKenzie comments, the covenant of Yahweh with David gathered into itself the covenant with Israel.[50]

Eissfeldt has demonstrated that the poems of Second Isaiah have been strongly influenced by the diction of Ps. 89, and comments that the seemingly hopeless position of Israel is resolved in a way that will bring a blessing to all the world and high recognition to Israel. The latter must not be minimized.[51]

In conclusion, one may point out that one of the fulcrums of the symbolism of Second Isaiah is the Zion imagery, reminiscent of the role of Zion in the psalms of the kingship of Yahweh and the royal psalms. In Second Isaiah there is some significance in the centering of attention on Zion rather than the "land" of Israel. It has been noted that the term *'erets* is normally used in Second Isaiah not to designate a specific geographical area of land, but in its cosmic connotation of earth as over against the heavens. So in over two score passages; e.g., 40:12, "dust of the earth"; 40:21-23, "foundations of the earth," "circle of the earth," "rulers of the earth"; 40:28; 42:10; 43:6; 45:22, "end(s) of the earth"; 44:23, "depths of the earth"; 44:24; 45:12, 18, etc. "earth" with "heavens" in creation context. The only two exceptions are 49:8, 19 and in the latter "your devastated land" refers to the territory of Zion, and the context is the repopulation and spread of the city. In Ezekiel, by contrast, *'erets* refers frequently to a geographical territory; see 6:14; 7:2, 23, 27; 8:17; 9:9; 11:15; 12:13; etc., and *'ᵃdhamah* is used thus more than two score times (7:2; 11:17; 12:19, 22, etc. [land of Israel]; 34:13, 27; 36:17, etc. [their land]). The word *'ᵃdhamah* does not occur in Second Isaiah.[52]

The centrality of the imagery of Zion in Second Isaiah may be taken as an aspect of the theocratic viewpoint of Second Isaiah.[53] Even when one might expect references to the repossession of the land in the Second Exodus, it is to Zion that the ransomed will come with singing after they have passed through the Sea (51:9-11). It is before Zion that the nations and peoples, the kings and queens, will bow down and lick the dust (49:22, 23). It is to Zion that the coming of the King is announced (40:9-11), and the new covenant with Zion will be more lasting than the mountains and hills (54:9, 10).[54] It is singular in the light of this that there is but one specific reference to the temple (44:28), and the originality of this has sometimes been questioned, although there are possible implicit references to the temple (52:11; cf. 60:7).

But this is all in keeping with the climactic theme of Second Isaiah—the whole world giving glory to Yahweh, and every knee bowing to him and acknowledging his sole Lordship and existence. This prepares the way for the universal *concern* of the Lord in the book of Jonah. The unknown author of Second Isaiah and the unknown author of the book of Jonah were each great spirits of their time. Who shall say that one is greater than the other?

NOTES

1. Edited by H. T. Frank and W. L. Reed, 1970, 80-107, 206-236.
2. "Were There an Ancient Historical Credo in Israel and an Independent Sinai Tradition?" 152-70. Indirectly related to the subject of this paper is Professor Hyatt's article, "The Sources of the Suffering Servant Idea," *JNES*, 3 (1944), 49-62.
3. See also H. M. Orlinsky, "The So-called 'Servant of the LORD' and 'Suffering Servant' in Second Isaiah," *SVT*, 14 (1967), 1-133; "The So-called Suffering Servant in Isaiah 53," in *Interpreting the Prophetic Tradition*, H. M. Orlinsky, ed., 1969, 225-274.
4. See discussion, R. E. Murphy, *A Study of Psalm 72 (71)*, 1948, 21-23, 45-98; G. W. Ahlstrom, *Psalm 89, Eine Liturgie aus dem Ritual des leidenden Königs*, 1959, 128-31. As has also been noted, it would not be out of harmony with Hebrew poetic imagery to visualize the relatively tiny kingdom of David in such universalistic terms: J. L. McKenzie, "Royal Messianism," *CBQ*, 19 (1957), 32.
5. F. C. Prussner, "The Covenant of David and the Problem of Unity in Old Testament Theology," in *Transitions in Biblical Scholarship;* J. C. Rylaarsdam, ed., 1968, 17-42; S. Sandmel, *The Several Israels*, 1971, 1-112; G. von Rad, *Old Testament Theology I*, tr. by D. M. C. Stalker, 1962, 3-92; G. W. Anderson, "Israel: Amphictyony: 'AM; KAHAL; 'EDAH," in *Translating and Understanding* . . . , 135-51; H. J. Kraus, *Worship in Israel*, tr. by G. Buswell, 1965, 179-236; Morton Smith, *Palestinian Parties that Shaped the Old Testament*, 1971.
6. *Translating and Understanding.* . . . , 135-136.
7. S. Sandmel, *Several Israels*, 17-18. It has been suggested that while the reference in 52:1 may be to ritual uncleanness, it is more likely to those who would come as attackers; J. L. McKenzie, *Second Isaiah*, AB, 20 (1968), 127.
8. See the studies of Second Isaiah by P. A. H. de Boer, *Second Isaiah's Message, OTS*, 11 (1956); N. H. Snaith, *A Study of the Teachings of Second Isaiah and Its Consequences*, *SVT*, 14 (1967), 135-264; especially 154-165; H. M. Orlinsky, "The So-called. . . . ," and "Nationalism-Universalism. . . . ,"; compare R. Martin-Achard, *A Light to the Nations*, tr. by J. P. Smith, 1962, 11-31. See also H. M. Orlinsky, "Nationalism-Universalism in the Book of Jeremiah," in *Understanding the Sacred Text: Essays in Honor of Morton S. Enslin on the Hebrew Bible and Christian Beginnings*, J. Reumann, ed., 1972, 61-83.
9. "The Literary Category. . . . ," 99. Abraham J. Heschel, *The Prophets*, 1962, 285-87. R. Martin-Achard, *A Light* . . . , 52.
10. *Nationalism-Universalism.* . . . , 228-31. Contrast G. von Rad, *Old Testament Theology*, II, 1965, 291-2, who is, however, correct in suggesting there is no wish here to see covenant and election severed from restriction to Israel.
11. The passage climaxes in v. 25, which as often elsewhere associates the glorification and restoration of Israel with the confession or recognition of Yahweh as the only God. See 45:14-17, and compare 45:17 with 45:25. See also 41:2-4; 49:6-7. See the discussion of Sheldon Blank, "Studies in Deutero-Isaiah," *HUCA*, 15 (1940), 12-18.
12. The only explicit allusion to the Jerusalem temple is in the intrusive poem in ch. 2.
13. See Zeph. 2:11, where "all the lands of the nations" will prostrate themselves before Yahweh "each in his own place"; cf. *JB*, "each on its own soil."
14. H. M. Orlinsky notes the terms evil (*ra'ah*) and violence (*ḥamas*) are those of the generation before the flood. For possible reflection from Jeremiah, see A. Feuillet, "Les sources du Livre de Jonas," *RB*, 54 (1947), 169-176.

15. The author of the book of Jonah transcends such cries of vengeance as occur in Jer. 50:15, 27-28; 51:35-40, and displays sensitivity to one of the universal horrors of war.

16. A. Feuillet, "Le sens du Livre de Jonas," *RB*, 54 (1947), 343-46; see also R. Martin-Achard, *A Light*. . . . , 51.

17. R. B. Y. Scott, *The Book of Isaiah, Chapters 1-39, IB*, 5 (1956), 160; J. P. Hyatt, *The Book of Zephaniah, IB*, 5 (1956), 790, 1104 ff.; "Zephaniah," *Peake's Commentary on the Bible*, M. Black and H. H. Rowley, eds., 1962, 640-42; H. G. May, *The Book of Ezekiel, IB*, 6 (1956), 200 ff., "The Biographer of Jeremiah," *JBR*, 10 (1942), 195-201.

18. Hyatt, *The Book of Jeremiah*, 1001-2. Cf. J. Bright, *Jeremiah, AB*, 21 (1965), 162-65, who believes Jer. 25:13b, 15-38 was attached "fairly early" as an appendix to the collection of Jeremiah's oracles against the nations, with vv. 15-38 composed of a prose passage (vv. 15-29) and two poetic pieces (vv. 30-31, 32-33). For other suggested arrangements, see G. Fohrer, *Introduction to the Old Testament*, tr. by D. E. Green, 1968, 397.

19. W. Zimmerli, *Ezekiel, BK*, 13, 1969, 579; Fohrer, *Introduction* . . . . , 414, 371-372, 400-401; S. Mowinckel, *He That Cometh*, tr. by G. W. Anderson, 1954, 146, 154.

20. W. Zimmerli, "Le nouvel 'exode' dans le message des deux grands prophètes d'exile," in *maqqel shaqedh, La branche d'amandier, Hommage à Wilhelm Vischer*, 1960, 216-227, mentioned in Zimmerli, *Ezekiel*, 580. Compare the seven oracles in Am. 1:3-2:16, thought by some to be secondarily expanded into seven, and prefixed by the later added "keynote" of 1:2, taken from Joel 4:16 (3:16), which might remind the reader of the eschatological context of the Joel passage.

21. H. G. May, "Cosmological Reference in the Qumran Doctrine of the Two Spirits and in Old Testament Imagery," *JBL*, 82 (1963), 9-14.

22. See Zeph. 2:10-11, a possible prose insertion in which Yahweh will destroy all the gods of the earth, and nations will bow down to him. See also Zeph. 3:8-10, where after the judgment on the nations, each will call on the name of Yahweh with a purified speech. See Hyatt, *Zephaniah*, 642, where this is interpreted as the conversation of the nations and compared with Isa. 19:18. Compare Zeph. 3:10 with Isa. 45:14 and Zec. 14:16-19. See N. K. Gottwald, *All the Kingdoms of the Earth*, 1964, 221-22.

23. Heinrich Gross, *Weltherrschaft als religiöse Idee im Alten Testament. BBB*, 6 (1953), 1-57; H. Schmöckel, *Jahwe und die Fremdvolker, BSTR*, 1934; Norman K. Gottwald, *All The Kingdoms*. . . . R. Martin-Achard, *A Light to* . . . ; S. Sandmel, *The Several Israels;* S. Blank, "Studies in Post-Exilic Judaism," *HUCA*, 11 (1936), 159-192; R. E. Murphy, *A Study of Psalm 72 (71)*, 1948.

24. Gross, *Weltherrschaft*. . . . , 20-65, 63-97.

25. Gottwald, *All the Kingdoms*. . . . , 332-341, 378-386. The P Source in the Pentateuch, which may come from the Persian period, reflects or is consonant with the ideal of a non-royal temple-centered theocratic eschatology. From the later period, in keeping with the non-messianic eschatology of the book of Daniel, the author of Dan. 7 presents the one like a son of man, the symbol of the saints of the Most High who will receive the Kingdom, as the one whom all dominions will serve and obey. The saints of the Most High are the people of God, and one is reminded of Second Isaiah's reinterpretation of the covenant with David, applying David's role to Israel. See C. H. W. Brekelmans, "The Saints of the Most High and Their Kingdom," *OTS*, 14 (1965), 305-329. Contrast M. Noth, "Die Heiligen des Höchstens," in *Gesammelte Studien zum Alten Testament*, 1957, 274-90.

26. N. C. Habel, "Yahweh, Maker of Heaven and Earth; A Study in Tradition Criticism," *JBL*, 91 (1972), 321-337, believes the title of El Elyon as creator or procreator of heaven and earth in Gen. 14 belongs to an archaic El tradition, and is a forerunner or prototype of Yahweh, maker of heaven and earth (Pss. 115:15; 134:3; 121:2; 124:8), an important reinterpretation of which occurs in Second Isaiah (45:18; cf. 44:24; 51:13). Whether El was an earth deity and Elyon a god of the heavens and the two are combined in El Elyon is uncertain. See M. H. Pope, *El in the Ugaritic Texts, SVT*, 2 (1955), 25-32, 49-54. Although Yahweh as creator of heaven and earth does not occur in the J narrative in Gen. 2:4b-25, the idea may be much earlier. Gen. 1:1-2:4b is based on an earlier undatable story of creation, H. G. May, "The Creation of Light in Genesis 1:1-3," *JBL*, 58 (1939), 203-11. See the discussion of G. Fohrer, *History of Israelite Religion*, tr. by D. E. Green, 1972, 179-82; and von Rad, *Old Testament Theology* I, 136 ff. Kingship and creation are often associated in the Psalms: e.g., 24; 89; 93; 95; 96; and 115 (see Ex. 19:5).

27. J. Gray, "The Hebrew Conception of the Kingship of God," *VT*, 6 (1956), 268-85; "The Kingship of Yahweh in the Prophets and the Psalms," *VT*, 11 (1961), 1-29; H. J. Kraus, *Worship.* . . . , 203-5; G. Fohrer, *History of.* . . . , 166-67.

28. Gordon, Anat #68 I:9, 10.

29. L. R. Fisher and F. Brent Knitson, "An Enthronement Ritual at Ugarit," *JNES*, 27 (1969), 156-67; L. R. Fisher, "Creation at Ugarit and in the Old Testament," *VT*, 15 (1965), 313-324 (conflict, kingship, order, temple building as a pattern of creation of the Baal types); P. C. Craigie, "Psalm XXIX in the Hebrew Poetic Tradition," *VT*, 22 (1972), 143-151; M. Pope, "Job," *AB* 15 (1965), 232, 237; see *Ugaritica V* (1968), 551 ff. Text RS 24.245.

30. J. B. Dumortier, "Un rituel d'entronization: le PS. LXXXIX 2-38," *VT*, 22 (1972), 176-96.

31. See P. C. Craigie, "Psalm XXIX. . . . ," 144; F. M. Cross, "The Song of the Sea and Canaanite Myth," *JThC*, 5 (1968), 1 ff.; J. M. Ward, "The Literary Form and Liturgical Background of Psalm LXXXIX," *VT*, 11 (1961), 321-39.

32. See discussion by R. E. Murphy, *A Study of Psalm 72 (71)*, 99-131; J. L. McKenzie suggests the king incorporates in himself the kingdom of Israel and its hope for the future in which the kingship of Yahweh will become universally effective; the historical king is the living pledge of the final realization of the kingdom of God, "Royal Messianism," *CBQ*, 19 (1957), 33-36; 51, 52. See also J. Fitzmyer, "Now this Melchizedek. . . . (Heb. 7:1)," *CBQ*, 25 (1963), 306-9.

33. R. B. Y. Scott, *Isaiah, chapters 1-39*, IB, 5 (1956), 230-234, 247-251. The context of Isa. 11:1-9 (vv. 10-16) is the world dominion of the Davidic Messiah.

34. A. R. Johnson, *Sacral Kingship in Ancient Israel*, 1955, 118-20; A. Weiser, *The Psalms*, tr. by H. Hartwell, 1962, 109-112; S. Mowinckel, *The Psalms in Israel's Worship*, tr. by D. R. Ap-Thomas, 1967, 55, 67; H. J. Kraus, *Psalmen I*, 1961, 14-16, "Die Weltherrschaft des Königs von Jerusalem." Cf. K. H. Bernhardt, *Das Problem der altorientalischen Königsideologie im Alten Testament*, SVT, VIII (1961), 246 ff., 263 ff.

35. J. Gray, "Sacral Kingship at Ugarit," *Ugaritica VI* (1969), 292-5; G. Fohrer, *History of.* . . . , 148. Compare also king Keret as the "son of El," which Gray plausibly interprets as singling out the king as the representative of the sacred community, illuminating the royal ideology of the Davidic dynasty.

36. H. G. May, "Some Cosmic Implications of *Mayim Rabbim*," *JBL*, 74 (1955), 11-12; B. W. Anderson, *Creation versus Chaos*, 1967, 132-34. Also, as G. W. Anderson notes, the heirs of the covenant promises made to David cannot be thought of

as petty rulers of an insignificant state: *Peake's Commentary*, 412-13. See the excellent discussion of "The David-Zion Tradition" by C. Loew in *Myth, Sacred History, and Philosophy*, 1967, 117-132. Not at all irrelevant to the concept of world dominion of both God and king is the cosmic symbolism of the temple, evident in the Bronze Sea and the twelve bulls beneath it, in the orientation of the temple, in the altar of burnt offering, in the two pillars before the temple, etc. See H. G. May, "Prolegomenon," in *Studies in Biblical and Semitic Symbolism* by M. H. Farbridge, *New Matter*, (1970), xxiv, xxxvii, and bibliography, liv, lvii.

37. M. Dahood, *Psalms I*, 289-90. S. Terrien, "The Omphalos Myth and Hebrew Religion," *VT*, 20 (1970), 315-38. Compare Ps. 110 where in the first four verses the motifs of Zion, the sacred mountain, the enthroned God, the enthroned King, the battle against the nations, the defeat and submission of the nations, and possibly a suggestion of the irrevocable covenant promise ("priest forever") are intertwined. See J. Fitzmyer, *CBQ*, 25 (1963), 308, 317.

38. There is an association of justice and kingship in the Ugaritic texts: see M. Dahood, *Psalms II*, 180; Gray, "Sacral Kingship at Ugarit," 298.

39. See the discussion in R. Murphy, *A Study of Psalm 72 (71)*, 21, 22, 79-98, concluding that the psalm is directly or literally messianic in the strict sense, concerned with the ideal king of the coming kingdom.

40. R. Murphy, *A Study of Psalm 72 (71)*, 27, 65-68.

41. V. 17b ("May men bless themselves by him, all nations call him blessed") is reminiscent of the promise to Abraham (Gen. 12:1-3), a promise to be fulfilled after the conquest of the Amorites (Gen. 15:16). Compare the role of the king's enemies in Pss. 2; 10; and in Ps. 89:24 (23), in the light of which 89:25 (24) is perhaps to be interpreted, and which is relevant to the meaning of 89:26 (25); cf. vv. 51, 52 (50, 51).

42. The hymn of praise thus begun fittingly ends in v. 19 (18) with the exaltation of Yahweh as Shield and King:
    Verily Yahweh is our Shield,
    the Holy One of Israel is our King!
See M. Dahood, *Psalms II*, 317.

43. Ahlström, *Psalm 89*, 112, 113. Cf. Ps. 82, where the kings of the nations are symbolized as gods in the council of El among whom God takes his place (is enthroned) and upon whom he passes judgment. See C. R. North, "The Religious Aspects of Hebrew Kingship," *ZAW*, 59 (1932), 26.

44. M. Dahood, *Psalms II*, 317; A. R. Johnson, *Sacral Kingship....*, 108 ff.

45. See also Isa. 60, 61: foreigners will build the walls of Jerusalem; the wealth of the nations will come to Israel, brought by men with their kings led in procession; aliens shall be Israel's plowmen and vinedressers; the nations that will not serve Israel will perish; Israel will be called the priests and ministers of our God, eating and glorying in the wealth of the nations; and Israel will suck the milk of nations and the breasts of kings. This breathes a somewhat different spirit from Second Isaiah. Although the theocratic overtones are prominent and the rebuilt temple and its offerings a concern of the author, ch. 60 at least presents a more politically oriented picture. See J. L. McKenzie, *Second Isaiah*, 177-78. G. Fohrer (*Introduction*, 386-87) says of chs. 60-62 that the author shows himself to be a descendant of earlier optimistic and nationalistic prophecy.

46. The eschatological defeat of the pagan nations by Israel would be somewhat incongruous in Second Isaiah. Isa. 41:15, 16 is probably not to be interpreted in terms of Israel's conquest of the nations, in contrast with Zec. 9:13-15, and is to be

taken symbolically (cf. Isa. 40:3-5). See J. L. McKenzie, *Second Isaiah*, p. 31; H. M. Orlinsky, *The So-called Servant. . . .* , pp. 34, 43-44. "And your descendants shall possess the nations" in 54:3b refers to dominion and not conquest, and the context shows the promise to the patriarchs was in the prophet's mind, for the nations to be dispossessed and possessed are in the Promised Land; 54:3b is parallel to 54:3c, where the "desolate cities" are the cities of Judah, and the address is to Zion. There are here overtones of world dominion, but not world conquest. See G. W. H. Jones, "Abraham and Cyrus," *VT,* 22 (1972), for the suggestion of Abrahamic (Gen. 14) typology in Isa. 41, which if true, would involve the implication that the conquests of Cyrus were on behalf of Israel, or in the place of Israel's conquests of the nations.

47. H. Wheeler Robinson, "The Council of Yahweh," *JTS,* 45 (1945), 151-57; J. Muilenburg, *Isaiah Chapters 40-66, IB,* 5 (1956), 40.

48. See Ps. 96:3-6; Yahweh is above both gods and idols.

49. D. Baltzer, *Ezechiel und Deuterojesaja,* 1971, 141-49.

50. *Second Isaiah,* 142-44.

51. O. Eissfeldt, "The Promise of Grace to David in Isaiah 55:1-5," in *Israel's Prophetic Heritage,* B. W. Anderson and W. Harrelson, eds., 1962, 196-207.

52. D. Baltzer, *Ezechiel und Deuterojesaja,* 41-48, "Die Bedeutung Zions und Jerusalems in der Heilserwartung Deuterojesajas." Cf. W. Zimmerli, *Ezechiel,* 874-75. R. de Vaux, "Jerusalem and the Prophets," *Interpreting the Prophetic Tradition,* H. M. Orlinsky, ed., 1972, 277-98.

53. E.g., 40:9; 41:27; 46:13; 49:14-26; 51:1-23; 52:1-12; 54:1-17.

54. Contrast Ezekiel: "I will bring you home into the land of Israel . . . and I will place you in your own land" (37:12, 14; see also 39:26, 28). This is not to ignore the primacy of the temple in Ezekiel.

PROBLEMS BETWEEN THE GENERATIONS IN THE OLD TESTAMENT

Hans Walter Wolff

Professor of
Old Testament at
the University of Heidelberg

Like every man and every human community, so also the university lives through and suffers through the tensions between old and young. It is good when the individual not only sees himself in contrast to representatives of another generation, but consciously reflects on the different phases of his own life. It is even better for a person when he enlivens and enriches such meditations from sources out of which not only our past originated, but also which arise in our present and future. The Old Testament scriptures are a result of this sort of meditation.

1. Let us begin with the question of the length of life expectancy in Old Testament Israel. The only source we have which gives exact and historically reliable statements concerning age covering several centuries is the court chronicles of the kings of Judah which have found their way into the Books of Kings. It is on the basis of these texts that we may study the chronology of the Davidides today with a reasonable amount of certainty that we can determine approximately the age of fourteen kings in the period 926 and 597 B.C.[2] We arrive at the following ages:

Rehoboam	56 years	Jotham	40 years
Jehoshaphat	55 years	Ahaz	35 years
Jehoram	38 years	Hezekiah	56 years
Ahaziah	21 years	Manasseh	66 years
Joash	45 years	Amon	22 years
Amaziah	38 years	Josiah	38 years
Azariah	66 years	Jehoiakim	35 years

The degree of accuracy may sometimes fluctuate one or two years. Also the statements concerning age in the period from Amaziah to Hezekiah (825-697 B.C.) in particular are doubtful. However, for our purposes the possible errors will be overlooked for the most part. It is worthy of note that the ages of these kings fluctuates between 66 and 21 and so the average age of these fourteen kings is not quite 44 years.[3] If we keep in mind that princes were given special care during infancy and early childhood, and that kings were protected in adulthood better than most of the other people, then we will have to assume that the average life expectancy of the common man was considerably lower, especially in view of the high infant mortality rate. In order to determine this, to a certain extent we may use modern statistics based on climatic and cultural conditions all the way to the life expectancy of living peoples. In the decade from 1951 to 1960 the average life expectancy was 42 years for men and 41 years for women in India, and 32 years for men and 39 years for women in Togo/Africa. The average life expectancy in ancient Israel was probably even lower than this, while it was 68 years for men and 73 years for women in 1968 in the Federal Republic of Germany.[4]

If a person survived his critical years in ancient Israel he could also live to be 70 years of age, which was the age of David according to the biblical tradition (2 Sam. 5:4), "or even by reason of strength" (*bigh^{e}bhûroth,* Luther: "at the most") 80 years of age (Ps. 90:10), as the History of David relates concerning the aged Gileadite Barzillai (2 Sam. 19:33 [32]). However, this is considered to be an extraordinarily old age, because none of the fourteen kings between Rehoboam and Jehoiakim reached the age of 70. The author of Ps. 90 sees a unique value in a person's reflecting on the limits of his life expectancy (v. 12):

> So teach us to number our days
> that we may get a heart of wisdom.

Outside the limits of historically precise comprehensible time there are other mythical standards in the Old Testament. Not only are the men before the great flood listed in Gen. 5 hundreds of years old,[5] but Dt. 34:7 states that Moses was 120 when he died. Like the patriarchs and a few other exceptions, the abundant blessings of the primeval period comply with the promised period of salvation, in which the youngest will die at the age of 100, according to Isa. 65:20.[6] At any rate, the Old Testament does not hold the view that the average life expectancy of man has been fixed irrevocably at a moderate level. Yet the contemporaries of the Old Testament writers must assume that man will live only a few decades.

2. That which the Old Testament tells us about the different periods of a man's life agrees with the idea that in Old Testament times there was a lower average life expectancy. The limitations of the length of service of the Levites at the sanctuary is very noteworthy. According to Nu. 4:3, 23 the Levite is to begin his work at the age of 30, and he must retire at the age of 50. Full maturity was necessary for the peculiar duties of this office, but also maximum energy.[7] A later revision[8] changes the age at which a Levite is to begin his work to 25, but does not raise the age of retirement fundamentally; those who are over 50 years of age are allowed to do only auxiliary work (Nu. 8:24-26). The later lowering of the age that one was to begin his Levitical tasks to 20 (1 Ch. 23:24, 27; Ezr. 3:8) was necessitated by the small number of candidates for this work in the oncoming generation. It is significant that it was considered to be impossible for a man to continue in this office in a full capacity after age 50.

In the earlier period, it was thought that full maturity for the complicated and responsible cultic service was not attained until one was 30 years of age, and yet generally speaking a person was considered to be completely responsible at the age of 30 (Nu. 14:29; 32:11), when he was obliged to enter into military service (Nu. 1:3, 18; 2 Ch. 25:5) and to be enrolled in the census (Ex. 30:14). At 60, generally speaking a person was not expected to have much strength for work (Lev. 27:7).

Lev. 27:1-8 gives us an interesting list indicating the way in which the Israelites looked on various phases of life. This passage is part of an appendix to the Holiness Code and comes from a time when people were no longer brought to the sanctuary as a gift to Yahweh, which had been the case at one time, as is indicated by the account of Samuel's dedication (1 Sam. 1:11, 24ff.). By now both the priestly tasks and the lower service had been in the hands of professional groups for a long time, and these groups were quite hesitant to admit those outside their own number into their ranks.[9] Consequently the people were told to give an amount of money equivalent to the value of a man's working ability rather than a man himself. The following price-list was drawn up for the various age groups, which gives us an indication of the value which Old Testament Jews placed on the working ability of people of different ages, and which also shows the distinction which they made between five stages of life:

Age:	Male	Female
First month of life	—	—
1 month to 5 years	5 shekels	3 shekels
5 to 20 years	20 shekels	10 shekels
20 to 60 years	50 shekels	30 shekels
Over 60	15 shekels	10 shekels

In reality, therefore, a newborn child up to one month of age was excluded from the price-list, because first of all the Jews wanted to wait a month to see how healthy the child would be. From one month to five years, the value of the child is set at 10% of the full working ability which he is expected to have later as an adult. At the age of 5 the value of the child triples or quadruples; from 5 on he is considered to be youthful and productive. A person is expected to be at his maximum capacity between the ages of 20 and 60. After 60 he declines quickly, an old man (about 35 shekels) more quickly than an old woman (about 20 shekels), who was considered to be quite useful as a grandmother in a large family. If a girl had only half the value of a boy, the old woman had ⅔ (66.6%) the value of the old man, while in the prime of life the woman had ⅗ (60%) the value of the man.

However, this list which appears at the end of the Old Testament period merely touches the surface in an investigation of the various stages of life and the evaluation of each stage in Old Testament thought as a whole.

3. Old Testament proverbs and narratives ably contrast *old and young with their respective peculiarities* in a very impressive way. In this essay we limit our study to the cases of tension between the two groups. I have selected seven striking examples.

a. After the miseries connected with the destruction of Jerusalem and the exile to Babylon, Zechariah paints the picture of a new period of peace for Jerusalem: "Thus says the Lord of hosts: Old men and old women shall again sit in the streets of Jerusalem, each with staff in hand for very age. And the streets of the city shall be full of boys and girls playing in its streets" (Zec. 8:4, 5). This contrasting scene includes everything which is necessary for a peaceful life. For the most part, the old and the young had to tolerate each other. Some can sit and rest and others can romp in the out-of-doors. Just as rest and frailty accompany old age, so playing and fulness accompany youth.

b. Prov. 20:29 contrasts youth and old age in a concise statement in an entirely different way:

> The glory of young men is their strength,
> but the beauty of old men is their gray hair.

Here the strength of youth is not contrasted with gray hair as a sign of declining energy, but as an honorable distinction for justice. However, we read in Prov. 16:31:

> A hoary head is a crown of glory;
> it is gained in a righteous life.

This brings out the confrontation between strength of the body and strength of judgment.

c. The scene from the life of the aging David in 1 Kgs. 1:1-4 reveals an entirely different side of the fulness of life: the heaviest blankets can no longer keep the aged warm in bed. Thus the council of David's servants seeks throughout the whole territory of Israel for a beautiful girl to care for the king. If this young girl could sleep in the king's arms, he would become warm. Soon they found Abishag of Shunem, who was very lovely. The solution is obviously successful, yet the narrator does not forget to emphasize: "but the king knew her not" (v. 4). Here the coolness and destitution of age comes into contact with the heat and ability of youth.

d. The narrator of 1 Kgs. 12 opens a whole package of new concepts. He sees the reason for the decay of the Davidic-Solomon empire as Rehoboam's unwise decision to reject the advice of the old men in preference for the advice of the young men. This passage presupposes that the tribes of Israel demanded that Rehoboam lighten the hard service with which Solomon had oppressed them more and more, or else they refused to support his accession to the kingship. Rehoboam retires for three days of deliberation. First he listens to the advice of the old men who had been his father's counsellors. They advise him to comply with the demands of the people. In fact, they suggest that the king should make himself a servant (*'ebhedh,* slave) of the people, and then the people would also be happy to serve him. Thus the old men have a spirit of conciliation, they reflect on the consequences of the decision which Rehoboam must make, and also obviously keep in view the best ancient Israelite traditions (God desires that Israel be free, and a king should serve this interest and not oppose it as in the final analysis Solomon had done). But Rehoboam turns to the young men for advice, i.e., to the contemporaries of the 41 year old Rehoboam (1 Kgs. 14:21). It is worthy of note that the narrator repeatedly refers to them as *yeladhîm,* "children" (1 Kgs. 12:8, 10, 14), a term by which he intends to characterize them as immature numskulls.[10] They advise the king to answer the people in this way: "My smaller thing is thicker than my father's loins. And now, whereas my father laid upon you a heavy yoke, I will add to your yoke. My father chastised you with whips, but I will chastise you with scorpions" (vv. 10b, 11). With such words, the younger generation shows implacable harshness which is expressed with strongly ostentatious boasting. But another thing should be noted. In the expression "my smaller thing is thicker than my father's loins," "the smaller thing" probably means the penis.[11] Thus here the younger generation is represented as obscene, ostentatious, and harsh in contrast to the discreet kindness of the older generation.

e. An oracle in Isaiah follows the same line of thought. Judgment threatens Jerusalem in the form of political chaos:

> And I will make boys their princes,
>> and babes shall rule over them . . .
> the youth will be insolent to the elder,
>> and the base fellow to the honorable (Isa. 3:4f.).

Arrogant disdain for age is regarded as a temptation into which the young fall quite easily.

f. Therefore the wisdom of Qoheleth advises a young person to realize at an early age that old age lies in his own future, and thus to recognize and to use the abilities of youth as gifts loaned to him by the creator. The infirmities of old age in the uniquely beautiful allegory in Eccl. 12:1-7 are listed for this purpose. (Perhaps this allegory was originally composed as a riddle).[12] While this poem was intended for the young, it appeals to every old person:

> [1]Remember also your Creator in the days of your youth,
>> before the evil days come,
> and the years draw nigh, when you will say,
>> "I have no pleasure in them."
> [2]Before the sun is darkened, and the light,
>> the moon and the stars,
> and the clouds return after the rain.[13]
> [3]In the day when the keepers of the house tremble,[14]
>> and the strong men are bent,[15]
> and the grinders cease because they are few,[16]
>> and those that look through the windows are dimmed.[17]
> [4]And the doors on the street are shut;[18]
>> when the sound of the grinder is low,[19]
> The voice of the bird 'is silent',[20]
>> and all songs are muffled.[21]
> [5]They are afraid also of what is high,
>> and terrors are in the way.
> Then the almond tree blossoms,[22]
>> the grasshopper drags itself along,[23]
>> and the caper bursts asunder.[24]
> Yea, man goes into his hidden house,[25]
>> and the mourners go about the streets.

> ⁶—Before the silver cord "breaks," [26]
> and the golden bowl "bursts," [27]
> or the pitcher is broken at the fountain,
> or the wheel broken at the cistern,
> ⁷and the dust "returns" [28] to the earth as it was,
> and the breath returns to God who gave it.

Thus step by step the youth is made aware of the fact that with advancing age the energies, the intellectual faculties, and all the manifestations of life become weaker and weaker. They are to be used well as gifts of the creator as long as they are vigorous.

g. Finally the picture of an individual may cast light on a particular characteristic. As a man gets older, in due course he can, and indeed should, be aware of his limitations. In the History of David, the aged 80 years old Barzillai appears in 2 Sam. 19:32-38 (31-37). He was a wealthy man and had given David provisions when he fled from Absalom. Now David wants to take him with him to Jerusalem and to care for him at the royal court as an expression of his gratitude for his help. But Barzillai answers the king:

> How many years have I still to live, that I should go up with the king to Jerusalem? I am this day eighty years old; can I discern what is pleasant and what is not? Can your servant taste what he eats or what he drinks? Can I still listen to the voice of singing men and singing women? Why then should your servant be an added burden to my lord the king? . . . Pray let your servant return, that I may die in my own city, near the grave of my father and my mother. (vv. 35ff. [34ff.]).

Then he suggests that a younger person go with the king in his place. So one who sees that his abilities to enjoy the pleasures of life, and especially who sees clearly that he can become a burden to another person, returns to his home. Unassumingly and content with his own lot in life, he turns things over to the oncoming generation.

However, this small collection of pictures of the old and the young should make us realize that by and large the Old Testament simply describes the very ambivalent character of both of these stages of life. The young are characterized by strength and beauty, but also by thoughtlessness and harshness; and the old are characterized by wisdom and kindness, but also by weakness and infirmity. And generally speaking it is almost impossible to know which of the two ages is to be preferred. There are numerous situations which occasion strife between the generations, and numerous opportunities for them to help one another. Who would change curse into blessing and blessing into curse here? (Blessing into curse: the one who regards himself as the final court of justice whether he be old or young; curse into blessing: the one who determines a man's gifts and limitations, and who gives him the knowledge and the desire to see his opportunities and possibilities to promote goodwill between the generations). Who would predict the sum and the differences?

4. As we attempt to deal with such questions, first we must allude to a phenomenon which is important to the Old Testament witness in different contexts. No biological rule is without exception. Yahweh, the God of Israel, who is responsible for the norms characteristic of the different age groups, also makes known by his own free will those individuals who are exempted from these norms. As a result, the relationship between the generations is even more complicated and diversified.

It is well known that in important portions of the biblical tradition coming from different periods, Yahweh chooses a young person and neglects or even rejects an old person. E.g., the older brothers of the young man Joseph treated him with animosity, but in the end he saved their lives and also the life of his aged father Jacob. Yahweh calls the young man Samuel and tells him to announce the coming judgment to the old priest Eli. Not only does Yahweh prefer the young man David above all his older brothers, but he chooses him in place of the rejected king Saul. Again and again Yahweh calls one to serve him in a special way who thinks of himself as incompetent and whose friends and neighbors consider him to be of little worth.[29]

The young man Jeremiah hesitates to accept Yahweh's commission to the prophetic office because he is inexperienced, and thus Yahweh says:

Do not say, 'I am too young!'
But to all to whom I send you you shall go!
  and whatever I command you you shall speak! (Jer. 1:6f.).

The Wisdom Literature has its own way of dealing with this theme. In the Book of Job, the young man Elihu stands up respectfully in the midst of the older Wisdom teachers, but demands to be heard:

I am young in years,
  and you are aged;
therefore I was timid and afraid
  to declare my opinion to you.
I said, 'Let days speak,
  and many years teach wisdom.'
But it is the spirit in a man,
  the breath of the Almighty,
  that makes him understand.
It is not the old that are wise,
  nor the aged that understand what is right.
Therefore I say, 'Listen to me;
  let me also declare my opinion.' (Job 32:6-10).

Here a young man comes forward in a group of older men courteously, but also determined to speak. It is not years, but the Spirit which determines truth. But God gives the gift of the Spirit freely to whom he will. Thus suddenly one's age becomes completely insignificant in light of the question, "Who is it that has the spirit of a child?"

Just as Yahweh can use youthful inexperience for his service, so he can also restrain the laws normally governing old age. Ps. 92 extols the righteous who flourish like a palm tree and grow like a cedar in Lebanon:

They still bring forth fruit in old age,
  they are ever full of sap and green,
  to show that Yahweh is upright;
    he is my rock and there is no unrighteousness in him (vv. 15f. [14f.]).

The prototype for this is the aged Moses, whose natural force was not abated as long as he lived (according to Dt. 34:7).

But not only does the Old Testament call man's attention to the gifts of Yahweh which do not follow the normal pattern and encourage him to accept them humbly, but also in this connection emphasizes the importance of man entering into dialogue with God continually. Even in hopeful confidence there can be a reversal of natural conditions, as Deutero-Isaiah states to the exilic generation:

> Even youths shall faint and be weary,
>   and young men shall fall exhausted;
> but they who hope in Yahweh shall renew their strength,
>   they shall mount up with wings like eagles,
> they shall run and not be weary,
>   they shall walk and not faint (Isa. 40:30f.).

Thus is the real man. Just as the limitations of various ages in general are clear, the unique individual in whom the unusual is to be accomplished is not so limited. In addition, Qoheleth summarizes the possible reversal of the norm in this maxim:

> Better is a poor and wise youth
>   than an old and foolish king,
>   who will no longer take advice (Eccl. 4:13).

The real wisdom of the young or of the old consists of one's willingness to hear, especially his willingness to hear testimony given by God himself, and in the final analysis this alone proves that a person is worthy of respect. This should give rise to an entirely new freedom in which the different generations would hear each other. Obviously this is altogether or not at all.

5. Instead, the natural differences between the stages of life all too frequently grow into tensions and full-fledged disputes. The Old Testament has a penetrating, reasonable view of this situation.

Now it is worthy of note that in the final analysis the responsibility lies with the older generation, since it is certainly responsible for educating the young. Quite frequently the Old Testament speaks of the "sins of the fathers" as the sins of the children, especially from the time of Jeremiah on (Jer. 2:5; 3:25; 11:10; etc.).[30] Even before this Hosea summons the children of Israel to bring charges against their adulterous mother (2:4f. [2:2f.]). Since parents are not the highest court of justice, but are subject to the word of Yahweh like their children, it is possible that the children might be faced with the responsibility of disobeying the demands and customs of their fathers. Thus we read in Ezk. 20:18:

> I said to their children in the wilderness:
> Do not walk in the statutes of your fathers,
>> nor observe their ordinances,
>> nor defile yourselves with their idols.

The Decalogue emphasizes the effect of the sins of the fathers on all four generations which live together in the large family (Ex. 20:5f.; 34:6f.; Dt. 5:9f.). The lamentations from the exilic period sigh:

> Our fathers sinned, and we are no more;
>> and we bear their iniquities (Lam. 5:7).

A "word of cynical protest"[31] circulated among the people of the exilic period (Ezk. 18:2; Jer. 31:29):

> The fathers have eaten sour grapes,
>> and the children's teeth are set on edge.

But Ezekiel delivered a new message. He says in the name of Yahweh:

> Behold, all souls are mine; the soul of the father as well as the soul of the son is mine: the soul that sins shall die (Ezk. 18:4).

Accordingly, each generation is responsible before God for the decisions which it makes in the scope of the freedom which God has granted to it:

> The son shall not suffer for the iniquity of the father, nor the father suffer for the iniquity of the son (Ezk. 18:20).

The opportunity of a new life is open to every generation.

Thus the Old Testament also speaks of the sins of the children (cf. Ezk. 20:21; Jer. 5:7). The Book of Proverbs speaks quite clearly about this matter in the framework of the family:

> A foolish son is a grief to his father
>   and bitterness to her who bore him (Prov. 17:25).
> A fool despises his father's instruction,
>   but he who heeds admonition is prudent.
> He who ignores instruction despises himself,
>   but he who heeds admonition gains understanding (Prov. 15:5, 32).

Once the book of Deuteronomy deals with an extreme case (Dt. 21:18-21). A son is so stubborn that he will not obey his father or his mother, and in spite of repeated chastisement he will not quit his stubbornness. It is worthy of note that in such an extreme case the parents have no legal authority to do more than chastise their son. The matter must be brought before the elders of the son's own city for judgment. Both parents together must bring their complaint before the elders. The parents do not have the right to punish their son. Their distress and the distress of their son is a part of the "evil" which affects "all Israel" (v. 21). Disputes can reach such heights when parents and children go to law against each other. 1 Sam. 2:12-14 describes the ill-bred sons of the priest Eli, 1 Sam. 8:1-3 the poorly trained sons of Samuel, and 1 Kgs. 1:6, e.g., the inadequate job that David did in raising his children.

The real end of tensions between the generations belongs to the eschatological age of salvation. Mal. 3:24 (4:6) expresses the expectation that the powerful prophet Elijah will return:

> And he will turn the hearts of fathers to their children and the hearts of children to their fathers, lest I come and smite the land with a curse.

Through the presence of Christ in his word, the New Testament community is to overcome conflicts between parent and child:

> Children, obey your parents in everything, for this pleases the Lord. Fathers, do not provoke your children, lest they become discouraged (Col. 3:20f.).

This statement assumes that both parent and child have already entered into a completely renewed life growing out of gratitude for the forgiveness which they had experienced.

6. On the assumption that the old and young alike have experienced this new life, the Old Testament gives provisional criteria for a *responsible relationship,* growing out of the realization that the differences in the generations have been established by the creator not as a curse, but as a blessing, i.e., for concrete reciprocal aid.

a. The experience of the parents ought to be beneficial to the children. There are three things in particular concerning ancient Israelite child raising which should be noted. (1) Important aspects of the Old Testament message, especially in the faith traditions and worship customs, were taught as responses to the *questions of children.* E.g., when children ask at the Passover, "What do you mean by this service?", the parents are to tell them (Ex. 12:24-27; cf. Dt. 6:20-25; Josh. 4:20-24). Thus the initiative for teaching did not come from the parents. (2) By and large the form of teaching was the *narrative.* The fathers related their own experiences and the experiences of their ancestors (Pss. 44:2ff. [1ff.]; 78:3ff.; Jgs. 6:13). They were more involved with their kinsmen before Yahweh in narrating what had happened than in repeating or making demands on their children. (3) When the parents did give concrete directions to their children, they *showed them the consequences* of wrong behavior and of right behavior, as the structure of Wisdom Oracles in particular shows.[32] These three things promote unity between the generations. Likewise, the basic attitude which the fathers manifest toward the young people in the family functions as a constant refuge in which they are able to discover all that is necessary for a secure life:

> In the fear of Yahweh one has strong confidence,
> and his children will have a refuge (Prov. 14:26).

In this way the parents can reduce the danger of severing communion between the generations.

b. But the younger generation can also contribute to this. First of all, the young can recognize that the advice of their parents is based on experience and is given with the child's interest in mind (Ex. 20:12). Also, the younger generation should be big enough to see its own faults and to guard against the danger of finding aging parents peculiar or even intolerable with more or less good reason. Thus, the book of Proverbs warns against the scornful look:

> The eye that mocks a father
> and scorns to obey a mother
> will be picked out by the ravens of the valley
> and eaten by the vultures (Prov. 30:17).

The responsibility of caring for the older generation, which was immense in the ancient world, also stands behind such words. It begins with opposition to the temptation to no longer respect the possessions of one's parents:

> He who robs his father or his mother
> and says, "That is no transgression,"
> is the companion of a man who destroys (Prov. 28:24).

Widows and orphans need very special protection (Isa. 1:17; Ex. 22:21 [22]; Dt. 16:11; 27:19; Jer. 7:6; Ezk. 22:7; Zec. 7:10).

When people cease to realize that the generations must strive to help each other, the prophets see the approach of the apocalyptic age:

> The son treats the father with contempt,
> > the daughter rises up against her mother,
> > the daughter-in-law against her mother-in-law;
> > a man's enemies are the men of his own house (Mic. 7:6).

This chaotic situation seems unavoidable when men consider themselves to be the final court of justice and put themselves in God's place, instead of living according to his good word, the word of unconditional reconciliation. With the appearance of Jesus Christ in human history and the opportunity for reconciliation which this offers, each person should look upon and deal with the difference between old and young at best as a penultimate stage in the relationship between the generations.

NOTES

1. Lecture given at the banquet on the anniversary of the Heidelberg Universität-Gesellschaft November 29, 1972.
2. Following A. Jepsen, *Untersuchungen zur israelitisch-jüdischen Chronologie. BZAW*, 88 (1964).
3. Because of other presuppositions L. Köhler, *Der hebräische Mensch* (1953), 30, concluded that the average age of these kings was 47 to 48 years.
4. According to *Brockhaus Enzyklopädie*[17], XI (1970), 232.
5. Here Adam lives to be 930 years of age, Methuselah lives the longest at 969, and Enoch the youngest at 365. In an old Babylonian list of kings who lived before the flood, Alalger lives to be 72,000 years of age, and the average age is 43,000 years. Here we must think of a "mythical transcending of the institution of kingship"; the primitive kings are like the gods; cf. C. Westermann, *Genesis. BK*, I, 478f.
6. According to an Egyptian Coffin Text the ideal age is 110 years, cf. V. Wessetzki, "Alter," *Lexikon der Ägyptologie*, I, 1 (1972), 154-156 (156).
7. Cf. the public appearance of Jesus at "about 30 years" in Lk. 3:23; cf. also 23:3.
8. Cf. M. Noth, *Das vierte Buch Mose. ATD*, 7 (1966), 63.
9. Cf. K. Elliger, *Leviticus. HAT*, I/4 (1966), 386.
10. M. Noth, *Könige. BK*, IX/1 (1968), 275, reads "playmates."
11. *Ibid.*, 267.
12. Cf. G. von Rad, *Weisheit in Israel* (1970), 267; on this text cf. also the commentaries of W. Zimmerli, *ATD*, 16/1 (1962), and K. Galling, *HAT*, I/18 (²1969).
13. As in late autumn and winter in Palestine.
14. The arms.
15. The legs.
16. The teeth.
17. The eyes.
18. The ears are hard of hearing.
19. The voice.
20. Cf. Galling on this passage.
21. One loses his ability to sing.
22. The hair becomes grey.
23. It will be hard to walk, one will not be able to jump.
24. No stimulant, no aphrodisiac can help the aged any more.
25. The rock tomb.
26. Cf. K. Galling on this passage.
27. Cf. K. Galling on this passage.
28. See *Biblia Hebraica*[3].
29. Cf. J. Conrad, "Die junge Generation im Alten Testament," *AzTh*, I/42 (1970).
30. Cf. E. Jenni, "'ābh, Vater," *ThHAT*, I (1971), 1-17.
31. W. Zimmerli, *Ezechiel. BK*, XIII (1969), 402.
32. Prov. 23:21: The drunkard and the glutton will come to poverty, and drowsiness will clothe a man with rags; 11:24: One man gives freely, yet grows all the richer; another withholds what he should give, and only suffers want; 15:15: All the days of the afflicted are evil, but a cheerful heart has a continual feast.

THE WRATH OF YAHWEH AND THE STRUCTURAL UNITY OF THE DEUTERONOMISTIC HISTORY

Dennis J. McCarthy

Professor of Old Testament
at The Pontifical
Biblical Institute, Rome

The deuteronomistic history is divided into sharply marked eras. This is obvious from the content: the smooth flow of the conquest is contrasted with the troubled time of the judges, and the monarchical era is something else again. There are said to be deep divisions too: in Judges a cyclic view of history, in Kings a linear one. Then, the tone of the narrative is different in different eras: there is an optimistic note in parts of Kings which is felt to accord ill with the general tone of the history.[1] Finally, divisions are clearly marked by a formal device: speeches and historical essays are used as structural keys.[2]

Naturally, these diversities have given rise to explanations based on a diversity of sources or of redactions. Such explanations are inevitable, though it is exaggerated to insist that diverse attitudes in different sections mean completely different sources.[3] Surely they can be explained more directly as resulting from the different aspects intrinsic to the stories of different periods. The idea of successive redactions in periods of hope and despair is more attractive.[4] However, hypotheses of diverse origins are not the only possible nor necessarily the most fruitful ways to approach the problems. One can also consider the fact of the deuteronomistic history as a rhetorical whole. By this I mean a unified structure of effective verbal expression, which the history certainly is, however it came to be. Study of the relationships within that structure and of the rhetorical devices which produce them can throw light on meaning, for, of course, the essential meaning of a text grows out of its structure as a present (synchronic) whole, not out of its diachronic aspect, its history in terms of its antecedent parts and their adaptation to form the present whole. This latter aspect is a legitimate object of study—indeed is overwhelmingly the most common one in biblical studies—but it is not my concern here. This is rather the former aspect. Consideration of it can usefully look to the problems already noted. They draw attention to questions caused by apparent difficulties in over-all coherence, that is, crucial questions of meaning. However, the immediate means will be the study of some significant means of expression, namely, the mentions of the wrath of Yahweh.

The deuteronomistic history has two basic phrases to speak of this wrath. In one "the anger of Yahweh blazes" (*ḥarah 'aph yhvh b^e*) or, simply, "Yahweh is angry" (*hith'annaph yhvh*). These are not merely cognates; rhetorically they are interchangeable. Over against this stands another phrase: "one provokes Yahweh to rage" (*hikh'îs 'eth yhvh*).[5]

Each formula has its own immediate associations. The anger formula is typically the climax of a stylized description of Israel's desertion of Yahweh; for example: "And the people of Israel did what was evil in the eyes of Yahweh, and served the Baals and the Ashtaroth, ... and they forsook Yahweh, and did not serve him, and the anger of Yahweh blazed against Israel."[6] It is part of a formidable set-piece, and the solemnity fits the content, for this is an assertion that the covenant is broken in terms of what this involved in the concrete: breaking the relation with Yahweh and forming one with another. Indeed, the description often includes an explicit affirmation that the covenant has been broken.[7]

Given the weight of this, the second characteristic association with the anger formula is not surprising. It is always tied to a proclamation of a divine judgment announcing a penalty. This is impressive. The formula is part of the expression of a law; revelation of divine anger demands a penalty which effectively halts the proper (independent) history of the people until repentance occasions salvation.[8] So absolute is the necessity of this sequence that, if anger is mentioned, the deuteronomistic history must complete the sequence or the story will come to a stop.[9]

In contrast, the link between the provocation formula and an announcement of a penalty is not so close. The formula is ominous enough in its own right, and it may be coupled with an announcement of a penalty, but this is not inevitable.[10] Neither is it so closely tied to the stylized description of infidelity involving the whole nation (see above, n. 5). Rather it forms part of its own statement, weighty enough but not so formidable as the context of the anger formula. Its typical context is the notice of the transgressions of kings.[11]

We have, then, a pair of formulæ for the divine wrath, each a rather forceful figure of speech in its own right, and each given added weight by regular association with a reinforcing verbal and conceptual context. But, be it noted, the latter feature clearly makes the anger formula a more formidable rhetorical instrument. These are the kinds of elements out of which larger rhetorical structures can be built. How is this done?

One fact leaps to the eye. The formulæ occur in clusters. We have already noted this for the provocation formula. It is at home in the notices of the kings of Israel from Jeroboam I to Ahaziah, and to a less noticeable extent after Manasseh in Judah. But the same phenomenon occurs with the more emphatic anger formula. It is common in the framework of Deuteronomy.[12] Another group of texts with the formula comes at the end of Joshua and the beginning of Judges.[13] Then, after a long extent of text where anger is hardly mentioned, it finally reappears at the end of the story of the kingdoms.[14]

Thus the references to divine anger are concentrated at certain key points, among them the major transitions from one to another of the eras which characterize the deuteronomistic narrative. But "transition" and "era" have an abstract sound. In fact, they are made very concrete, for it is the passing of a man, a leader, which marks the transitions.

This occurs in Deuteronomy. Simply because they are there the mentions of Yahweh's anger are associated with Moses's last discourses. But there is more here than simple association. The wrath motif is explicitly tied to Moses's death in Dt. 31:16-19. The dying leader knows that the people will fall away from Yahweh when he is gone. In a way there is a paradox in this, for the danger is not really immediate. The penalty which makes the threat of the anger so real is the exile, so far distant in fact from this literary context.[15] All the clearer for this is the intention to link the anger with the passing of the leader which marks the transition to the conquest era.

Again, the aged Joshua's admonition to fidelity (Josh. 23:16) and the editorial description of what followed upon his death (Jgs.

2:14, 20; echoed in 3:8) connect mention of Yahweh's anger and the departure of a leader. And now the danger is immediate, not something foreseen for the distant future. This offers the opportunity for a different rhetorical effect from that achieved in different circumstances in Deuteronomy. Because the death of each judge is a new, explicit occasion for danger (Jgs. 2:19-20), the threat of divine anger hangs over the whole period. However, the concentration of explicit mention of the anger attaches it emphatically to the major transition opening the era. All transitions are said to be dangerous, and the major transition is made to appear most dangerous of all.

In view of all this emphasis on the connection between the threat of divine anger and major transitions, it is all the more striking when the next such point is reached and anger is not mentioned. The climax of the story of the introduction of the kingship, Samuel's address and dialogues in 1 Sam. 12, should, according to its parallels in Deuteronomy and Judges, be full of references to divine anger, but it is not. This is all the more notable because 1 Sam. 12 has such unpropitious immediate antecedents, connecting as it does with the condemnation of the people for deserting Yahweh to seek a king "like the gentiles." One would expect this to reinforce the tendency to associate key transitions with the anger of Yahweh. Yet the text speaks not of anger and ruin, but of renewal. In spite of an express reprobation of the self-willed demand for a king (1 Sam. 12:8-12), it turns into a reaffirmation of covenant.

Here there are three points to note. Firstly, v. 13 marks the climax of the formulation, and it reverses the history of sin. The king is no longer the sign of a great infidelity; he is Yahweh's gift.[16] Secondly, vv. 14-15 place the people (and the king) under a renewed possibility of blessing or curse, which is the equivalent of the renewal of the covenant state.[17] Thirdly, this reaffirmation is confirmed explicitly in v. 22, an allusion to the so-called *Bundesformel*.[18] Reconciliation is complete.

This major transition to the monarchical era, then, is at once similar in genre and diverse in tone and content from the parallel earlier passages. Like them it is marked by an admonitory address from the leader in the old order. But in contrast to them it avoids the rhetoric of the anger of Yahweh.

So far the use of the anger formula marches to a considerable degree with Noth's observation about structure in the deuteronomistic history and with von Rad's point about the diversity between the story of the judges and that of the kings. That is to say, the emphatic clustering of the formula serves to reinforce some of the key speeches and essays in their function of structuring the narrative. Thus it contributes to the impression of over-all unity. In addition, the breaking of the established connection between the danger of divine anger and key transitions makes one notice the transition to the monarchy. Thus it too works toward defining structure. Further, the absence of reference to anger here contributes to the notable difference in tone between the era of the judges and that of the kings. This is *what* happens, but in it all is a clue as to *why* it happens, and this is in terms of leadership.

Now, the kind of leadership involved in an era is clearly one of the factors which characterizes the era in the deuteronomistic history. A Joshua makes things different from a series of judges, and a succession of kings is something else again, but the use of the anger formula in conjunction with this points to something more than the vagaries of empirical political structures. There is a religious dimension involved. The changes of leadership, even if it is a question of transfer from a Moses to a Joshua, are occasions of danger associated with the anger of Yahweh. However, with Saul's accession this changes, and not merely at the point of accession. The story of the kingdoms is organized in terms of regular successions to power. So far it is not unlike the era of the judges and, as von Rad argues, the whole story might have been constructed in terms of ups and downs or troubles, but it is not. Not just one change but the changes in general are out from under the sign of the divine anger. No doubt this is not uninfluenced by the fact that the sources, royal annals, archives, and, especially important, king lists,[19] were already organized in an unbroken sequence. Influence from this direction may have worked on the formal factor of the sequence, but it does not account for the omission of the anger formula and announcement of troubles it brings. Rather the reverse is true, for mention of divine anger is royal style![20]

To understand what is going on, one must consider the leadership factor, for we are confronted with a change not of leaders, but of the form of leadership. The monarchy is per se an ongoing institution. The sequence of kings goes on without break. This is true even without smooth dynastic succession. A usurper of seven days, a Zimri, can keep the sequence going as well as a legitimate prince. Hence, in the deuteronomistic presentation of the monarchy the dangerous crisis represented by a change in leadership is no longer acute.

The force of this fact, sequential presentation, is enhanced by explicit reference to continuity. 1 Sam. 7:1-16 is part of the pattern of key texts which set up and explain the monarchical era.[21] This text looks directly to continuity, for it is the charter not of a king but of a royal line. Its effectiveness is reiterated even in the face of difficulties (1 Kgs. 11:13). And the same point is made for the kings of Israel in the person of Jeroboam I (1 Kgs. 11:38).[22] In this way attention is focused on the kingly line. God deals directly with it so that a gift to it affects the people, and this is another new element relating to leadership. Contrast the situation with previous leaders: the gift (the word of God, victory in war) goes to the people through them. They do not receive for themselves; they are the means through which others receive. This difference is pointed up by the way prophetic activity is represented. In Kings, prophets characteristically speak to kings. What they have to say concerns them, and especially their threats which allude to penalties affecting the royal family. Contrast Jgs. 6:7-10, where the people, their conduct and their fate, is the direct object of prophecy.

And here we can return to the wrath of God theme, for it too works to the same effect. Notice the most striking cluster of the provocation formula—half of the eighteen examples concentrated in only eight chapters—in the reports of the kings of Israel from Jeroboam I to Ahaziah. These kings provoke Yahweh, but when a penalty is mentioned it normally affects royalty itself.[23] This is the case in the series of prophetic trial speeches and fulfilment notices in I Kgs. 14:9-10; 15:3; 16:2, 13; 21:21-22. The mention of wrath and its effects thus ties in to the actions of the prophets in marking out the special role of royal leaders. In this perspective the fact that mention of wrath stops with Joram becomes meaningful. His is the first regnal notice which mitigates the condemnation of a king of Israel, and after him one never again finds the extended condemnations characteristic earlier. Neither does one find the sort of prophetic text which we have just discussed and which the history associates with the earlier reigns. Improved leadership is accompanied by diminished insistence on the danger of wrath.[24]

A further device in connection with these provocation formulae helps focus attention on the royalty and turn it away from the people. The provoking sin, the worship at Jeroboam I's shrines, is bad enough in deuteronomistic eyes. Still, it never turns into the stereotyped description of the destruction of the covenant relationship by "forsaking Yahweh and going after other gods," despite the fact that the phrase which so often triggers this description in other contexts, "do evil in the eyes of Yahweh," is always present in the regnal notices where the sin is mentioned. Given deuteronomistic writing habits, this is striking. One feels in a positive way the avoidance of the allusion to the covenant with its direct (though in this context threatening) reference to the people as such. The focus on the kings tempers the danger for the people.

But we have not yet said the last word on the function of the wrath formulae. An era ends when finally the royal leadership is hopelessly corrupted. This is the significance of the last cluster of wrath texts in the reports of the last reigns. The kings provoke Yahweh, they insistently lead the people to provoke him, and the result is the anger of Yahweh and the inevitable penalty. The combination of the two expressions emphasizes the gravity of the situation and the failure of the monarchy. The office seems to have held off divine wrath, but its ultimate failure becomes the ultimate failure of the people.

It is thus that the threats in Moses's last discourses are finally realized. Once more the theme of wrath functions structurally to round off the story, tying beginning to end. This works in several ways. There is a recurrence of atmosphere, a brooding opening and a gloomy close. There is intentional direction: the beginning looks directly to the end. And there is an echo effect: even without explicit reference back to the beginning, in fact the reader "hears" it unreflectively when the wrath theme returns.

To sum up, we find that the wrath theme works in the formation of a well-knit structure in the deuteronomistic history. In Deuteronomy it helps create a troubled atmosphere of foreboding at its beginning, and its intentional direction points to the final catastrophe. Between these limits it helps distinguish eras in the story. Before the monarchy, transitions in leadership are points of threat; afterwards, this threat is deflected and a new era is marked out. At the last, it serves to characterize the final corruption of royal leadership and the consequent final catastrophe. This is an intrinsically coherent structure. It is differentiated, not as a haphazard collection, but as a meaningful, nuanced construction. It speaks directly to our original problems. The use of the wrath formulae emphasizes leadership as a central factor. It points to a coherent explanation of the diversities that have troubled scholars. Differences in the kind of leadership are in back of the cyclic view of a troubled era and the linear view of a more settled one. They also work toward producing a difference in tone, now of gloom and now of hope.

The "rhetoric of wrath" itself even points to a final hope. The cycle: anger, penalty, repentance, salvation, is not an accidental element in the story of the judges. It is an iron law which must take its course. Hence anger cannot be mentioned in connection with an era where a penalty is not applied, so much so that if it is, the cycle must be completed at any price, as we have seen in the case of 2 Kgs. 13:4-6 (see above, n. 9). But is this law not also an opportunity? Precisely because it is a law whose parts *always* hang together it means that salvation on condition of repentance is still an open possibility after 587 B.C. If it had to run its course, so much so that it forced intrusions into the story before that, it should run its course after that.

So all the deuteronomistic history becomes a call to hope and repentance, as Wolff (see above, n. 1) has argued on somewhat different grounds.

NOTES

1. See G. von Rad, *Old Testament Theology*, I, 1962, 347, 345, and "The Deuteronomistic Theology of History in the Books of Kings," *Studies in Deuteronomy*, 1953, 74-91, on these problems; for the note of hope in the history, see H. W. Wolff, "Das Kerygma des deuteronomistischen Geschichtswerkes," *ZAW*, 73 (1961), 171-186.

2. Cf. M. Noth, *Überlieferungsgeschichtliche Studien*, 1957, 5-6; D. J. McCarthy, S.J., "II Samuel 7 and the Structure of the Deuteronomic History," *JBL*, 84 (1965), 131-138.

3. Cf. G. Fohrer, *Introduction to the Old Testament*, 1968, 194: ". . . . it is impossible to think of the books Judges-Kings as parts of a work composed by a Deuteronomistic author or redactor." This is because Judges has a cyclic course of history, Kings a linear.

4. Cf. F. M. Cross, Jr., "The Structure of the Deuteronomic History," *Perspectives in Jewish Learning*, III, 9-24, accepting a basic over-all unity, and positing an "optimistic" redaction under Josiah and a "pessimistic" exilic redaction.

5. For convenience I call phrases with *hikh'îs* provocation formulae, those with *ḥarah 'aph/hith'annaph* anger formulae, and the two together constitutes the wrath formulae or theme. This refers strictly to the literary facts: the usages are stereotyped, formulaic, in the deuteronomistic history. It does not claim (or deny) that we are dealing with technical formulae from other spheres, e.g., law or cult.

6. Jgs. 10:6-7. The description varies in details (the addition of phrases, "go after other gods," "bow down to them," e.g.) but it is clearly a set-piece associated with the divine anger. It occurs ten times with the anger formula (Dt. 6:12-14; 7:4; 11:16; 29:24-26 [25-27]; 31:16-17; Josh. 23:16; Jgs. 2:19-20; 3:7-8; 10:6-7 with *ḥarah 'aph*, 2 Kgs. 17:15-18 with *hith'annaph*), it is alluded to in connection with the formula twice (Dt. 9:7-21 [note vv. 7-8, 18]; 1 Kgs. 11:9-11, both with *hith'annaph*), and it is used with the anger and provocation formulae together once (Jgs. 2:11-14). There is one baroque expansion of the description with the provocation formula (2 Kgs. 21:2-6), and three allusions to it with that formula (Dt. 4:25; 31:29; 2 Kgs. 22:17).

7. Dt. 29:24 (25, *'azabh berîth*); 31:16 (*parar berîth*); Josh. 23:16; Jgs. 2:20 (*'azabh berîth*); 2 Kgs. 17:15 (*ma'as berîth*).

8. Deuteronomy itself is an apparent exception: anger is often mentioned, but there is no interruption of history. However, the anger *cum* penalty is really the object of prediction. When it actually blazes much later, the penalty, the exile, does interrupt the history!

9. Cf. 2 Kgs. 13:3-6 where the application of the law explains the intrusion of vv. 4-6, which puzzle commentators because they break the narrative flow and have no historical referent. They are not historical narration but theological explanation of the fact that the history continues. Cf. D. J. McCarthy, S.J., "2 Kings 13:4-6," *Bibl*, 54 (1973), for full discussion.

10. See 1 Kgs. 16:26, 33; 22:54(53); 2 Kgs. 21:6 for the provocation formula with no mention of a penalty. The omission is especially striking in the case of Ahab. Even though the author evidently loathes him, he does not mention a penalty. And note the case of Manasseh also.

11. 1 Kgs. 14:9; 15:30; 16:2, 13, 26; 21:22; 22:54(53); 2 Kgs. 21:6; 23:19. Of course, the formula occurs in other contexts too. It is occasionally tied to the description of covenant breaking (see above, n. 6) and to the sins of the people (1 Kgs. 14:15; 2 Kgs. 21:15; 22:17; 23:26). However, these latter examples are all

tied closely to the sins of the kings. Thus twelve of nineteen examples relate to kings so that in terms of frequency as well as repetition within a relatively short compass of text the royal connection of the formula stands out.

12. Dt. 4:21; 6:15; 7:4; 9:8, 19, 20; 11:17; 29:19, 23, 26, 27(20, 24, 27, 28); 31:17.

13. Josh. 23:16; Jgs. 2:14, 20; 3:8.

14. 2 Kgs. 17:18; 23:26; 24:20, and include here also 22:17 on the basis of the use of ḥamah which is a rhetorical equivalent for the anger formula (cf. Dt. 29:27 [28]).

15. The reference to exile is explicit in Dt. 29:24-27 (25-28); it is implicit in 6:15; 7:4; 31:16-19, which use the same language as 2 Kgs. 23:26-27; 24:19-20, texts where the exile is explicitly in question. The import of Dt. 29:19 (20) is obscure, but it could refer to individual exile. There is no question of exile in 4:21; 9:14, 19; but these are reports of the past, not threats with either present or future reference. This leaves 11:16-17 (drought) as the only threat which is clearly not connected with exile.

16. For the force of v. 13, see J. Muilenburg, "The Form and Structure of the Covenantal Formulations," *VT,* 9 (1959), 363. For the literary (not historical) analysis of the whole chapter showing its positive import, see A. Weiser, *Samuel, FRLANT,* 81, 1962, 79-88; also H. J. Boecker, *Die Beurteilung der Anfänge des Königtums in den deuteronomistischen Abschnitten des I. Samuelbuches. WMANT* 31, 1969, 60-88; M. Tsevat, "The Biblical Narrative of the Foundation of Kingship in Israel," *Tarbiz,* 36 (1966), 99-109 (Hebrew, English summary) is good on the *sic et non* structure which ties chs. 8-12 together, but fails to note the resolution of the tension in ch. 12.

17. V. 14 is to be read as a full benediction: *vihyithem . . . 'aḥar yhvh* is the apodosis which is to be interpreted "you will be of the party of Yahweh." For the sense of the phrase see the analysis of Boecker, *Beurteilung . . .* , 79-81, but note that the parallel passages point especially to the attachment of followers to a chief, not vice versa as he argues.

18. See R. Smend, *Die Bundesformel. ThSt,* 68, 1963; N. Lohfink, "Dt. 26, 17-19 und die 'Bundesformel'," *ZkTh,* 91 (1969), 517-553.

19. On the special importance of the lists as such in forming the deuteronomistic history, see S. R. Bin-Nun, "Formulas from Royal Records of Israel and of Judah," *VT,* 18 (1968), 423.

20. Cf. the Mesha Stone, 11:5-6; discussion in McCarthy, "2 Kings 13:4-6," *Bibl* (1973).

21. Cf. McCarthy, "II Samuel 7 . . . ," *JBL* (1965).

22. Of course, it is commonly held that the dynastic principle was not easily admitted among the Hebrews and that this fact has left its traces in the deuteronomistic history. This may be so, but here one must not confuse historical background with literary fact. The problems with dynasty belong to the reconstructed background. In the text, the direct assertion of the deuteronomistic history, the monarchy is dynastic.

23. One exception: 1 Kgs. 14:15, but note also the further evidence for the connection of anger and penalty with dynasty: the condemnation of Solomon, 1 Kgs. 11:9-13 (with *hith'annaph*).

24. H. Weippert, "Die 'deuteronomischen' Beurteilung der Könige von Israel und Judah und das Problem der Redaktion der Königsbücher," *Bibl,* 53 (1972), 301-339, sees the change in the use of the provocation formula as part of the evidence

for successive redactions of Kings. I am not directly concerned with such questions of origins, but I would like to suggest that the interpretation of the change noted here points up a meaning for the differences between the two sets of passages built on the logic of the immediate narrative context. In addition, the differences are functional in a larger narrative structure. Should not such considerations modify our eagerness to see change always in terms of sources?

THE PROPHET AS PARADIGM

SHELDON H. BLANK

Emeritus Professor,
Hebrew Union College—
Jewish Institute of Religion

A "paradigm" is a bore we tolerate when we approach a new language by way of deductive grammar; it is a declension of a representative noun or a conjugation of a typical verb, designed to serve as a sample of what normally happens to such vocables in the language under review. A "paradigm" is also, in a broader and less tiresome sense, an example or a standard, as when, for example, one speaks of a Job as a paradigm of virtue wronged: "Have you considered my servant Job? You will find no one like him on earth, a man of blameless and upright life, who fears God and sets his face against wrongdoing" (NEB).

A puzzle which confronts a student of the biblical Book of Jeremiah is the presence in that context of the compositions known to the trade as "confessions." On inspection these "confessions" turn out to be Jeremiah's private prayers and it seems strange to find such personal musings included in a collection of his prophecies. If they appeared in the Book of Psalms, we would undoubtedly wonder about this or that detail, but we would not question their appropriateness in that devotional context.

The obvious difference between the prophecies and the prayers in Jeremiah is the addressee. Predominantly in prophetic literature the speaker is the prophet and he addresses his people—or certain persons among them, a king, a merchant prince, a priest or liar-prophet. To be sure, prophet and God here speak as one; but the addressee is normally people or the people. This is not the case in the prayers. There Jeremiah the prophet speaks for himself only and the addressee is God, his refuge or his adversary. It is a private matter between them—Jeremiah and God—and we hardly expect to find it reported along with the prophecies. Moreover, what the prophet says to his God is not in the public domain. No one else was there, and if Jeremiah had not himself put his words on record we would have no access to them.[1]

Why did Jeremiah tell his prayers? I suggest that in doing so he made of himself a paradigm.

In essence the confessions are prayers, and the one praying is Jeremiah. Until recent times these two statements were unchallenged assumptions; today they are questioned.

The confessions under consideration are those usually so called: parts of Jeremiah 11; 12; 15; 17; 18 and 20.[2] We must say: they are prayers "in essence," because in two of the confessions a prefatory verse[3] introduces the prayer itself, and because a response[4] follows close on three of the prayers—and implicitly a fourth (20:11)—but the confessions are essentially prayers. These prefatory verses and discovered responses are intimately linked to the respective prayers in thought or phrase. A "therefore so God says" (*lakhen koh 'amar yhvh*) joins 11:21-23 to the foregoing prayer and promises the precise vindication which the prayer demands. The symmetry in 11:20 and 22 corresponds to the symmetry in 20:10 and 11. In the former, the promise: "I will punish them" (*hinenî phoqedh ^{a}lêhem*, v. 22) is an orderly response to the plea: "Let me see your vengeance on them" (*'er'eh niqmath^{e}kha mehem,* v. 20), and in the latter, the assurance "But God is with me . . . therefore my persecutors will stumble and fail" (*vayhvh 'ôthî . . . 'al ken rodh^{e}phai yikkash^{e}lû v^{e}lo' yukhalû, v. 11*) properly balances—even with a form of the same verb—the complaint: "(They say) 'Perhaps we can beguile and overpower him'" (*'ulai y^{e}phutteh v^{e}nûkh^{e}lah lô*, v. 10). Incidentally this comparison is particularly instructive, suggesting the route by which the answer comes to one who prays. The response in 20:11 is only implicit; it is not introduced as in 11:21 by a "Therefore so God says." It is a "this-I-know" conclusion. The speaker simply concludes his prayer with the serene assurance that he has been heard, God is with him. He does not need to be told; he knows.

In the confessions in chs. 15 and 12 we note again the symmetry between plea and response. In the one, the response (15:19-20) is linked to the prayer with a "Therefore so God says," while no such phrase joins 12:5 to the prayer in vv. 1-4. The prayer is over. "You" is no longer God in v. 5: "Running with men you get all worn out; how, then, will you race with horses? If only in a land at peace you could feel safe, how will you do in Jordan's dense thicket?" This is as surely a response to the preceding prayer as is the one explicitly so labeled in 15:19-20.

The symmetry here in chs. 15 and 12 is also obvious, but it is on a level different from that of the preceding pair. The response now is not supportive and reassuring. God does not here promise ruin for the adversaries, vindication for the petitioner; he makes new demands, tightens the reins. But rebuke is an appropriate response to both prayers. The speaker has said to God: "Know that for your sake I have borne disgrace" (15:15), "I sat alone because of your irresistible power" (15:17), "You indeed behave towards me as a deceptive stream, as undependable waters" (15:18)—to which evasive tactics ("copping out") the response attributed to God seems a proper reaction: "Therefore so God said: 'If you come back I will receive you; you may minister to me.'" In ch. 12 the rebuke already quoted (v. 5) follows the expression of similarly evasive sentiments. The speaker points the finger at God, an arbitrary power: "You have to be in the right, O Lord, if I argue with you," he says; "nevertheless I must bring certain cases to your attention," and then as in ch. 15 he claims that justice is awry and God has let him down. Hence the discovered response.

As the three responses, and the fourth, are linked with the prayers, so also are the two prefatory sentences, 15:10 and 18:18. These are joined by common matter with the prayers they introduce. Before the petitioner turns in prayer to his God in 15:11 he complains to his mother about his bitter lot. Before he condemns his adversaries and demands justice of God in 18:19-23 he describes in 18:18 their reprehensible behavior, the occasion for his prayer. We therefore join to the prayers, for the exploration to follow, these prefatory verses as well as the responses. When we speak of "confessions", these are what we mean.

The prayers are prayers, and the human component in the dialogue (prayer and divine response) is a prophet, Jeremiah.

The prayers are prayers. A man speaks to God, puts into words his intimate concerns, pleads with his lord and defender, and waits. We find this sense in all six of these prayers. In each confession, at the outset (twice following a prefatory verse), in the opening words of his prayer, the man calls on God by name (with a vocative: "Lord"—*yhvh*) and continues then to address him with second person pronouns: "you."[5] He tells his story, says in declarative sentences why he needs God's understanding and help: "I have stood before you to speak good on their behalf." "They have dug a pit to take me." He asks God to intervene, addressing him now in the imperative mood or with a rhetorical equivalent: "Give heed to me," "Deal with them," "Is good to be rewarded with evil?" And he voices his confidence in the God to whom he directs his plea: "You are the object of my praise . . . my refuge in a day of distress." Each of the prayers has the form and features of prayer[6]—not of prophecy.

We are assuming that these prayers belong to Jeremiah. Not all scholars agree. We are assuming that they are personal prayers. Not all agree.

As to the first assumption, it is true that prophets rarely address God in prayer or engage him in dialogue. They do so in a prophet's intercessory plea in time of national crisis (Am. 7:1-6), or in a vision narrative, the prophet's claim to authenticity (Isa. 6; Jer. 1), and occasionally besides. As we have mentioned, the place to expect such prayers is the Book of Psalms, and there is a marked resemblance between certain psalms and the prayers of Jeremiah. Since Hermann Gunkel's basic work on psalm typology,[7] scholars have recognized the undeniably close relationship between the prayers of Jeremiah and the "Klagelieder des Einzelnen"[8]—the individual laments among the Psalms. Those prayers and these laments correspond feature by feature, sometimes in language as well as vocabulary, and the question is not whether, but how, they are related. The relationship is not necessarily one of dependency. Neither Jeremiah nor the author of a psalm of this type in the Book of Psalms is clearly imitating the other. In form and language roughly, and in intent undoubtedly, the lament antedates both Jeremiah and the psalmists. The presence of Babylonian equivalents[9] attests to the antiquity of the form, and Ugaritic parallels are evidence for the age of the language.[10] Both Jeremiah and the authors of the Psalms may well have followed ancient patterns—assuming that Jeremiah is the author of the prayers attributed to him in his book.

Gustav Hölscher is a forthright representative of scholars who would deny the confessions to Jeremiah. He collided with Gunkel. Hölscher's work *Die Profeten* appeared in 1914. That was the first year of World War I. Another German scholar, Hans Schmidt, was occupied on the Eastern front, so that Hermann Gunkel "in herzlichen Bereitschaft" wrote the three "Introductions" to Schmidt's *Die Grossen Propheten* to appear in 1915. Gunkel and Hölscher did not agree. Hölscher denied the confessions to Jeremiah: these "psalmartige Dichtungen" were "sekundäre Stücke."[11] Gunkel deplored this recent trend in Jeremiah scholarship: "Ebenso irrig ist es freilich, wenn man neuerdings diese Lieder des Jeremia, die sich so eigentümlich mit den Psalmen berühren, für unecht erklärt hat."[12] In a second edition (1923, LXI) he named names: the recent author of the false opinion was "G. Hölscher."

Against Hölscher, Gunkel held that this most individual of all prophets, Jeremiah, found at hand for his personal need a new literary form, the individual lament.[13] Jeremiah was not the father of this form (common in Psalms and already known to the Babylonians and Egyptians); he merely adopted it. For his prayers he shaped the form to his needs; the prayers are his own.

Scholars before Hölscher had denied not the totality, but parts of these prayers to Jeremiah. B. Duhm had insisted that Jeremiah could not have harbored such thoughts of vengeance as appear in 11:21-23; 17:18 and 18:21-23.[14] These passages (but curiously not 12:3b or 15:15)[15] were supplied by a later reader who did not share the prophet's true spirit. At the same time as Hölscher, Buttenwieser maintained Duhm's less radical view, saying of Jer. 18:21-23: Jeremiah "certainly could not give vent to such implacable and fanatic hatred."[16] Referring to Duhm's position, George Adam Smith[17] observes: "In contrast with its boldness in textual criticism a curious timidity of sentiment has set through recent O. T. scholarship in Germany from which the older German scholars were free." The writings of Knobel,[18] Graf,[19] Keil,[20] and especially Graf suggest that they were somewhat less squeamish, but it is also proper to note that even as Smith was publishing this observation, Hans Schmidt[21] was repeating in a second edition (1923) his earlier observation about prophets:

They are passionate men, hating and loving, subject to error and failure. . . . They are no saints, but for that very reason they are guides for those who seek. Also Volz, a little later,[22] could not take exception to Jeremiah's "so humanly comprehensible" indignation. Contemporary scholarship is similarly willing to let Jeremiah react in human fashion to the indignities he suffered.

I am glad to find myself in agreement with James Muilenburg who counts the "confessional laments" among the passages which may "with some confidence" be assigned to Jeremiah "unglossed."[23] In the context of this volume I am especially glad to accept J. Philip Hyatt's thought that one factor enabling Jeremiah to maintain his sanity was the circumstance that "he did not hesitate to give vent to his feelings of despair and bitterness."[24]

As a matter of fact, these vindictive cries are so dominantly characteristic of the individual lament[25] that if they were absent from Jeremiah's prayer-laments we would probably insist that some editor had expunged them to clear Jeremiah's character of such "un-Christian" thoughts. Jeremiah was not so free of literary convention that he could ignore the pressure to include in a lament a demand for the humiliation of his adversaries and the vindication of God and his own self.

Moreover, although Jeremiah did not invent the private lamentation, he gave it a distinctive flavor. He did not simply use the form, he personalized it. Far more clearly than in the Psalter, the prayers in Jeremiah partake of the nature of a plaintiff's plea in a court of justice. In quite the same way as a wronged man would approach a human court in Bible times, Jeremiah approaches God as his judge. We do find this concept in the Psalms; there too God is judge of all the earth and the Psalmist calls on him for justice.[26] But the words and phrases with a legal flavor are nowhere so abundant as they are in Jeremiah's confessions.[27] This is one distinctive feature.

Another concerns the identity of the plaintiff and his adversaries. Attempts to identify the "enemy" in the Psalter founder; the language is simply conventional, stereotyped. The enemy there is the "bad guy." So too the psalmist, the speaker, lacks identity and his cause for lamentation is one of a selection of standard complaints.[28] Like all summary statements, these concerning the psalmist and his "enemy" present an oversimplification—but they are right when they are balanced against the Jeremianic confessions.

We should not overstate the case for the Jeremiah material. For his prayers Jeremiah does adopt the inherited form and he freely employs the conventional phrases.[29] And yet he builds himself and his trials into his prayers; his adversaries (unnamed) are more than conventional expressions. When we read the confessions in the context of the considerable biographical information which the book of Jeremiah provides, we can with a degree of assurance identify the speaker, and to some extent the adversaries as well. The interlocutors in the confessions are a person and God, and the person is a prophet, and the prophet is Jeremiah. Gunkel lists in a footnote[30] the most obvious marks of identification: "As God's mouth" (15:19),[31] "to stand before God" (18:20), "Anathoth" (11:21, 23), and "Jeremiah" (18:18). The list could be longer: "You shall not prophesy" (11:21), "We will smite him on the tongue and hear no more of his words" (18:18), "They say to me: 'Where is this word of God? Let it come to pass'" (17:15), "When your words presented themselves I devoured them; your word was a pleasure to me" (15:16), "You filled me with indignation" (15:17), "The word of the Lord has become for me a constant source of shame and disgrace" (20:8), "If I say: 'I will not . . . speak any more in his name' it is in me as a raging fire" (20:9), "I stood before you to speak good on their behalf" (18:20; cf. 15:19), "I have interceded with you" (15:11). The man of the prayers is consistently the injured prophet, the prophet from Anathoth, Jeremiah—consistently, except that being Jeremiah,[32] he also twice refers to himself in his prayers as interceding for his people. He is not faceless.

His enemies, too, are persons, the jeering crowd, the men of Anathoth, the Pashhurs (20:1) and Hananiahs (28:1) and all the other named and unnamed opponents of the prophet in the biographical matter. Attempts[33] to attach each of the confessions to a particular event in the lifetime of the prophet are hazardous, to say the least, yet the confessions are clearly not unrelated to their narrative context and the persona of the prayers are real persons. We cannot agree with the Hölscher school who see in the confessions only misplaced psalms, interpolations in the book of Jeremiah.

Unlike Hölscher, Henning Graf Reventlow[34] has sought not to excise the confessions, in whole or in part, but to convert them. They undergo a sea change and become liturgies. Jeremiah speaks in them but not as a messenger-prophet; he prays, but not on his behalf. Instead, he plays an intercessory role, laying his people's concerns before God. A confession is in fact "eine Klageliturgie, in der ein repräsentativer einzelner, der Prophet, als Vorbeter und Fürbitter die Not des Volkes vor Gott bringt."[35] The erroneously so-called "confessions," he argues, say next to nothing about Jeremiah the prophet, his pain, his love, his indignation—only that as a *shaliaḥ tsibbûr* (public prophet) he approaches God on behalf of his people.

Now, prophetic literature is not entirely void of occasions where prophets display an intercessory capacity. Twice when Amos sees in visions disaster sweeping over Jacob, he intercedes and averts the catastrophe (7:1-3, 4-6); Ezekiel twice approaches God with a similar plea (9:8; 11:13); on two occasions the king or people of Judah appeal to Jeremiah to exercise his intercessory function in their time of doubt (21:2; 42:2f.); twice Jeremiah mentions the circumstances that God forbade his interceding (7:16; 14:11), implying that otherwise he would speak for the nation; and twice in the confessions themselves he reminds God that, with or without permission, he has interceded for his people (15:11b; 18:20). Intercession was undoubtedly a prophetic function; the only question is whether that is Jeremiah's activity in the confessions. Is he there a cultic functionary representing the community in a public liturgy, as Reventlow would have it? Or is he himself, the prophet, bringing his personal grief to the attention of his God and seeking relief and vindication?

Reventlow deals with four of the six listed confessions[36] and he labels three of these four without question prophetic liturgies. The three are 15:10-21; 17:12-18 and 12:1-5. He is less certain about the fourth: 11:18-20; 12:6; 11:21-23. He does not make his case without efforts. Embarrassing terms and phrases[37] confront him, and to make any kind of a case he must frequently resort to a forced exegesis. It takes strenuous mental gymnastics to make of the messenger prophet Jeremiah a cult functionary and to convert his prayers into prophetic liturgies.

Two capable recent works have given Reventlow's proposal the attention it deserves; an essay by John Bright[38] and a book by John M. Berridge.[39] Bright concludes (p. 214) that Reventlow "arrives at his conclusions only by forcing or ignoring evidence." Berridge (p. 210) rejects Reventlow's view that the "I" of the confessions is no more than "the embodiment of the community which the prophet Jeremiah, as the holder of a cultic office, represents." On the contrary, he notes "numerous expressions of a self-conscious individual who bore the name Jeremiah." To this we would add the thought that if the pieces of a chapter which includes a confession do build up to a liturgy as Reventlow contends, the arrangement of the pieces is the work of a liturgist, not of Jeremiah.

Except for the view of Hölscher which, by denying that Jeremiah wrote the confessions, removes them entirely as a source for the understanding of the man Jeremiah, Gerstenberger[40] goes farthest, in his treatment of Jeremiah 15:10-21 and his closing questions there: "Can the other individual complaints in Jer also be explained as compositive elements in some larger textual unit? Can the complaints in Jer thus be shown to be later insertions into an existing collection of prophecies?" (p. 408). Gerstenberger's conclusion goes beyond Reventlow. Their works appeared in the same year (1963), and I have seen no evidence that either was acquainted with the other's views. They go a long way together but Gerstenberger goes farther. Both interpret the confession in Ch. 15 as a prophetic liturgy, but whereas Reventlow holds that Jeremiah is the author and (in his role as cult functionary) the reader of the liturgy, Gerstenberger holds that the whole liturgy is a compilation by a liturgically oriented Deuteronomist (pp. 407f.). Gerstenberger's, too, is a forced interpretation.

I cannot speak for Phil Hyatt but, as for myself, despite Reventlow and Gerstenberger, I am unreconstructed and still see personal prayers and the answers to prayers in the confessions of Jeremiah. These are available as primary literary sources for the understanding of Jeremiah, the messenger prophet.

The problem that I still face is how to account for the presence of these "documents of self-revelation"[41] in their prophetic context. Berridge (who asks the same question) answers: "Each 'confession' has more than merely a private validity." (p. 158), and he refers to von Rad,[42] and also to Stoebe[43] whom he quotes (p. 157) to the effect that the confessions "im Bewusstsein Jeremias eine über die eigene Erfahrung hinausgehende Allgemeingültigkeit gehabt haben müssen." Somewhat earlier Martin Buber asked our question in this form: ". . . why does he make known to us complaints and pleadings, and even resentments and shouts of vengeance?" "Obviously," he continued, "because he thinks all these supra-personally important."[44]

What renders them especially important to a prophet like Jeremiah is the fact that at the end of several of the prayers there came to him what he heard as a divine response, a communication,[45] an oracle. Such communications are, of course, the impulse which sends a prophet on his prophetic way; when he is the recipient of the word, he wearies himself in vain to contain it (Jer. 20:9). At the first God had said to him: "Whatever I command you you shall speak," and had put words in his mouth (1:7, 9; cf. 26:12). Undoubtedly the responses to his prayers, a renewal of the original impulse, were a quantity that lent his confessions significance—more than personal significance. We assume that it was these responses which prompted Jeremiah to share with his people his unshared prayer experience. God's word to him was a word for them. Berridge[46] puts forward "the thesis that Jeremiah's 'confessions' were . . . spoken in public, constituting a part of his proclamation"—his "proclamation," the message which he, the prophet, must bring. Whether or not Jeremiah indeed spoke his prayers "in public," which seems improbable, Berridge is right that these answers were what prompted him to somehow get the confessions into the record.

A passage in Jer. 16 is a prime example of a word to the prophet which, though personal, had more than private significance. This passage should now open the way to the theme: prophet as paradigm.[47] Here preparing to make public what he had heard, he says: "The word of the Lord came to me (*vay^{e}hî dh^{e}bhar yhvh 'elai,* v. 1)" and then continues with the word: "You shall not marry and have children in this place." It is a private word, having to do with his private life, but as he develops the thought it reeks with shuddering dread. "For so the Lord said of children born in this place and their parents in this land: They shall die diseased and lie unburied like dung on the ground, be ravaged by sword and famine, food for carrion birds and beasts." The private word has implications broad as the land, and Jeremiah, advised not to marry and beget, has become a paradigm for the people. The pattern appears three times within the first nine verses of this chapter: private word and its broad implications, the prophet a paradigm. Here follows the third, a further word to Jeremiah (vv. 8f.): "A house of feasting too you shall not enter, to sit with them to eat or drink." And then its application: "In this place, before your eyes in your own time, I will bring to a close the sounds of joy and mirth, the sounds of bridegroom and bride." With the mention of marriage in the concluding phrases, the thought returns to the beginning of the passage and Jeremiah's private life. He serves as analogy and paradigm, and it is for such a purpose that he makes public what might be regarded as nobody's business.

Jeremiah was not the first prophet to use his marriage (or failure to marry) as an analogy. In an earlier century Hosea, to whom Jeremiah is otherwise kin, starts with similar words: "The Lord said to me" (*vayyo'mer yhvh 'elai*), and proceeds to publish God's instructions to him in person: "Again go, love a woman, unfaithful and adulterous" (Hos. 3:1), a private matter which he lets stand as a paradigm for the relation between God and Israel.

Jeremiah's contemporary, Ezekiel, quite consciously acts out his analogies, and incidentally supplies a Hebrew equivalent for our word "paradigm." In his marathon lying on public display, first on one side unturned and then on the other, he paradigmatically represents the slow discharge of Israel's guilt, and of Judah's.[48] He does not here vicariously "bear the iniquity of the house of Israel" ($v^e nasa'tha$ $^a von$ $bêth$ $yisra'el$), he makes of himself a paradigm. His performance in 5:1-5, the treatment of his shaven hair, a paradigm for the fate awaiting Jerusalem's inhabitants ($zo'th$ $y^e rûshalaim$, "this is Jerusalem," v. 5) is similar; and 12:1-14 is an explicit example which reveals the Hebrew term for his device: In their rebellious mood, the people close out the sights and sounds which might otherwise instruct them (v. 2), and to convey his message the prophet must find a new medium. He enacts in person "before their eyes"[49] the stages of the disaster—the defeat and exile—which he knows to be in store for Jerusalem. He does this publicly, properly expecting his public to demand an explanation. When they do so he is to say: "(I am glad you asked me) $'^a nî$ $môpheth^e khem$, I am your paradigm. What I have done will be done to them.[50] They will experience captivity and exile" (12:11). In this context the word $môpheth$ ("sign," "token," "omen," "portent") seems to have the meaning we here give to the term "paradigm." It has this meaning in Ezk. 24, where again, like Jeremiah and Hosea, Ezekiel involves his public in matters related to his own marriage. At the death of his wife he omits signs and rites of mourning. When he is asked, as was to be expected, to explain the omission, he develops his implicit analogy, equating the death of his wife, the delight of his eyes, with the destruction of the Jerusalem sanctuary, the people's joy. Then God draws the conclusion: "Ezekiel shall serve you as a paradigm ($l^e môpheth$); all that he did you will do" (vv. 15-24). Ezekiel goes a step beyond Hosea and Jeremiah; in these and other presentations he adds a visual element.[51] The people have eyes. If they were willing they could see. Jeremiah is subtler. He only puts on record his confessions. These must suggest the message to such as can read.

Did an event in Jeremiah's life with Baruch dispose Jeremiah to preserve his confessions? Imagine the prophet and his disciple sitting quietly alone. Jeremiah hears the young man sigh. He looks at him and Baruch speaks: "Alas! and Woe! God has added misery to my pain; I am worn out with sighing and find no respite." Jeremiah reflects. The complaint is familiar. Has he himself not given voice to such impatient despair? Repeatedly he had laid his own grief before God in reproachful lamentation. His friend is only mirroring his mood. What comfort now can he bring to Baruch? What comfort indeed had his praying brought him? The distilled essence of what Jeremiah learned in prayer is what he now offers as God's word to Baruch: "What I, myself built I am about to demolish. I am about to uproot what I planted. Would you seek advancement? Desist! I will bring disaster to all flesh, God says, but I will give you your life as reward wherever you go" (Jer. 45). This much Jeremiah says to Baruch. His overtones convey a further query, and a thought: Have you really such good reason, friend, to be so sorry for yourself? Did you suppose it would be easy? We must carry on.

As he replied to Baruch, did Jeremiah open wide his eyes, recognizing a broad truth? Had he suddenly caught sight of the paradigmatic nature of his own experience with God? He saw meaning in that encounter for Baruch; could it be helpful to his whole people? It is hazardous to weave history with slender threads; we may be writing fiction. Yet the possibility exists that, moved by some such reflections as these, Jeremiah first recorded his meetings with God in prayer, putting his prayers in words, perhaps for Baruch to intersperse among his prophecies, perhaps even communicating them by word of mouth—prayer plus discovered response—to some gathering of persons like the elders of Judah who sat before Ezekiel.[52] This proposal may stand as an alternative to the Hölscher-type interpolation theory,[53] or the confession-as-prophetic-liturgy explanation of Reventlow[54] or Gerstenberger.[55] It is like, but not identical with, the confession-as-proclamation hypothesis of Berridge.[56] It emphasizes the paradigmatic nature of the confessions, comparable with, but more subtle than, the acted-out communication of Ezekiel.[57]

There is no apparent logic in the distribution of these pieces across the chapters of Jeremiah's book—just as there is none for the distribution of the other literary units in chs. 1 to 20. Nor are the six confessions arranged in any meaningful order, except perhaps that the first three, in chs. 11; 12 and 15, are in the form of dialogue: prayers complete with discovered responses, while the second three, in chs. 17; 18 and 20, are monologic. I am not willing to guess at the significance of this observation, if indeed there is any.

Putting on record his confessions, Jeremiah set in motion the process by which he became a paradigm. The theme of prophet as paradigm does not end with Jeremiah and Ezekiel. The writer known as the Second Isaiah and the author of the book of Jonah carried it on, developed it further.

According to what is, in my opinion,[58] the most satisfying interpretation of the "servant" figure, the Servant of God is

> a personification
> of the people Israel,
> as a prophet
> after the manner of Jeremiah.

The servant is not a person, but a personification, a figure of speech. Second Isaiah was a master at the craft of personification. Babylon becomes for him a pampered queen (Isa. 47) and Zion climbs her high hill and raises her voice with glad tidings (40:9). The servant figure is an extended sample of his art.

The servant of God is his people Israel personified, an ethnic community given a corporate personality, a people with assigned work to do, therefore a "servant."

Israel's mission is so like that of a prophet that the servant's features are the features of a prophet: an ear to hear, a mouth to speak and a message to bring to the nations, prophetic *torah* to impart to the peoples of the earth. Like certain prophets the servant is exposed as well to all the tribulations of a truth speaker.

The prophet-servant figure so resembles the prophet Jeremiah in one particular after another that without a doubt the Second Isaiah chose, as paradigm for the servant, the life and work of Jeremiah. He obviously had before him the book of Jeremiah, whether in written form or as oral tradition. His source included the confessions along with the third person narratives, and he found just there the model for the figure of his "servant," a man whose life experience matched his people's lot and destiny.[59]

There is so clear a correspondence between the servant and Jeremiah that this conclusion is safe. The implications of the conclusion bear intimately on our theme. Second Isaiah did not overlook the meaning of the confessions among the Jeremianic matter. He sensed their paradigmatic purport. Possibly Ezekiel's way of employing his personal behavior as a paradigm for his people's fate helped Deutero-Isaiah make the connection between prophet and Israel[60]—although it is not Ezekiel but Jeremiah who sits for the portrait of the servant. We cannot say who first perceived why Jeremiah put down for the record his dialogic encounters with God; the reason for his doing so may have been quite obvious to the prophet's disciples, those responsible for the preservation of his words. But it is Second Isaiah, two generations after Jeremiah, who clearly articulated, effectively employed, broadened and transmitted the theme of prophet as paradigm. He was not the last to do so in the Bible.

The author of the book of Jonah put the theme in story form. Jonah, in the title role, is a prophet, like prophets told to go, sent to make proclamation, his destination a distant land, his aim to avert a national calamity. But Jonah demurs; he goes, but in the wrong direction, runs away, putting into action Jeremiah's unacknowledged craving. God counters Jeremiah's craving with a rebuke: "If you come back—," "How will you do in Jordan's dense thicket?" After the truant Jonah he sends a storm and a fish. And Jeremiah sobered, and Jonah redirected, again assume the mantle of prophecy, Jeremiah to be God's mouth and to speak to Jerusalem, Jonah to go and proclaim the doom of Nineveh.

The author of Jonah appears to reach back to the paradigmatic prophet Jeremiah and his dialogic prayers. But to get to Jeremiah he had to look past Second Isaiah, and this has affected his vision: Jonah is as much a "servant" as he is a Jeremiah. Like the 'ebhedh, Jonah is a prophet as paradigm. He stands for the generation of Israel whom the author of Jonah knew as contemporaries. And the story calls the people back to their destined mission to the nations, the Ninevehs of the world. Jonah dramatizes the prophet-as-paradigm theme, announced by Jeremiah and incarnated by Second Isaiah.[61]

If one were inclined to ask what place an essay on the prophet as paradigm has in a volume on Old Testament ethics, the key word in the answer might be "responsibility." What Jeremiah learned in his dialogue with God had to do with individual responsibility. It did not relieve him of his duties; it returned him to his task, impressed him with the need to subordinate private peace and comfort to the broader goals. His being chosen as a prophet yielded him a certain assurance of divine concern so that he might well expect to survive and do God's work, but this choice entailed no warrant that the going would be easy. Jeremiah's word of spare comfort to Baruch had the same intent—if anything it is still more direct: "Would you seek advancement? Desist; . . . I will give you your life as reward," but no more. In the chapters in Isaiah God amply reassures his prophet-people Israel—consolation is the prime ingredient in the proclamation of Second Isaiah—but we note, of course, that the people is personified as "servant," chosen to serve, assigned a task and sent on a broad mission. And finally, Jonah is depicted as one who suffers but survives. I have been translating *hahêtebh ḥarah lakh* in Jonah 4:4 and 9: "Are you very angry?" But the NEB gets just the right amount of casual irony into God's voice with its reading: " 'Are you so angry?' said the Lord." The point of the paradigm may be just there: "Are you so angry?" Who said it would be easy?

NOTES

1. And I would not be writing this paper as tribute to a man for whose insights I am grateful and whose admiration for the man Jeremiah I share.
2. Meaning specifically: 1) 11:18-23 with 12:6 added after 11:18; 2) 12:1-5; 3) 15:10-11 plus vv. 15-20; 4) 17:14-18; 5) 18:18-23; 6) 20:7-11. I dealt with aspects of this material in a paper entitled "The Confessions of Jeremiah and the Meaning of Prayer," *HUCA,* 21 (1948), 331-354, and then more fully in *Jeremiah Man and Prophet,* 1961.
3. 15:10 and 18:18.
4. 11:21-23; 12:5; 15:19-20.
5. It is only in 20:7b-10 that he adopts the oblique form of meditative prayer.
6. Not that these features appear in a fixed order; the address does come among the opening words of the prayer, but otherwise the elements freely mingle.
7. *Einleitung in die Psalmen,* 1966.
8. Gunkel, *Einleitung,* 172-265.
9. Literature listed in Gunkel, *Einleitung,* 6f.
10. Matitiahu Tsevat, *A Study of the Language of Biblical Psalms, SBL* Monograph 9, 1955, 47-51, 57f.
11. Hölscher, *Profeten,* 394.
12. Schmidt, *Die Grossen Propheten,* 1915, LXIV.
13. Schmidt, *Propheten,* 1923, LXI.
14. Bernhard Duhm, *Das Buch Jeremia,* 1901, 158f.
15. Duhm, *Jeremia,* 115, 135.
16. Moses Buttenwieser, *The Prophets of Israel,* 1914, 112.
17. *Jeremiah,* 1923, 330 n. 2.
18. August Knobel, *Der Prophetismus der Hebräer,* 2, 1837, 263.
19. K. H. Graf, *Der Prophet Jeremia,* 1862, 269.
20. Carl F. Keil, *Bibl. Comm. über den Propheten Jeremia,* 1872, 225.
21. *Propheten,* 1923, 275; 1915, 269.
22. Paul Volz, *Der Prophet Jeremia,* 1928, 200f.
23. "Jeremiah the Prophet" in *IDB* II, 1962, 832, 824.
24. *IB,* V, 1956, 783.
25. Cf. Pss. 7:16f. (Eng. 15f); 28:4f.; 35:4-8, 69:23-29 (22-28); 109:7-20 (6-19); et al.
26. Pss. 9:17(16); 58:12(11); 94:2; 35:1; 109:7(6).
27. For a detailed development of this observation, see my *Jeremiah,* 112-128, especially 119-121.
28. Cf. Laurence A. Martin, *A Study of the Individual Psalms of Lament* (Unpublished Dissertation, Hebrew Union College), 1972, 157, 217f.
29. The uninhibited cursing of one's enemies may have been the routine and conventional thing to do—especially, we may suppose, if one was trying to influence the court.
30. In Schmidt's, *Die Grossen Propheten* (1923), LXI, n. 5.
31. On the expression $k^e ph\hat{i}$ $thihyeh,$ see n. 37 below.
32. Who did on occasion "stand before" God to present to him his people's need (21:2; 42:2f.).
33. Like those of Moses Buttenwieser, *The Prophets of Israel,* pp. 89f.
34. *Liturgie und prophetisches Ich bei Jeremia,* 1963.
35. Reventlow, *Liturgie,* 225.

36. Pp. 205-257. He does not analyze the two in chs. 18 and 20.
37. He finds $k^ephî\ thihyeh$ in 15:19 troublesome (pp. 226-228).
38. "Jeremiah's Complaints: Liturgy or Expressions of Personal Distress?" in *Proclamation and Presence, Old Testament Essays in Honour of Gwynne Henton Davies,* ed. by Durham & Porter, 1970, 189-214.
39. Prophet, People, and the Word of Yahweh, *An Examination of Form and Content in the Proclamation of the Prophet Jeremiah,* 1970. Cf. also Georg Fohrer, *Introduction to the Old Testament,* 1968, 395.
40. Erhard Gerstenberger, "Jeremiah's Complaints. Observations on Jer. 15:10-21," *JBL,* 82 (1963), 393-408.
41. S. Blank, *Jeremiah,* 65 ff.
42. *Theologie* 2, 212 (ff).
43. Hans Joachim Stoebe, "Seelsorge und Mitleiden bei Jeremia," *WuD* 4, 131.
44. *The Prophetic Faith,* 1960, 180 (first English edition 1949).
45. See above, pp. 3-5.
46. *Prophet,* 157.
47. I had chosen the theme and title of this paper before I came upon the word "paradigmatic" in von Rad, *Theologie,* 2, 216; Gerstenberger ("Complaints," 407); and Berridge (*Prophet,* 148). I am glad for the company.
48. Ezk. 4:4-6 plus 8.
49. The phrase $le^‘ênêhem$ occurs here no fewer than 7 times in the compass of 5 vv. (12:3-7).
50. Note Isa. 8:18, where the prophet and his sons are called $môph^ethîm$. The unexpected change from second to third person is in confused recognition of the fact that God is still instructing Ezekiel concerning his reply to "them."
51. He becomes the very model of a maker of metaphors, a $m^emashshel\ m^eshalîm,$ 21:5 (20:49).
52. As in Ezk. 8:1; 20:7; cf. 33:30f.
53. See above, pp. 116-117.
54. See above pp. 120-121.
55. See above, p. 121.
56. See above, p. 122.
57. See above, pp. 123-124.
58. I have defended the opinion in *Prophetic Faith in Isaiah,* 1958, 49-160.
59. See Blank, *Isaiah,* 77 and 100-104. My observations were anticipated in part by Otto Eissfeldt, *Der Gottesknecht bei Deuterojesaja,* 1933, who lists on pp. 16ff. some of the contacts between the servant and Jer. which I have listed on pp. 101-104 and in the pertinent footnotes 54 to 70 on pp. 218-220. The tenth century Jewish philosopher Saadia reputedly went the whole way and identified the servant as the prophet Jeremiah himself; cf. S. R. Driver and Adolf Neubauer, *The Fifty-third Chapter of Isaiah according to the Jewish Interpreters,* I, 1876, 43 and II, 1877, 19.
60. At least for certain other insights Second Isaiah was indebted to the writings of Ezekiel; cf. Blank, *Isaiah,* 123-132.
61. See Blank, *Understanding the Prophets,* 1969, 129-138.

A PROBLEM OF THEOLOGICAL ETHICS IN HOSEA

WILLIAM F. STINESPRING

Emeritus Professor,
Duke Divinity School

Professor Hyatt was one of my dearest friends and I wish to honor his memory by discussing a subject on which we formerly had some friendly disagreements, but later came closer together.

In an article published in 1950, entitled "Hosea, Prophet of Doom,"[1] I took the view that the prophet was almost exclusively a prophet of doom like Amos, Isaiah, Micah, and Jeremiah, holding out little or no hope that the punishment on Israel could be averted, since there had been no repentance. It was claimed that the happy endings in chs. 1; 2; 11; and 14, and all of ch. 3, are Judean interpolations from the exilic or post-exilic periods, when words of rehabilitation were in order and much of the prophetic literature was supplemented with hopeful oracles to fit the new conditions. Likewise today, many books are revised or supplemented to bring them into line with new conditions and new needs.

It was also pointed out that if Hosea had promised success and salvation for the Northern Kingdom, he would have been a very poor predictor, for that kingdom fell, never to rise again. Somehow, the prophet's original book found its way to the South, where it was revised by Judean editors, who had taken over the name "Israel", applying it to the kingdom of Judah and later to the province of Judah and its people in the Persian period. This added material, however, constitutes no more than one-fifth of the total book as it now stands, so that the doom theme remains dominant to the reader who looks at the whole book, and not just at certain comforting parts.

One of the main points of contention was 11:8-9, and especially v. 9b, which I insisted could only be translated "I will not *again* destroy Ephraim," arguing that Hosea could not have said "again" before Ephraim had been destroyed the first time. Professor Hyatt in his *Prophetic Religion* had translated this line "I will not *turn* to destroy Ephraim," arguing that vv. 8 and 9 are genuinely from Hosea and that thus Hosea was a prophet of hope, though the hope "was contingent upon the repentance of Israel."[2] My view was that Hosea came to feel that Israel would not repent, and hence had no final hope message. It was with great regret that I had to part company with my friend on this point, especially since I greatly admired this particular book of his and agreed with it in almost every other particular.

At that time, nearly everyone disagreed with me, and I was looked upon as a sort of heretic who had tried to convert a soft-hearted prophet into a hard-hearted one like Amos. As a matter of fact, I regarded Amos and Hosea as two like-minded prophets who said much the same thing to the same people at about the same time. They were both somewhat soft-hearted and would have liked to have Israel repent and be saved, but there came a time when it was too late. My heresy was compounded when I cast doubts on the authenticity of all five vv. of ch. 3, the favorite passage of those exegetes who prefer to regard the book of Hosea mainly as a personal romance of love lost and regained by forgiveness.[3]

Now it is time to examine what some more recent writers have said, to see if any new insights have been gained. But first, a backward glance at J. Lindblom's *Hosea literarisch untersucht,* 1927. This provides a good summary of Hosea scholarship up to that time. It excludes entirely the last chapter, 14:2-10 (1-9), from consideration as a later interpolation, also 2:1-3 (1:10-2:1) and 2:18-25 (16-23). But Lindblom salvages 11:8-9 by connecting it with 2:16-17 (14-15) and putting it early in the married life of Hosea while he was still in a forgiving mood. He retains ch. 3 by considering it likewise as from early in Hosea's career. In his later book in English, *Prophecy in Ancient Israel,* 1962, Lindblom comes out more strongly with his view that any hope belonged to the early period only (p. 365):

> But these hopes were confined to a brief period of Hosea's life. The light went out, and after the flagrant adultery of Gomer the prophet became convinced that conversion was impossible and that the annihilation of the Northern Kingdom was inevitable. . . . The names given to the two last children, 'Not-pitied', 'Not-my-people', refer to the final form of Hosea's prophetic message.

Some other writers tend to put Hosea's forgiving mood at the end of his career, thus making him finally a prophet of hope, saying that

Hosea and even God had changed their minds, and that Israel would be saved, presumably without repentance.

We come now to N. Snaith's *Mercy and Sacrifice,* 1953. Snaith has read Hosea more carefully than most, and has consequently arrived at some clear insights. E.g. (p. 48):

> It is sheer sentiment of the most dangerous type which suggests that God, because of his love for Israel, is going to let Israel off from paying the price of her sin. . . . For Hosea, God's mercy has come to an end.

And on p. 50, I read this, with surprise and approval: "We think that the whole of chapter 3 is late and not from Hosea." Very few recent writers have been willing to say that, for it cuts out the heart of the sentimental notion of buying back the wayward wife as a historical fact in the life of Hosea rather than a figure of speech for God's treatment of post-exilic Judah. Moreover, Snaith also rejects 2:1-3 (1:10-2:1), the happy ending of ch. 1. But by retaining 2:16-25 (14-23), the happy ending of ch. 2, 11:8-11 (the happy ending of ch. 11), and all of ch. 14 except the last verse, he manages to present a picture very similar to that of most other interpreters. E.g., on p. 55:

> Thus Hosea knew that God also was prepared to begin again with Israel and to enter into another covenant with her. He knew this because of his own love for his erring wife; not all her adulteries could destroy his love for her.

He even has a whole chapter (IV) on "The Second Marriage," though this idea in earlier exegetes was usually based on ch. 3. So Snaith gets nowhere by his rejection of ch. 3, and, like his predecessors, ends up with an over emphasized theology of hope, national and individual, that has no connection whatever with the historical events of the time of Hosea, especially the total end of Israel, the Northern Kingdom.

The only oracles of hope that make clear sense to me historically are oracles on the restoration of Judah after the exile.⁴ Snaith rejects these when they appear in Hosea, and in the process makes some very good remarks on the subject (p. 50).

> Thus we would say that 2:1-3 (1:10-2:1) is not from Hosea ben Beeri. This is not because it is full of hope, but because it looks forward to a hope of an Israel and a Judah unified with one common head. This is a southern expectation. No northerner could possibly look forward to anything of this kind. The vision of a united kingdom with a Davidic king belongs to the south. All dreams of a Davidic Messiah are southern dreams. . . . No northerner in his senses would write or say a thing like that. The oppression of the north in the time of Solomon would prevent any thought like that for ever, and even more the actual expression of any such thought.⁵

Yet Snaith is very willing to accept a hope passage in Hosea if it can be interpreted as hope for Israel alone. But Israel fell forever, and the Ten Lost Tribes are really lost. Snaith's Hosea was indeed a poor predictor, who failed utterly in discerning the will of God for Israel. Hosea may have forgiven his wife, but God let Israel go down to extinction as Amos and the presumably real Hosea said he would. Whatever Hosea was talking about, it was not the restoration of Judah after the Babylonian exile. Yet this is what most of the "hope" passages in the prophetic books are talking about, and Hosea could never have even dreamed about such a thing, according to Snaith.

H. H. Rowley, 1956,⁶ defending the traditional view, concludes his article thus:

> Like Another (meaning Jesus), he learned obedience by the things that he suffered, and because he was not broken by an experience that has broken so many others, but triumphed over it and in triumphing perhaps won back his wife, he received through the vehicle of his very pain an enduring message for Israel and for the world.

After Hosea there was no Israel in Hosea's sense to receive the "enduring message"; and to drag in Christian theology and soteriology distorts even more the historical message of the historical Hosea. To be sure, the book as it now stands has a soteriology for exilic or postexilic Judah, now calling itself Israel, and this has been often twisted into support for a Christian soteriology of the individual. But what has all that to do with Hosea and his problem with his condemned nation?

George A. F. Knight, 1960,[7] really goes to extremes in reading Christian theology into Hosea. Some of his section headings are: "The Cross in the Heart of God," "I Love You Still," "The Gospel according to Hosea," "Life from the Dead," and "The Creative Grace of God's Ways." Knight has some good ideas on Christian theology, but appears to have no conception of what happened to Israel about 722 B.C.

In 1961,[8] *In* ran a symposium on Hosea, consisting of four articles as follows:

1. "The Holy One in Your Midst," by Walther Eichrodt
2. "Guilt and Salvation," by Hans Walter Wolff
3. "God's Conversion," by Dietrich Ritschl
4. "The Love Story of God," by Wilhelm Vischer

The last article was labeled "A Sermon," which sets the tone of the series and ends by quotation of 11:8-9 in a traditional translation, followed by this supposedly explanatory remark (p. 309):

> Nothing and no one can kill the love of God which is in Jesus Christ. It bursts forth from the grave and rises from the dead on the third day.
> Who, in the long run, can withstand this love?

As a believing and confessing Christian, I like this conclusion, but I do not think that it follows at all from the historical Hosea. The method by which this sermon is drawn from this text is rather well described by Ritschl in his comment on 11:8-9 (p. 303):

> Hosea's words proved to be lies, did they not? Ephraim was made like Admah and Zeboi'im. But Judah later claimed this

chapter and the whole Northern tradition for its own, in the same way in which we (Christians) say that Israel's tradition belongs to us.

Of course, I think that Judah not only borrowed, but also edited the "Northern tradition." Yet this theological process is not too bad if the eschatology of the individual (resurrection of the dead, etc.) is not included. In other words, it seems to me that the redactional part of the book of Hosea, and other similar passages, can be used by Christians to support their idea of the high place of the Church in God's designs. But the resurrection of dead individuals is barely mentioned in the Old Testament (Dan. 12:2; Isa. 26:19?), and theologizing about it should be placed in the historical context of the intertestamental literature and the New Testament.

Also in 1961 appeared Hans Walter Wolff's large commentary.[9] Wolff's basic stance was set forth in his article in *In*. In his commentary he immediately (p. viii) tells us that he seeks to find "that place at which the prophetic word elucidates the Christ event as a word of God today." Thus, in ch. 3 of Hosea he rejects only the words "and David their king" and "at the end of the days" in v. 5 as "additions of the Judean redaction" (p. 70). He regards 2:1-3 (1:10-2:1) as from Hosea in content, though not in form (p. 29). He does have doubts (p. 58) about 2:18-25 (16-23), but none about 11:8-9 (p. 261), which to him means that God changed his mind and decided to forgive Israel. Obviously this exegesis does not fit the time of Hosea, but Wolff overlooks the historical facts as he moves on to his sermonette on intimations of Christian love.

The article on Hosea by J. D. Smart in *IDB*, 1962[10] marks an advance in understanding of the historical context and in cautious treatment of the text. E.g., (p. 649, col. 2):

> The acceptance of chs. 4.13 as basic in understanding Hosea makes impossible the kind of erratic judgments concerning him . . . which build him up as the prophet of God's tender love in sharp contrast to Amos as the prophet of God's unquenchable wrath.

Smart also describes accurately "the romantic theory" of recent years and recognizes a considerable amount of Judean interpolation. He warns against "imaginative reconstructions" and determines to be swayed only by "solid evidence." Yet in the end he defends the genuineness of 2:3, 16-25 (1, 14-23); 3:1-4; 14:2-9 (1-8) and so comes out with "Hosea's final word" as this: "When she (Israel) had tasted the bitterness of judgment, he (God) would intervene and open the way for restorations of the covenant and a new future." Unfortunately, God did no such thing, and this hope for restoration seems to me to be putting into the mind of Hosea what Smart himself described as "Judean" and from "a hand other than Hosea's."

The comprehensive and impressive commentary by Wilhelm Rudolph, 1966,[11] must be considered. It is an enormous mine of detailed information on the whole book, no matter what interpretative stance one takes. Rudolph starts off well (p. 24):

> The repeatedly expressed opinion that his marriage and love life became determinative for his message has easily led to the result that people view Hosea too sentimentally and thereby distort the picture of his personality.

On the next page he again speaks clearly:

> The literary legacy of Hosea has plainly been preserved from oblivion or complete destruction by the fact that after the fall of Samaria it was brought safely to Judah and there fashioned into the present book of Hosea. *That the catastrophe of the Northern Kingdom so often announced by him had so quickly come to pass authenticated him as a true prophet of Yahweh.*[12] That was sufficient reason for the circle of faithful prophets of Yahweh in the Southern Kingdom to preserve his heritage and to utilize it for their own proclamation, especially since Hosea himself had already made reference to Judah several times.

Surely Rudolph is saying here that the story of Hosea has been oversentimentalized and that Hosea was primarily a prophet of doom.

But does he maintain this stance throughout his book? He does not. On p. 217 he finally decides that 11:8-9 is a genuine Hosean hope passage, though he worries about the contradiction thus introduced. So he goes off into theology to relieve his embarrassment and decides that God is somewhat ambivalent, but in the end is almost sure to come out in favor of mercy rather than judgment. Thus (p. 218) he preaches a sermon on "I am God and not man" (11:9c), concluding "Hier ist Evangelium in Alten Testament." So it is if one takes these verses as a text for a sermon on the hope for the individual or the church of God; but the historical Hosea was thinking of something else, namely the doomed Northern Kingdom.[13]

James M. Ward's *Hosea: A Theological Commentary,* 1966, may be described in somewhat the same terms as Smart's article in *IDB.* Ward is well aware of the danger of sentimentalizing, yet he says (p. 194): ". . . Hosea's promises do not negate his threats." To be sure, Ward's book is a search for a theology for all mankind. Necessarily, therefore, he must use the entire book of Hosea in order to get a complete system of sin, punishment, repentance, and restitution. The book of Hosea as it now stands has such a complete system for Judah, and Ward simply and legitimately expands the promise and offers it to all mankind. His mistake (in common with others) is in attributing too much of this complete system to the historical Hosea. It is the concern of this paper to probe the problem of what the historical Hosea said to the historical northern Israel, and not to project a theological plan for the whole human race. Ward has attempted the latter task and has produced an interesting and helpful book. It is to his everlasting credit that he confines himself to group eschatology within this world and does not bring in the resurrection of dead individuals or try to make Hosea a prototype of Jesus Christ, in spite of the fact that the title of his last chapter is "From Death to Life."

The latest work on the subject that I have found is *Hosea, A Commentary* by J. L. Mays, 1969. It is a conscientious study, but rather conventional in its findings. Ch. 3 is accepted, save for the phrases "David their King" and "at the end of the days" in v. 5, which are considered too "Judahistic" or "Judean." Otherwise, the chapter is attributed to the latter part of Hosea's career, thus making his final message one of hope. 11:8-9 are accepted and interpreted as usual, with this comment:

> Yahweh's refusal to destroy Israel is no concession to their sin, no curtailment of discipline; but it is a declaration that his relationship in history with Israel shall not end because of their sin and his wrath. The call of the son (11:1) shall have its fulfillment in a future which unfolds out of the identity and power of God himself.

But Hosea's Israel did not remain "in history"; so perhaps when Mays speaks of "fulfillment in a future" he was thinking of the whole human race, as was Ward; but he should have said so. Immediatley after, he rejects v. 10 as the work of "a later Judahistic theology of salvation." This is a good phrase and might well have been used of some other hopeful passages in the book, such as vv. 8-9 preceding.

Mays ends with his commentary on ch. 14. Vv. 2-4 (1-3) are skillfully interpreted as Hosea's final plea to apostate Israel as it is about to fall. Israel did not repent, yet somehow "Yahweh's word of salvation begins" in v. 5 (4). On the very last page Israel is universalized into all mankind and bad history becomes good Christian theology, derived through Judean editors, though Mays seems unaware of that:

> In Yahweh alone Israel may find life! That has been the message of Hosea in all his oracles—and the word of the Lord which he leaves as a heritage for all who read his prophecy.

The last v. of this final ch. is quite properly treated as an addition of a later time by someone "schooled in the reflections of Wisdom."

So, perhaps the problem of theological ethics in Hosea is this: Would it have been more ethical for God to declare that Israel would be destroyed and then let it happen, or to declare destruction, then change his mind and not let it happen? I opt for the first alternative because I think it was right and because I think it happened that way. But I have a way of choosing the less popular side, and I have little interest in romantic fiction.

After reflection upon the enormous volume of literature on this subject, most of it not even mentioned herein, it seemed fitting to look again at what might be called the first definitive work on the subject in English, namely W. R. Harper's volume on Amos and Hosea in ICC, 1905. Harper did a thorough job, his bibliography running to more than two hundred items, most of them not in English. He probably spent too much space in trying to make a contrast between Amos and Hosea and in ferreting out minor interpolations. Much has been learned since 1905 from archaeology, textual criticism, and all the rest. Yet Harper in his overall view is perspicacious. In discussing the message of Hosea he says (p. cxlvii):

> There is . . . the question whether to Hosea or to later writers we shall ascribe the strongly expressed teaching of Israel's restoration, which is found in the book as it is now constituted. The most careful consideration seems to show that this thought is non-Hoseanic.

And again (pp. clix and clxi):

> It is impossible to reconcile with Hosea's situation and declarations certain passages referring to Israel's future, the so-called Messianic allusions. . . . These passages . . . are entirely inconsistent with Hosea's point of view, and directly contradict the representations which are fundamental in his preaching.

Thus he rejects the happy endings of chs. 1; 2; 11; and 14 and deals with ch. 3 (minus v. 5) as Lindblom did later, by putting it in the early period of Hosea's career. For an interpretation done nearly seventy years ago, this is very good. It is a pity that Harper did not have more followers. But sentimentality and romantic illusions die hard.

The other preexilic prophets from Amos through Jeremiah can easily be accepted by modern "critical" scholars as heralds of doom, yet the severest of them all, perhaps because he was just that, was turned by the Judean editors into the most forgiving spokesman of divine love. But can we not say that the editors were theologically right for their times and for the future, while at the same time admitting that Hosea was historically and theologically right for his time, with a warning for the future which Israel did not heed and a lesson which Judah did not learn?

Finally, a word should be said about Jeremiah, who stood in the South in a position comparable to that of Hosea in the North, namely on the brink of destruction. Few would deny that Jeremiah proclaimed a clear message of doom. As in Hosea, the doom material far outweighs the hope material, and many exegetes seem to be aware of this fact. A considerable number are even willing to consider the "new covenant" passage (31:31-34) and the relatively few similar passages as additions of post-exilic redactors.

Formerly, Professor Hyatt attributed this passage to Jeremiah "as the logical development and outcome of Jeremiah's teaching."[14] But on September 4, 1972, in an appearance in Los Angeles before a section of the Society of Biblical Literature in connection with the International Congress of Learned Societies in the Field of Religion, he indicated that mature reflection had caused him to experience a feeling of doubt on this matter. Thus in the end he moved closer to my own position and this pleases me because of the great feeling of fellowship between us for many years. Both of us would of course have agreed that much of this exilic and post-exilic redactional material is of the utmost importance in the development of later Jewish and Christian theology. Exegetes should no longer apply a derogatory term like "spurious" to this material merely because its authors and editors were modestly anonymous. The fact of postexilic Judean redaction should be recognized and properly utilized for historical and theological research.[15]

NOTES

1. *Crozer Quarterly,* 27 (1950), 200-207.
2. J. P. Hyatt, *Prophetic Religion,* 1947, 102. But there was no repentance, so how could Hosea's final message be one of hope? It is at this point particularly that I find many exegetes to be inconsistent.
3. For similarly drastic views, see C. H. Toy, *JBL,* 32 (1913), 75-79; P. Haupt, *JBL,* 34 (1915), 41-53; L. W. Batten, *JBL,* 48 (1929), 257-273; R. E. Wolfe, *ZAW,* N. F. 12 (1935), 93; H. G. May, *JBL,* 55 (1936), 285-291; R. E. Wolfe, *Meet Amos and Hosea,* 1945, 83-87.
4. Excepting, of course, the preexilic false prophets of prosperity and military success who were opposed by the genuine prophets of their own time; e.g. in 1 Kgs. 22:1-28; Hos. 4:5; 9:7-8; Mic. 2:6-11; 3:5-7; Jer. 23:9-40; 28:1-17; Ezk. 13:1-16.
5. The opposite opinion can perhaps be supported analogically by the concern of Amos to go north to Israel in an attempt to save it. One can also say that Hosea himself fled to the south, became converted to the Judean viewpoint and himself inserted at least some of the Judean type of hope material. So argues R. Gordis, "Hosea's Marriage and Message: A New Approach," *HUCA,* 25 (1954). This idea is not new. It was suggested by H. Ewald, *Commentary on the Prophets,* I, 1875, 210.
6. "The Marriage of Hosea," *BJRL,* 39 (1956), 233.
7. *A Christian Theology of the Old Testament.*
8. *In,* 15 (1961), 261-309.
9. *Dodekapropheten I, Hosea. BK,* XIV, part 1; revised in 1965 without basic change.
10. *IDB,* 2, 648-653.
11. *Hosea. KAT,* XIII, part 1.
12. Emphasis mine; by W. F. S.
13. T. H. Robinson turns 11:8-9 into a doom passage by translating 11:9ab,d as questions expecting the affirmative answer: "Shall I not carry out the heat of my anger? Shall I not return to destroy Ephraim?" etc. Yet he also insists that Hosea "could still not bring himself to postulate that the divine love for Israel would be surrendered forever." See *Die Zwölf Kleinen Propheten, HAT,* XIV, 1938, 4, 44.
14. *Prophetic Religion,* 107. In his commentary on Jeremiah, *IB,* V, 1956, he was less certain. On p. 786 he says the passage is probably authentic"; on p. 1038, while admitting that the wording may not be Jeremiah's, he insists that "the thought is essentially his." In *Jeremiah, Prophet of Courage and Hope,* 1958, 105-107, he was again a bit more positive. In any case, in these two works and in several articles, Hyatt had made himself a respected specialist in Jeremiah studies.
15. My friend's appearance in Los Angeles occurred only a short time before his lamented death. It is regretable that there was no opportunity for discussing with him the full implications of his altered viewpoint, giving more credit to postexilic redactional activity.

ETHICS IN A CULTIC SETTING

JOHN T. WILLIS

Associate Professor
of Old Testament at
Abilene Christian College

In view of Professor Hyatt's interest in the message of the prophets,[1] and of the fact that he once wrote an article on Mic. 6:8,[2] it seems fitting to include in a volume honoring his memory an essay on two psalms which many scholars connect with the prophetic message, and particularly with Mic. 6:6-8, viz., Pss. 15 and 24. A study of articles and commentaries on these psalms since the works of Mowinckel,[3] Gunkel,[4] and Galling[5] in the 1920s shows that by and large Old Testament scholars have attained a consensus as to their nature and function. To be sure, they disagree on specific details, but still they assume that the genre and the *Sitz im Leben* of these psalms are well established. Perhaps this consensus is well-founded! Nevertheless, there seem to be sufficient legitimate alternate ways of looking at these psalms to warrant caution in accepting the prevalent view without careful scrutiny. Thus, in this paper the present writer casts himself in the role of the *advocatus diaboli,* not with a view of proposing a new interpretation of Pss. 15 and 24 at this point, but of reopening an old question which has been considered closed long enough.

What are the fundamental questions which must be answered in analyzing Pss. 15 and 24? By getting these before us, perhaps we will be in a better position to evaluate the strengths and weaknesses of hypothetical alternating interpretations. These may simply be listed for consideration and for easy reference throughout the course of this study.

1. What is the structure of Pss. 15 and 24:3-6?

2. Who asks the questions in Pss. 15:1 and 24:3? What kind of questions are they?

3. To whom or for whose benefit are these questions asked?

4. Who is responsible for giving the answers to these questions in Pss. 15:2-5b and 24:4? How is one to explain the differences in the number of answers given in each psalm?

5. How are Ps. 15:5c and 24:5 to be interpreted?

6. What role is played by Ps. 24:6?

7. What is the *Sitz im Leben* of Pss. 15 and 24:3-6?

8. How is one to explain the relationship of Ps. 24:3-6 to vv. 1-2 before it and vv. 7-10 following it?

I.

With these issues in mind, it seems proper first to sketch the most prevalent view held in scholarly circles. Several scholars find a twofold division in Ps. 15: a question in v. 1, and its answer in vv. 2-5.[6] But the majority of critics see three parts: a question in v. 1, its answer in vv. 2-5b, and a promise of blessing (inviolability) in v. 5c.[7] This view is undoubtedly influenced by the analysis of the structure of Ps. 24:3-6, which is usually divided into three parts: a question in v. 3, its answer in v. 4, and a promise of blessing in v. 5; since it is generally agreed that Ps. 15 and 24:3-6 are similar in structure and content.

The questions in 15:1 and 24:3 are spoken by pilgrims or worshippers who wish to enter the temple (at Jerusalem) to worship and thus ask the appropriate priest(s) at the temple gate what is required of those seeking entrance. Occasionally it has been suggested that temple singers actually spoke or sang these questions in behalf of such pilgrims.[8] The reply in 15:2-5b and 24:4 is given by the appropriate priest. Most scholars do not specify which priest gave this answer, but Galling suggests that it was the *Schwellenhüter*, a priest of third rank.[9] As the worshippers proceed to enter the sanctuary, the officiating priest pronounces a blessing upon them: 15:5c and 24:5, assuming they have met the conditions specified in the reply.[10] Thus, these texts reflect a dialogue which took place between the laity and the clergy. Emphasizing the desire of the pilgrims to "enter" the sanctuary for worship, they may be called "Entrance Liturgies"; emphasizing the regulations (*toroth*, "laws," "instructions") given by the priests, they may be characterized as "Torah Liturgies"; or emphasizing the pilgrims' affirmation that their hearts and lives are in harmony with these conditions and thus are worthy to enter the sanctuary, they may be termed "confession mirrors" (*Beichtspiegel*).[11]

This view rests on several plausible arguments. First, many religions in the ancient world required worshippers to meet certain conditions before allowing them to enter into the sanctuary. There is ample evidence of this and of high moral ethics similar to that found in Pss. 15; 24:3-6 in Phoenician, Greek, Hittite,[12] Babylonian,[13] and Egyptian literature.[14] Although requirements for entrance into sanctuaries in these religions usually consisted of ritualistic demands, high ethical standards do occur.[15]

Secondly, there are several examples of pilgrims or worshippers entering into dialogue (*Streitgespräch, Disputationswort, Diskussionswort*) with priests or (cultic?) prophets, in which the priest or prophet gives ethical instructions. Dt. 26:1-15 describes a dialogue between those who brought their firstfruits to the Lord and the priest; vv. 13-14 in particular resemble the high moral standards in Pss. 15 and 24:3-6. According to Isa. 33:14-16, "the sinners of Zion" ask the prophet which of them can dwell with the devouring fire and with everlasting burnings; his reply consists of high ethical norms. Mic. 6:6-8 may be understood as containing a series of questions by a worshiper or worshipers asking what kinds of sacrifices or ritualistic acts would please God (vv. 6-7), followed by the prophet's reply stating that God requires the highest type of ethics (v. 8).[16] Jer. 7:1-11 might be interpreted to mean that Yahweh told the prophet to stand at the gate of the temple where the priest normally stood to give the people cultic instructions, and to give them ethical instructions. According to Hag. 2:11-13, the prophet asks the priests certain questions and receives a reply; this passage seems to presuppose that it was customary for people to go to a priest for instruction. Zec. 7:2-3 tells how the people of Bethel sent Sharezer and Regem-melech and their men to ask certain priests and prophets what they should do about fasting in the fifth month; again it appears that such a practice was customary. In Mal. 2:7-9 the prophet rebukes the priests because they did not instruct the people as they should.[17]

Thirdly, there are several texts in the Old Testament which indicate that priests, Levites, and/or gatekeepers refused to allow worshippers entrance into the temple if they were unclean, which would require a prior investigation of those seeking entrance.[18] According to 2 Ch. 23:19 Jehoiada "stationed the gatekeepers at the gates of the house of the Lord so that no one should enter who was in any way unclean." Dt. 23:2-5 (1-4) explicitly names certain kinds of people who were forbidden to enter the "assembly of the Lord." 2 Sam. 5:8 declares that "the blind and the lame shall not come into the house," which could very possibly mean "the house of the Lord," i.e., the temple, as the context shows. In Ps. 118:19ff., one speaker asks for entrance into the gates of righteousness and another replies that the righteous shall enter through the gate of the Lord.[19]

Finally, the terminology in Pss. 15 and 24 points to a cultic situation, and most likely to the Jerusalem temple. To some extent, this argument is linked with the view that Ps. 24 is a unit, and not two separate psalms (vv. 1-6 and 7-10) which have been put together accidentally or liturgically.[20] The unity of this psalm is defended on the following grounds: a) the key concepts in the psalm are introduced interrogatively: "Who shall ascend the hill of the Lord?" v. 3, and "Who is the King of glory?" vv. 8, 10;[21] (b) Yahweh's "hill" and "holy place" in v. 3 and the "gates" or "ancient doors" in vv. 7, 9 point to the Jerusalem temple;[22] (c) vv. 1-2 and 7-10 refer to Yahweh's rule over the whole earth; the creator of vv. 1-2, as king, defeats the powers of chaos, vv. 7-10;[23] (d) the concepts of entering into God's presence for worship (vv. 3-6) and of Yahweh as king (vv. 7-10) are also combined in Ps. 95:1-7;[24] (e) those who enter the temple precincts to worship (vv. 3-6) must do so with a realization of the awesomeness and majesty of God whom they approach (vv. 1-2, 7-10);[25] and (f) the opening of the gates to allow the ark entrance (vv. 7-10) was the signal that the worshippers who sought entrance (vv. 3-6) could enter also.[26]

Assuming, then, that Ps. 24 is to be taken as a unit, several arguments (primarily based on terminology) point to a cultic setting of Pss. 15 and 24. (1) *har qodsh^{e}kha* (15:1) or *har yhvh* (24:3; note the parallelism with *m^{e}qôm qodhshô*) also occur in Pss. 2:6; 48:2 and Isa. 2:3; 30:29 respectively, where the contexts refer explicitly to Zion and/or Jerusalem.[27] (2) *'ohel* (15:1) is used of the temple in Pss. 27:5-6 (see v. 4); 61:5 (see vv. 7-8); and Isa. 33:20.[28] (3) the verb *'alah* (24:3) is a *terminus technicus* for a procession "going up" to a hill sanctuary for worship (1 Sam. 10:3; 1 Kgs.

12:33—Bethel), and particularly to Zion or Jerusalem (2 Sam. 6:12, 15; 1 Kgs. 8:4; Ps. 47:6 [see v. 9]).[29] (4) The verbs *biqqesh* and *darash* (24:6) are *termini technici* (used with or without *panîm*) for approaching God at a sanctuary for worship (2 Sam. 12:16; 21:1, Am. 5:5; Hos. 5:15).[30] (5) The terms appiled to Yahweh in 24:7-10 are connected with the ark in other Old Testament texts, indicating that an ark procession is intended here. *kabhôdh* is identified with the ark in 1 Sam. 4:21-22 (cf. 1 Kgs. 8:9-11). Yahweh is thought to be "sitting enthroned" as King above (upon, between) the cherubim of the ark in 1 Sam. 4:4; 2 Sam. 6:2; etc. The phrases "Yahweh strong and mighty, Yahweh mighty in battle" point to a war setting typical of texts involving the ark. The expression *yhvh tsᵉbha'ôth* (v. 10) is a divine title connected with the ark, as e.g., in 1 Sam. 4:4 and 2 Sam. 6:2; and all these terms have a peculiar connection with the Jerusalem cult.[31] (6) Contrary to the earlier view of Wellhausen and his followers, there were priests who were just as concerned with ethical matters as were the prophets and the wise men. As Koch puts it:

> Eine solche Sorge um die Reinheit der Beziehung Mensch-Gott erinnert zwar an die Profeten der späteren Königszeit und an das Deuteronomium, ist aber kein hinreichender Beweis für irgendwelche Abhängigkeit der priesterlichen Gattung von profetischem Einfluss, sondern erklärt sich hinreichend aus innerkultischen Bestrebungen.[32]

Critics who maintain the common position are unable to agree on the *Sitz im Leben* of Pss. 15 and 24. Apparently one of the earliest views is represented by the heading of Ps. 24 in the *Tes mîas sabbaton;* in conjunction with this Snaith thinks that it was a Sabbath Day Psalm.[33] Many scholars avoid connecting these psalms with a specific historical event, and attempt to determine the kind of cultic situation to which they belong. These include the Feast of Tabernacles (or Booths), the New Year Festival, the Festival of Yahweh's Enthronement, and the Covenant Renewal Festival, festivals which are often equated.[34] Kraus denies the existence of a Festival of Yahweh's

Enthronement in Israel for several reasons. First, *yhvh malakh* does not mean "Yahweh *has* become king," but "Yahweh *is* king." Secondly, since Yahweh has no image, there is no way that he could have been "enthroned" as the Babylonian deities were. Thirdly, Israel's concept of Yahweh would not allow her to accept the idea that each year the deity died (in winter), was carried into the Underworld, and later was resurrected (in spring). Finally, the very psalms which are used most frequently to defend the view of Yahweh's annual enthronement (93; 96-99) emphasize that Yahweh continues to rule as king without interruption. Thus Kraus assigns Ps. 24 to the Feast of Booths, but denies that this includes or is to be equated with the Festival of Yahweh's Enthronement.[35]

On the strength of Ps. 24:7-10, it is generally thought that Ps. 24 (and even Ps.15[36]) was sung in connection with an ark procession which originated at some point outside the temple precinct (possibly at the foot of Mt. Zion) and terminated with the depositing of the ark in the Most Holy Place of the temple. In addition to what was suggested above concerning the ark, this view is based on a particular interpretation of *pithhê 'ôlam* in vv. 7 and 9, and of the "kind" of battle assumed in the phrase *gibhôr milḥamah* in v. 8.

pithhê 'ôlam has been interpreted in at least three different ways. (a) *'ôlam* is a divine appellative, and thus this expression should be translated "gates of the eternal." Accordingly, the "gates" could be real earthly gates of the temple enclosure or heavenly gates, "personified" in this context.[37] (b) *'ôlam* means "ancient," thus indicating that the "gates" intended here had been in existence for a very long time when this psalm was written.[38] (c) *'ôlam* is a cultic term meaning "heavenly" or "everlasting, eternal." As in other ancient Near Eastern religions, the Israelites believed that there was a heavenly temple with its "gates for the heavenly King (Ps. 29:9-10) corresponding to or contiguous with the earthly (Jerusalem) temple and its gates.[39] As long as these "gates" are understood as "temple gates," they may be connected with an (annual cultic) ark procession to the Jerusalem temple.

It is usually assumed that the phrase *gibbôr milḥamah* in Ps. 24:8

indicates that Yahweh has just returned from a successful battle against his enemies. But does this allude to a terrestrial or to a celestial battle? Ordinarily critics who interpret Ps. 24 as a cultic psalm sung at an annual ritual understand it as a cosmic battle between Yahweh and the powers of chaos, which they associate with the view of Yahweh as creator who was victorious over the Sea in the hymn of creation (vv. 1-2).[40] That which takes place between Yahweh and his enemies in the heavenly sphere is reflected in that which takes place between Israel and her enemies on the earthly plain.

Nevertheless, there is a variant view among scholars who assign Pss. 15 and 24 to a cultic setting. Several connect the inception of these psalms with a specific historical event, which (at least in part) was commemorated in the cult when these psalms were sung. (a) A few scholars interpret the phrase "Lift up your heads, O gates!" in 24:7, 9 as a call to surrender issued by the Israelite army as they besiege an enemy city. When the enemy surrenders, Yahweh will enter through the "city gates" and make it his own.[41] (b) Others argue that Ps. 24:7-10 is an ancient hymn written by David or one of his contemporaries to commemorate his conquest of Jerusalem against the Jebusites, 2 Sam. 5.[42] (c) The Babylonian Talmud, Sanhedrin, fol. 107b, Mo'ed Katan, fol. 9a, and Sabbath, fol. 30a, connect Ps. 24:7-10 with Solomon bringing the ark into the Holy of Holies (1 Kgs. 8:1-11),[43] and Deissler thinks that Ps. 24 was written to commemorate this event.[44] (d) Some scholars think it was written in connection with the rededication of the temple by Judah Maccabaeus in 165 (164) B.C. This view is based on a number of interesting arguments. It would not have been appropriate to refer to the "gates" of the temple as "ancient" (24:7, 9) in the time of Solomon, or even after the second temple was completed in 516 B.C. "Lord mighty in battle" (v. 8) and "Lord of hosts" (v. 10) suggest a wartime setting, which did not exist when Solomon finished the temple or when Zerubbabel finished it. The summons "Lift up your heads, O Gates:" and other details in 24:7-10 are borrowed from Callimachus's *Hymn to Apollo*, 6-7 (258-247 B.C.). The Maccabees rejected all human kings and proclaimed that God alone was king, which fits 24:7-10 very well. The expression "King of Glory" in 24:7-10 is borrowed from the Book of Enoch. Those who lift up their souls to vanity (v. 4) are sinful Jewish priests who participated in the worship of Zeus in the time of Antiochus IV Epiphanes. The phrase "clear hands and a pure heart" sounds very Hellenistic and was probably taken from the Greek tragedians.[45] (e) Critics rarely connect Ps. 15 with a specific historical event or setting. Kapelrud dates Pss. 15 and 24 in the eighth century B.C. because they are so similar to many statements in Isaiah and Micah.[46] Briggs dates Ps. 15 in the Persian period because the reference to mental truthfulness in v. 2b is typical of Persian ethics, and this psalm would be a forceful reply to the Samaritan demand that the Jews allow them to participate in the rebuilding of the temple (Ezr. 4:2f.).[47] Gunkel and McCullough date this psalm in the postexilic age because the psalmist knows Dt. 23:20 (19); Lev. 5:4; 25:36-37.[48]

While differing in details, scholars have made a good case for interpreting Pss. 15 and 24 as Entrance Liturgies or Torah Liturgies or the like, in which worshippers approach a priest or priests at the gate of the Jerusalem temple, ask for the conditions of entrance, and are given a divine reply through the instruction of the priest(s). It is plausible that they were used in connection with the ark procession at the annual New Year Festival, Festival of Booths, Festival of Yahweh's Enthronement, or Covenant Renewal Festival, as the case may be. And yet, there are alternate explanations of these psalms which are just as plausible, and which should caution one against dogmatism in interpretation.

II.

Still assuming that the questions in 15:1 and 24:3 are straightforward and that those who ask them are seeking information, it could be argued that these are Psalms of Asylum.[49] While the "cities of refuge" were designed for those accused of manslaughter and claiming accidental or unintentional homicide and offered extended asylum,[50] sanctuaries may have been designated as places of refuge for "lesser" crimes and may have offered temporary asylum to those who claimed to be innocent. This would be appropriate to the idea that Yahweh did not want his temple to be used as a "den of thieves" (Jer. 7:11). The verb *gûr* in 15:1 could very easily be taken to mean "find refuge (asylum)," a concept which could be derived from Pss. 27:5 and 61:5 (4).[51] It seems to have been customary for Israelites in a certain area to go to the same sanctuary all the time (see e.g., 1 Sam. 1:3, 21; 2:19). Thus it would not be necessary to ask conditions of entrance *for worship,* since they would already know them.[52] But if they committed a crime or were accused of doing so, it would be necessary to learn the requirements under which the sanctuary allowed one to seek refuge there lest they profane it.[53]

III.

The general analysis of Pss. 15 and 24:3-6 suffers from a lack of symmetry. These sections are divided into three parts, the first spoken by the worshipers (15:1; 24:3), and the last two (15:2-5b, 5c; 24:4, 5-6) by the priests. Galling recognized this lack of balance and tried to compensate for it by suggesting that 24:6 is an assertion of innocence uttered by the people after the priest had finished his response in vv. 4-5, and that the assertion of innocence which surely stood at the end of Ps. 15 in its original form was replaced by v. 5c when this psalm was separated from the cult.[54]

But if it is assumed that worshipers who frequented a certain sanctuary were expected to know the conditions for entrance or *leges sacrae* of that sanctuary, these psalms can be analyzed in a different way. The initial speaker is a priest asking those seeking entrance for worship to demonstrate their worthiness by repeating the requirements (15:1; 24:3). The worshipers reply by repeating the conditions for entrance, which were put in a form easy to remember (a decalogue form in 15:2-5b and a threefold form in 24:4). Then the priest indicates that they may enter into the sanctuary by pronouncing a divine blessing upon them (15:5c; 24:5-6). According to this view, a symmetrical A-B-A pattern emerges.[55]

IV.

If one considers the questions in 15:1 and 24:3 to be rhetorical,[56] several other plausible interpretations of these psalms appear. It seems quite possible that they (or at least that portions of them) were sung antiphonally.[57] This being the case, they may have been written by priests or temple singers or other cutlic personnel to be sung during the worship (not necessarily in preparation for worship) for the edification of the people.

V.

It is clear that Pss. 15 and 24 have strong didactic propensities.[58] The high ethical standards which they advocate are quite similar to those found in the Wisdom Literature, as in Job 29; 31; and in passages scattered here and there throughout the book of Proverbs. Furthermore, Wisdom teachers frequently used rhetorical questions as a teaching method to introduce a thought on which they wished to elaborate (see e.g., Pss. 25:12ff.; 34:13ff. [12ff.]; 94:16ff.; etc.). Thus, it is possible that Pss. 15 and 24 originated in circles of Wise Men who wished to instruct their students or the people in ethical norms.

VI.

Pss. 15 and 24:3-6 are similar to a number of prophetic oracles in structure and content, especially Isa. 33:14-16 and Mic 6:6-8; and this is the case whether the questions introducing the instruction are regarded as straightforward or rhetorical. Consequently, a good case can be made for the view that these psalms come from prophetic circles or that their authors were strongly influenced by prophetic thought.[59] In harmony with the Wellhausenian concept of a rigid dichotomy between prophet and priest in ancient Israel, a concept enthusiastically maintained by Begrich in an article which has had a great impact on some scholars who have studied Pss. 15 and 24,[60] it is sometimes argued that if priests had given the "answers" in 15:2ff. and 24:4ff., they would have stated ritualistic or cultic requirements for entrance into the temple, certainly not ethical requirements,[61] and therefore these psalms must come from prophetic spokesmen.

However, such an extreme view[62] is not necessary to defend the thesis that these psalms are of prophetic origin. Even admitting that priests were concerned with ethical (as well as their ritual) matters, and that Israel had high ethical ideals early in her history, it is still possible that Pss. 15 and 24 come from prophetic circles. Texts like Am. 5:21-24; Hos. 6:4-6; Isa. 1:10-17; Mic. 6:6-8; Jer. 7:1-11; and Isa. 58:1-8 seem to imply that priests at local sanctuaries or even at the Jerusalem temple allowed all sorts of wicked people to enter the holy place to worship, and that it was for this reason that the prophets had to discharge the function which belonged to the priests of appealing to the worshipers to live the kind of life morally required by the kind of God whom they professed to serve.[63]

There is no way that the priests could know whether pilgrims or worshipers kept some of the conditions specified in Pss. 15:2ff. and 24:4f., and thus there was no legitimate reason for them to keep them from entering the temple grounds for worship. For example, a priest could hardly know whether a particular worshiper "spoke truth from his heart" (15:2) or "had a pure heart" (24:4).[64] And it is difficult to see how this can be explained away by the theory that worshipers were so afraid that they would be cursed if they entered the sanctuary unclean that requirements for entrance uttered by a priest would cause them to turn back.[65] Surely they would not even take the trouble to approach the sanctuary in the first place if they felt they would not be accepted. Thus it appears that Pss. 15 and 24 are intended for audiences who must decide for themselves how to respond to the instruction contained in these psalms, and a situation in which a prophet speaks to an audience guilty of the crimes assumed here is suitable.

biqqesh and *darash* in Ps. 24:6 are used in connection with God, not in connection with a sanctuary or temple, a situation similar to that found in Am. 4:4; 5:4-6, 14-15. These verbs are used frequently in the Old Testament to mean "be converted, approach God in prayer, etc." They may very well have this meaning in 24:6, and thus do not necessarily convey the idea of entering a sanctuary for worship.[66] The statements in 15:5c ("he who does these things shall never be moved") and 24:5 ("he will receive blessing from the Lord, and vindication from the God of his salvation") do not fit the questions in 15:1 and 24:3 if they are understood to pertain to entering a sanctuary for worship. But if the questions are interpreted in a setting involving a prophetic reply, the concluding statements are appropriate.[67]

VII.

In spite of the fact that the view has not enjoyed wide reception, one cannot entirely exclude the possibility that Ps. 24 (and even 15) has an eschatological intention.[68] The ark is not mentioned by name in 24:7-10, and the terms used here to justify connecting this psalm with an ark procession can be interpreted in a different way, as is apparent from comparing them with Isa. 40-66 and Ezekiel. The description of Yahweh as a man of war or mighty warrior is not limited to early texts, but appears in Isa. 42:13; 51:9; 63:1-6; 66:15-16. The idea of the "glory" of Yahweh entering the temple through a gate appears in Ezk. 43:1-5 apart from any connection with the ark. Yahweh is said to be "king" in Isa. 41:21: 43:15; and 44:6. Ps. 24:3-6 is similar to Isa. 33:10-16, which is an eschatological text referring to the Last Days or the End Time. The concept of "ascending the hill of the Lord" (24:3) is used of the nations coming to Jerusalem "in the latter days" to learn his ways and to walk in his paths (Isa. 2:2-3). $b^e rakhah$ and $ts^e dhaqah$ (24:5) are words which appear in Isa. 40-66 as synonyms of "salvation" (cf. Isa. 44:3; 45:8; 51:6-7; 65:23), and thus may have an eschatological ring. Consequently, it is possible to number Ps. 24 (and perhaps 15) among exilic and postexilic prophetic eschatological texts which envisioned a bright future through Yahweh's intervention in the Last Days.

VIII.

The views of Pss. 15 and 24 suggested thus far have assumed that they were intended for a rather large audience such as worshipers, students, and sinful people or people thought to be guilty of sin. But these psalms take on a different hue if it is supposed that they were designed for a special person or group in Israelite society.

Koole has advanced the theory that Ps. 15 is a *Königsritual* applied not to Yahweh, but to an earthly king. The purpose of the cult is to expiate sins; thus, a liturgy of entrance requiring a person to be clean *before* he is allowed to enter the sanctuary is out of harmony with the very heart of the cultic concept. The verbs *gûr* and *shakhan* (v. 1) hardly apply to a "visitor" at the sanctuary; rather, they refer to one who "lives" there. This fits the king very well because his royal palace joins hard onto the temple precinct. The high ethical demands in vv. 2-5b agree with similar demands made of the king in Ps. 101, a text which is frequently compared with Pss. 15 and 24. The promise that the person(s) addressed "shall never be moved" in 15:5c has a striking parallel in Ps. 21:8(7), where it is explicitly applied to the king. For a setting appropriate to Ps. 15 (or even 24), Koole suggests that it might well be the choral accompaniment of the "testimony" given to the king at the time of his coronation (2 Kgs. 11:12).[69]

However, it is also possible that Pss. 15 and 24 are addressed to priests by prophets, wise men, or other priests. Indeed, Ps. 15 has been called a "Liturgie des Amtsantritts."[70] It seems certain that only priests (and in certain circumstances Levites) were allowed to enter the Jerusalem temple proper,[71] and the same was probably true of all local sanctuaries in Israel. So if "tent" (15:1) and "holy place" (24:3) mean the main sanctuary, it is hardly likely that these psalms have the common people in mind. According to the Egyptian "Ritual of the Festival Days," the priests had to make a confession pertaining to ritual and moral sins before entering the temple; and the Edfu Temple contains two "unofficial" inscriptions written by workers and decorators of that temple as "instructions" for priests and other temple servants, which contain strong ethical norms.[72] To say the least, it is logical that there would be those in Israelite society (priests, prophets, wise men, etc.) who would feel that priests that placed great emphasis on ritual purity needed to be charged to live according to high ethical standards. *gûr* (15:1) may be used more easily of a priest who lives in temple chambers than of pilgrims who "visit" for a brief time to worship or even the king who actually "lives" or "dwells" in his own place.[73] *qûm* (24:3) also is more appropriately said of priests than of pilgrims.[74]

One might conceive of Pss. 15 and 24 as polemics of the Zadokite priesthood in Jerusalem against its rival, the Elide priesthood, that had been located at the Shiloh temple. The sons of Eli had brought reproach on their father's good name by committing ritualistic and ethical sins (1 Sam. 2:12-17, 22-25; see 2:27-36). The temple at Shiloh was destroyed and Eli and his sons were killed because of these sins (1 Sam. 3:11-14; cf. Jer. 7:13-14; 26:4-6, 9; Ps. 78:59-64). Later the Elide priesthood failed to transport the ark successfully to Jerusalem. Perhaps in imitation of the Philistines (1 Sam. 6:7-11), they carried the ark on a *new cart* (2 Sam. 6:3-4), and not on their shoulders with poles as had been commanded (see 2 Sam. 6:13; 1 Ch. 15:2, 15). Abiathar was allowed to serve as priest along with Zadok under David (apparently in a strained relationship), but in due time he was banished to Anathoth by Solomon (1 Kgs. 2:26-27). In contrast to this, Zadok and his descendants were held in high esteem and finally received the priesthood alone for themselves. In the process, however, there must have been a struggle for power and prestige, and Pss. 15 and 24 may very well reflect the tension. If it may be assumed that the Elide priests gave great emphasis to cultic matters and were guilty of ethical sins, it is reasonable to propose that the Zadokite priests charged them to practice high moral principles.

Although *'ohel* is used for the temple in certain passages, its more natural meaning is "tent" (see 2 Sam. 6:17; 7:2, 6). In fact, critics often point out that the reason the Jerusalem temple is called *'ohel* is that Old Testament writers were intentionally attempting to connect it with the "tent" that had housed the ark before Solomon built the temple.⁷⁵ Ugaritic texts now show that it was quite possible for Yahweh to be called "king" (Ps. 24:7-10) before the conquest and settlement of Canaan (cf. Jgs. 8:22-23), and for Israel to think in "universalistic" terms (Ps. 24:1-2) at a very early time.⁷⁶ "Yahweh Sebaoth" (Ps. 24:10) was a divine title used in connection with the ark at Shiloh (1 Sam. 1:3; 4:4), and the concept of Yahweh as a mighty warrior appears quite early in Israelite religion (cf. Ex. 15:3).⁷⁷ Thus there is nothing in Pss. 15 and 24 to prevent one from interpreting them as polemics against or ethical charges to a ritualistically inclined priesthood such as the Elide priesthood at Shiloh.

IX.

The present study has attempted to show that the nature and setting of Pss. 15 and 24 are not as certain as is generally assumed. Perhaps this will stimulate scholars more mature and perceptive than the present writer to take another hard look at these psalms in an attempt to remove some of the obscurities which still seem to remain. But it is interesting that irrespective of the view scholars have taken, they all agree that these two psalms reflect a very high ethical standard present in Old Testament religion. In 1938, Buttenwieser issued this warning concerning Ps. 15:

> The treatment Psalm 15 has received at the hands of present-day interpreters is anything but adequate. Preoccupied with its literary type more than with its spiritual content, they have missed the spirit and purpose of the psalm and have underrated its ethical standard.⁷⁸

This is indeed a justifiable criticism of the present study. Thus it seems fitting not to conclude without making some remarks concerning the ethical norms set forth in Pss. 15 and 24.

"One of the most penetrating of biblical questions, next in importance to the question as to the nature of God, is, What does God require of His worshipers?"[79] Ps. 24 answers this with a broad principle ("he who has clean hands and a pure heart") applied first to one's relationship with God ("who does not lift up his soul to what is false," i.e., to idols), and then to his relationship with his fellowman ("and does not swear deceitfully," i.e., commit perjury). Ps. 15 answers with a decalog of divine requirements, all pertaining to man's relationship to his fellowman. Possibly v. 2 lays down the broad principles governing man's actions ("He who walks blamelessly, and does what is right, and speaks truth from his heart"), then vv. 3-5b list certain practical expressions of these principles. Here one is forbidden to slander, do evil to, or malign another (v. 3), or to charge interest on loans to the poor and needy or accept bribes against the innocent (v. 5a-b), and is exhorted to despise a reprobate, honor those who fear the Lord, and be true to his word irrespective of the consequences which he might have to suffer (v. 4). It is worthy of note that there is no specific reference to any of the Ten Commandments (Ex. 20:1-17; Dt. 5:6-21) in these requirements. This could be because the people for whom these psalms were originally intended were not guilty of violating the Ten Commandments, or because they took pride in their adherence to these commands as a license to commit the crimes which are condemned (cf. Mt. 19:16-22), or because the crimes condemned were so prominent in their lives when these psalms were first written, or because they had been sufficiently taught these commandments, or for some other reason.

Pss. 15 and 24 raise the question of the proper relationship between worship or cult and ethics. Must one be ethically pure in order to worship acceptably, or is worship a means of motivating (or even enabling) one to improve his moral behavior? Koch argues that in the preexilic period (represented by the "Liturgies of Entrance" including Pss. 15 and 24) the sinner had to be made righteous before he was allowed to enter the sanctuary, but in the postexilic period the sinner was encouraged to enter the sanctuary in order to be made righteous.[80] However, this is an oversimplification. The facts appear to show that cult and ethics stood side by side throughout Israel's religious history, although at different periods more emphasis was placed on one than on the other. Sacrifices, assemblies, singing, praying, etc., *were* considered to be effective, but *"only* when (they were) the organ of the spirit."[81] After all, it is just as possible for man to abuse ethical norms as it is for him to abuse ritualistic acts, if he makes ethical norms works of merit![82] The more complex view seems to be the more valid one:

> Righteousness is *both* a condition *and* result of blessing. A man must cleanse himself so far as in him lies before God will receive him: then the blessing bestowed consists mainly in the power given to attain a deeper and more abiding purity.[83]

Pss. 15 and 24 call for more than "right actions" in or out of the cult. They encourage, yea demand, "right motives." They challenge men to "speak truth *from the heart"* (15:1), to "have clean hands and *a pure heart"* (24:4). For Israel's nobler thinkers, "sin" was not basically a violation of explicitly stated ritualistic or ethical laws, but a struggle of the human heart and will against the heart and will of God. Thus right living consisted of far more than external cultic and ethical acts or words; it had to do with the motive or intention lying behind them.[84] No doubt, many Israelites did not take this sort of religion seriously, but it can hardly be doubted that the authors of Pss. 15 and 24 (whatever the setting to which they belong) were "dead serious" about the quality of religion that they held before their respective audiences.

NOTES

1. See e.g., J. P. Hyatt, *Prophetic Religion,* 1947; and "The Book of Jeremiah. Introduction and Exegesis," *IB,* 5 (1956), 777-1142.
2. J. P. Hyatt, "On the Meaning and Origin of Micah 6:8," *ATR,* 34 (1952), 232-239.
3. S. Mowinckel, *Psalmenstudien,* II. "Das Thronbesteigungsfest Jawhes und der Ursprung der Eschatologie" (1922), 118-120; V. "Segen und Fluch in Israels Psalmendichtung" (1924), 58-60; "L'origine du décalogue," *RHPR,* 4 (1926), 409-433, 503-525, especially pp. 508-511, 517.
4. H. Gunkel, *Die Psalmen. GHKAT,* 1926, 47-50.
5. K. Galling, "Der Beichtspiegel. Eine gattungsgeschichtliche Studie," *ZAW,* 47 (1929), 125-130.
6. Galling, "Der Beichtspiegel," 128-129; H. Schmidt, *Die Psalmen. HAT,* 1934, 23; P. C. Boylan, *The Psalms. A Study of the Vulgate Psalter in the Light of the Hebrew Text,* I, 1936, 47-48; H. Lamparter, *Das Buch der Psalmen, I. BAT,* 1961, 83-86; G. W. Anderson, "The Psalms," *Peake's Commentary on the Bible,* 1962, 415; A. S. Kapelrud, "Salme 15, en paktsfornyelsessalme," *NorTT,* 66 (1965), 40-41; A. Deissler, *Le Livre des Psaumes. Verbum Salutis. Ancien Testament,* I, 1966, 77; F. M. Th. Liagre Böhl, *De Psalmen,* 1-89, 1968, 124; and Roland E. Murphy, O. C., "Psalms," *The Jerome Biblical Commentary,* I, 1968, 574, 578; etc. O. García de la Fuente, "Liturgias de entrada, normas de asilo o exhortaciones proféticas" A propósito de los Salmos 15 y 24?" *Aug* 9 (1969), 281-282, 84; J. A. Soggin, "Il Salmo 15 (Volgata 14)," *BeO,* 12 (1970), 87-88, 90; L. E. Toombs, "The Psalms," *The Interpreter's One-Volume Commentary on the Bible,* 1971, 265; etc.
7. C. A. and E. G. Briggs, *The Book of Psalms. ICC,* I, 112; J. P. Peters, *The Psalms as Liturgies,* 1922, 121-123; Gunkel, *Die Psalmen,* 48-49; F. James, *Thirty Psalmists,* 1938, 239-241; E. A. Leslie, *The Psalms,* 1949, 187-189; S. Terrien, *The Psalms and their Meaning for Today,* 1952, 102; W. S. McCullough, *IB,* IV, 1955, 78; H. J. Kraus, *Psalmen,* I, BK, 110-117; A. Weiser, *The Psalms. OTL,* 1962, 168; J. L. Koole, "Psalm XV—Eine königliche Einzugsliturgie?" *OTS,* 13 (1963), 98; E. J. Kissane, *The Book of Psalms,* 1964, 59-60; J. H. Eaton, *Psalms. TBC,* 1967, 56-57.
8. So e.g., Kapelrud, "Salme 15," 40, who distinguishes sharply between the temple singers (who were influenced by the prophets) and the priests, p. 44.
9. Galling, "Der Beichtspiegel," 126, n. 1, referring to 1 Sam. 4:18 and 1:12; and S. Mowinckel, *The Psalms in Israel's Worship,* I, 1967, 177, referring to 2 Kgs. 25:18. Eaton, *TBC,* 80, says such were "priests of the highest rank."
10. So i.a., Gunkel, *Die Psalmen,* 47-49, 102; Galling, "Der Beichtspiegel," 125; Schmidt, *Die Psalmen,* 23, 42-43; Boylan, *The Psalms,* 47-48; James, *Thirty Psalmists,* 239-241; Leslie, *The Psalms,* 187-189; Terrien, *The Psalms,* 102; McCullough, *IB,* IV, 77, 131; K. Koch, "Tempeleinlassliturgien und Dekaloge," *Studien zur Theologie der alttestamentliche Überlieferungen* (1961), 46, 51; Lamparter, *BAT,* 84; Anderson, "The Psalms," 415; Weiser, *OTL,* 167-168, 233; Koole, "Psalm XV," 98; Deissler, *Le Livre des Psaumes,* 77; Kraus, *BK,* 111-112, 194, 196; Eaton, *TBC,* 56, 80; Mowinckel, *The Psalms in Israel's Worship,* I, 178-179; Murphy, "Psalms," 578; and Toombs, "The Psalms," 265, 269.
11. So Galling, "Der Beichtspiegel," 125-130; followed by Kraus, *BK,* 111; Koch, "Tempeleinlassliturgien und Dekaloge," 50, 51; Weiser, *OTL,* 234; and de Liagre Böhl, *De Psalmen,* 124, 148. Before Galling, B. Duhm, *Die Psalmen. KHAT,* XIV, 1922, 56 referred to Ps. 15 as a *Beichtspruch.*

12. See Galling, "Der Beichtspiegel," 125; and García de la Fuente, "¿Liturgias de entrada . . . ?" 270-271.

13. So the names of the twelve gates of E-sagila, see Galling, "Der Beichtspiegel," 125; the humility of the king on the night of the Day of Atonement, see de Liagre Böhl, *De Psalmen,* 124-125; the Surpu Tablets II, III, and VIII, the Counsels of Wisdom from ca. 1500-1000 B. C., the Shamash Hymn from ca. 1000 B. C. or later, the Sumerian Prayer to Any God from ca. 2000 B.C., and other Confessions of Penitent Ones, see Kraus, *BK,* 111; de Liagre Böhl, 125; García de la Fuente, "¿Liturgias de entrada . . . ?" 271-272; and D. Winton Thomas, editor, *Documents from Old Testament Times,* 1961, 104-117.

14. So ch. 125 of the Book of the Dead, see Galling, "Der Beichtspiegel," 130; Koch, "Tempeleinlassliturgien und Dekaloge," 50; and García de la Fuente, "¿Liturgias de entrada . . . ?" 279, 286; the Ritual for Festival Days, and now in particular the Inscriptions on the Edfu Temple, dating in the third to the first centuries B.C., see García de la Fuente, "¿Liturgias de entrada . . . ?" 275-283, 286.

15. Koole, "Psalm XV," 101, e.g., incorrectly states that requirements for entrance into sanctuaries in the ancient Near East outside Israel were *only* ritualistic.

16. For a detailed presentation of the various interpretations of this passage, see J. T. Willis, *The Structure, Setting, and Interrelationships of the Pericopes in the Book of Micah,* PhD Dissertation, Vanderbilt Divinity School, 1966, 262-263, n. 3; and "Review of Th. Lescow, *Micha 6,6-8," VT,* 18 (1968), 273-278.

17. Scholars cite many other passages to justify the commonly held view of Pss. 15 and 24:3-6, including 2 Sam. 21:1ff.; Isa. 1:10-20; 56:1-7; 58:1-8; 66:1-4; Hos. 4:1-3; Jer. 22:1-5; Ezk. 18:5-9; 33:13-14; Job 31:1ff.; Pss. 5:5-8 (4-7); 18:21-25 (20-24); 50:16-20; 101; 119:101-102; 134:1-2; Lk. 17:14; etc. However, it seems to the present writer that the passages mentioned above make the strongest case.

18. "Temple" within the context of this view must be understood in the broad sense, including the inner and outer court (or courts). H. C. Thomson, "The Right of Entry to the Temple in the O.T.," *TGUOS,* 21 (1965/66), 25-34, has shown that the priests (and in some texts the Levites) alone were allowed to go into the "temple proper."

19. Lev. 21:16-24 forbids *the descendants of Aaron* to "draw near" to God under certain conditions, and may have some relevance here.

20. The unity of Ps. 24 is denied by such scholars as T. K. Cheyne, *The Book of Psalms,* 1904, 101-102; Gunkel, *Die Psalmen,* 101-102, who argues for three original psalms (vv. 1-2, 3-6, 7-10) which were combined later; Schmidt, *Die Psalmen,* 44; and M. Buttenwieser, *The Psalms Chronologically Treated,* 1938, 206.

21. M. Treves, "The Date of Psalm XXIV," *VT,* 10 (1960), 433, n. 1; Kraus, *BK,* 194; de Liagre Böhl, *De Psalmen,* 148; cf. the admissions of Gunkel, *Die Psalmen,* 102; and Schmidt, *Die Psalmen,* 44, at this point.

22. See below.

23. McCullough, *IB, IV,* 134-135; Treves, "The Date of Psalm XXIV," 434; Anderson, "The Psalms," 418; Weiser, *OTL,* 235; Eaton, *TBC,* 79-81; Mowinckel, *The Psalms in Israel's Worship,* I, 178; and de Liagre Böhl, *De Psalmen,* 148.

24. Kraus, *BK,* 195-196.

25. Cheyne, *The Book of Psalms,* 101, 103; W. T. Davison, *The Psalms, I, CentB,* 130; Mowinckel, *Psalmenstudien,* V, 59; Terrien, *The Psalms,* 106, 109; Weiser, *OTL,* 233, 236; and Deissler, *Le Livre des Psaumes,* 119, who says appropriately, "Celui qui franchit le seuil du sanctuaire doit être en accord avec la sainteté de celui qui est Seigneur du Temple."

26. Leslie, *The Psalms,* 190; and Kraus, *BK,* 205-206. Cheyne, *The Book of*

Psalms, 101-104, argues that originally vv. 1-6 and 7-10 were two separate psalms, and that later they were combined because of the references to Jerahmeel, a lunar deity, in vv. 4, 6, 7, and 9, in the "original text." Scholars have rightly ignored Cheyne's preoccupation with Jerahmeel and the Jerahmeelites, which appear in many (quite unexpected!) places in his works.

27. Briggs, *ICC,* 113; Gunkel, *Die Psalmen,* 48; Schmidt, *Die Psalmen,* 23, 42; Leslie, *The Psalms,* 186; Kapelrud, "Salme 15," 41; Kraus, *BK,* 112, 196; and Toombs, "The Psalms," 265.

28. Briggs, *ICC,* 113; Duhm, *KHAT,* 57; Schmidt, *Die Psalmen,* 23; Leslie, *The Psalms,* 186; Kapelrud, "Salme 15," 41; Kraus, *BK,* 111-112; Murphy, "Psalms," 578; and Toombs, "The Psalms," 265.

29. Kraus, *BK,* 196.

30. Galling, "Der Beichtspiegel," 129; Kraus, *BK,* 193, n. c, 197; and García de la Fuente, "¿Liturgias de entrada . . . ?" 273, who points out that *biggesh* and *darash* correspond to the Akkadian *se-'u,* which is also used in cultic settings.

31. For penetrating studies of these terms, see J. R. Porter, "The Interpretation of 2 Samuel VI and Psalm CXXXII," *JTS,* 5 (1954), 161-173; O. Eissfeldt, "Silo und Jerusalem," *KlSchr,* III, 417-425; and especially G. H. Davies, "The Ark in the Psalms," *Promise and Fulfilment,* ed. by F. F. Bruce, 1963, 51-61; cf. also Gunkel, *Die Psalmen,* 103-104; Schmidt, *Die Psalmen,* 44; Deissler, *Le Livre des Psaumes,* 118; Kraus, *BK,* 194-195, 201, 204-206; and de Liagre Böhl, *De Psalmen,* 149. According to J. D. Smart, "The Eschatological Interpretation of Psalm 24," *JBL,* 52 (1933), 176, the first scholar to recognize the connection between the divine title "Yahweh Sebaoth" and the ark was von Lengerke in 1847.

32. Koch, "Tempeleinlassliturgien und Dekaloge," 52; cf. also pp. 51, 55-56, 59; Leslie, *The Psalms,* 187; Kapelrud, "Salme 15," 42; Deissler, *Le Livre des Psaumes,* 77; Kraus, *BK,* 114; and Murphy, "Psalms," 580. Schmidt, *Die Psalmen,* 43, writes pointedly concerning Ps. 24:3-6: "Wenn wir die Kritik der Propheten über den Kultus des israelitischen Volkes lesen, können wir mitunter den Eindruck gewinnen, also sei dieser ganze Kultus nur äusserliches Tun und Lippendienst (Amos 5 23 Jes 29 13 f.). Liturgien wie die hier genannten zeigen, dass das nicht allgemein berechtigt ist."

33. According to Kraus, *BK,* 195.

34. "Dass Ps. 24 ein Festprozessionslied, und zwar eins zur Prozession des grossen Herbst- und Thronbesteigungsfestes Jahwä's ist, darf als sicher betrachtet werden," Mowinckel, *Psalmenstudien,* V. 58; cf. Gunkel, *Die Psalmen,* 104; Schmidt, *Die Psalmen,* 44-45; Leslie, *The Psalms,* 188; R. Rendtorff, "Sammlung und Sendung," *Vom Auftrag der Kirche in der Welt. Festausgabe für Prof. D. H. Rendtorff,* 1958, 121-129, especially pp. 122 and 126; Kapelrud, "Salme 15," 39-40, 42; McCullough, *IB,* IV, 131-132; Anderson, "The Psalms," 418; Eaton, *TBC,* 79; and Toombs, "The Psalms," 269. Lucidly, Kapelrud, "Salme 15," 42, refers to the festival presupposed in Ps. 15 as "den kombinerte host- og nyarsfest og paktsfornyelsesfest."

35. Kraus, *BK,* 201-205.

36. So Kapelrud, "Salme 15," 40.

37. M. Dahood, *Psalms I, AB,* 1966, 153.

38. Davison, *CentB,* 131; Gunkel, *Die Psalmen,* 104; McCullough, *IB,* IV, 132; and Kraus, *BK,* 195.

39. "The Egyptians believed that when the *doors* of the earthly temple opened the portals of heaven (eternal gates) swung wide as well, and the ps. may reflect a similar concept," Toombs, "The Psalms," 269; cf. also Eaton, *TBC,* 80; Kraus, *BK,*

205; and the special study of M. Metzger, "Himmlische und Irdische Wohnstatt Jahwes," *UF,* 2 (1970), 139-158.

40. Cheyne, *The Book of Psalms,* 103; Leslie, *The Psalms,* 189; McCullough, *IB,* IV, 134; Eaton, *TBC,* 79; de Liagre Böhl, *De Psalmen,* 149; Mowinckel, *The Psalms in Israel's Worship,* I, 178; and in particular F. M. Cross, Jr., "The Divine Warrior in Israel's Early Cult," *Biblical Motifs: Origins and Transformations,* ed. by A. Altmann, 1966, 11-30, especially pp. 21-27. Weiser, *OTL,* 235, holds the same view, but argues that it is sufficient to connect this psalm with a divine theophany in the cult, and thus it is not necessary to connect it with an ark procession. Kraus, *BK,* 116, finds a reference to association of the celestial realm with the terrestrial in the phrase "shall never be moved" in Ps. 15:5c.

41. Cheyne, *The Book of Psalms,* 103, identifies this city as the capital of the Jerahmeelites. Davison, *CentB,* 131-132, thinks it is the city of the Jebusites which David conquered and made his capital, Jerusalem, 2 Sam. 5. He says the gates are said to be "ancient" because Jerusalem was a very old city when David captured it.

42. See Terrien, *The Psalms,* 107; Eissfeldt, "Silo und Jerusalem," 420, 422-423; "Psalm 132," *KlSchr,* III, 482, 484; Kraus, *BK,* 206; and Cross, "The Divine Warrior," 21, 24. Eissfeldt argues that Ps. 132:6-9 is an early poem commemorating an event concerning the ark prior to the time it was carried to Jerusalem, which was later incorporated into Ps. 132; and that Ps. 24:7-10 is an early poem commemorating David's bringing the ark to Jerusalem, which was later incorporated into Ps. 24.

43. For the text and an English translation, see I. W. Slotki, "The Text and the Ancient Form of Recital of Psalm 24 and Psalm 124," *JBL,* 51 (1932), 220-221.

44. Deissler, *Le Livre des Psaumes,* 118-119.

45. Seemingly Duhm was the first scholar to suggest the Maccabean Age as the setting for Ps. 24, see Kraus, *BK,* 195. The arguments here are those of Treves, "The Date of Psalm 24," 428-432.

46. Kapelrud, "Salme 15," 43-44.

47. Briggs, *ICC,* 113-114.

48. Gunkel, *Die Psalmen,* 49; McCullough, *IB,* IV, 78.

49. G. Pidoux, "Quelques allusions au droit d'asile dans les Psaumes," *Maqqel shaqed. Hommage à W. Vischer,* 1960, 191-197, finds allusions to the right of asylum in Pss. 7; 11; 17; 26; 27; 31; and 71.

50. M. Greenberg, "The Biblical Conception of Asylum," *JBL,* 78 (1959), 125-132, limits his discussion to the matter of manslaughter as it is treated in Ex. 21:12-14; Dt. 19:1-13; Nu. 35:9-34; and Josh. 20:7-8.

51. On this see Gunkel, *Die Psalmen,* 48; Weiser, *OTL,* 168; Deissler, *Le Livre des Psaumes,* 77; and Soggin, "Il Salmo 15," 83, 88.

52. Mowinckel, *The Psalms in Israels Worship,* I, 177, is sensitive to the difficulty here, and argues that at an early period pilgrims who came to various sanctuaries had to ask the conditions for entrance. But "in the course of time these natural practices would, as so often happens, develop into a fixed form, a rite; in such and such a way people were to ask, and thus they were to be answered on given occasions, even if everybody knew the answer beforehand."

53. In essence this is the view defended by L. Delekat, *Asylie und Schutsorakel am Zionheiligtum,* 1967, 166-169; and vigorously rejected by García de la Fuente, "¿Liturgias de Entrada . . . ?" 269-270, 295-297, with a careful study of the Hebrew terms involved.

54. Galling, "Der Beichtspiegel," 128-129.

55. This view is considered a live option by Terrien, *The Psalms,* 102; and is

mentioned as plausible but not defended by de Liagre Böhl, *De Psalmen*, 148; and García de la Fuente, "¿Liturgias de Entrada . . . ?" 281.

56. See the appropriate remarks of García de la Fuente, "¿Liturgias de Entrada . . . ?" 268, n. 18; 292; especially with regard to the rhetorical nature of the questions used to introduce ritualistic and ethical teachings on the inscriptions of the Edfu Temple in Egypt, p. 283.

57. This has been suggested by such scholars as Davison, *CentB*, 129; Treves, "The Date of Psalm XXIV," 433; Weiser, *OTL*, 235; Dahood, *AB*, 151; Kraus, *BK*, 194; and de Liagre Böhl, *De Psalmen*, 148-149. Slotki, "The Text and the Ancient Form of Recital of Psalm 24 and Psalm 124," 214, 217, 219-220, emphasizes this point. He thinks that the written psalm is an abbreviated form of what was actually sung in the cult, and uses this as justification for adding whole lines to achieve what he believes to be good symmetry. His view is too subjective to gain approval.

58. This has been pointed out by Briggs, *ICC*, 112; McCullough, *IB*, IV, 77; Koole, "Psalm XV," 98; Dahood, *AB*, 83; and others.

59. "Man erkennt hierin deutlich den Einfluss der prophetischen Bewegung, welche die Opfer und heiligen Brauche ganz beiseite geschoben und die Sittlichkeit an ihre Stelle gesetzt hatte," Gunkel, *Die Psalmen*, 48. García de la Fuente, "¿Liturgias de entrada . . . ?" 270, contends vigorously that these psalms are "Prophetic Exhortations," i.e., "instrucciones besadas en la doctrina de los profetas sobre las disposiciones morales y espirituales que debe tener toda persona que desee sacar provecho de un acto de acto de culto." See also Leslie, *The Psalms*, 188.

60. J. Begrich, "Die priesterliche Tora," *Gesammelte Studien zum Alten Testament*, *ThB*, 21, 1964, 232-260 (the article was first published in 1936).

61. See e.g., Smart, "The Eschatological Interpretation of Psalm 24," 179; Koole, "Psalm XV," 100; and García de la Fuente, "¿Liturgias de entrada . . . ?" 289.

62. Here I feel compelled to differ with my esteemed teacher, Dr. J. P. Hyatt, "The Prophetic Criticism of Israelite Worship," *Interpreting the Prophetic Tradition*. LBS, 1969, 203-224, who believes that the great prophets of Israel felt that the cult was detrimental to or stood in the way of true service to God.

Koch and Lescow have devoted special studies to an attempt to reconstruct the history of the Torah Liturgy in the Old Testament. Koch, "Tempeleinlassliturgien und Dekaloge," 45-60, thinks that originally worshippers approached a sanctuary and asked the appropriate priest(s) for conditions of entrance, and that the priest(s) replied with a rather stereotyped threefold statement in participial form (pp. 53, 56). At a later period, statements in the perfect tense were added to the original participial statements to be used by priests in the cultic community as a "decalog" of requirements for entrance such as we find in Ps. 15 (p. 53). Still later, prophets borrowed these cultic instructions when they were approached by persons seeking information as to how to behave in a specific situation, thus explaining Isa. 33:14-16 and Mic. 6:6-8. Concerning the latter, Koch thinks that the prophet's point is that "Opfer und Riten *in der gegenwartigen Stunde* keineswegs das sind, was Gott wunscht" (p. 55). Finally, passages like Ezk. 18:5-17 represent a stage in which the perfect tense was used almost exclusively, and in which the decalog pattern was rigidly followed (pp. 57-58).

Th. Lescow, "Die dreistufige Tora. Beobachtungen zu einer Form," *ZAW*, 82 (1970), 362-379, tries to show that originally in Israel there was a Priestly Torah Liturgy composed of three parts: (1) a general introduction, not necessarily in interrogative form; (2) a body with concrete statements pertaining to cult and ethics, always to be reduced to three statements or lines; and (3) a conclusion, usually in the form of a promise (pp. 362-363). As different situations arose, this Liturgy was applied in different ways, sometimes to a priestly "Liturgy of Entrance" as in Pss. 15 and 24 (pp. 364-365), sometimes to a prophetic oracle as in Jer. 7:1-15 (pp. 365-366), sometimes to foreigners as in Isa. 33:14-16 (pp. 367-368), sometimes to a prayer for torah as in Isa. 58:1-8 (pp. 369-370), etc., but none of these represents the original form or *Sitz im Leben* of the Priestly Torah Liturgy (p. 368).

These views represent careful scholarship, but are too neat to be compelling. For example, there is no reason why instructions consisting of three requirements could not have existed side by side with instructions patterned after or like the Decalog in priestly or prophetic circles. But for the present study, it is significant that neither scholar is embarrassed by assigning ethical ideals to priests or by concluding that Old Testament prophets frequented the cult and drew important portions of their messages from cultic priestly instructions.

63. Cf. Koole, "Psalm XV," 100; and García de la Fuente, "¿Liturgias de entrada . . . ?" 289-290.
64. Cf. Davison, *CentB*, 130; Kraus, *BK*, 115; Kapelrud, "Salme 15," 42, 45; and Gracía de la Fuente, "¿Liturgias de entrada . . . ?" 289.
65. Cf. Mowinckel, *The Psalms in Israel's Worship*, I, 177-179.
66. See the careful study of the use of these terms in the Old Testament by García de la Fuente, "¿Liturgias de entrada . . . ? 292-298, with bibliography.
67. García de la Fuente, "¿Liturgias de entrada . . . ?" 291.
68. E. G. King, Stade, and Cheyne make statements which point toward this interpretation, but it is developed most extensively by Smart, "The Eschatological Interpretation of Psalms 24," 175-180, from which most of the following points are derived.
69. Koole, "Psalm XV," 102, 105-111; cf. also the observations of de Liagre Böhl, *De Psalmen*, 124-125.
70. Koole, "Psalm XV," 102.
71. Thomson, "The Right of Entry to the Temple in the O.T.," 31-32, 34.
72. See the extensive treatment of the pertinent texts by García de la Fuente, "¿Liturgias de entrada . . . ?" 275-283.
73. Koole, "Psalm XV," 99, 103-104; Deissler, *Le Livre des Psaumes*, 77.
74. Treves, "The Date of Psalm XXIV," 433.
75. See Briggs, *ICC*, 113; McCullough, *IB*, IV, 78; Kraus, *BK*, 112; Lamparter, *BAT*, 84, n. 3; Anderson, "The Psalms," 415; Weiser, *OTL*, 168; Kapelrud, "Salme 15," 41; de Liagre Böhl, *De Psalmen*, 125; and Murphy, "Psalms," 578.
76. See Kraus, *BK*, 198-200; and J. T. Willis, "The Song of Hannah and Psalm 113," forthcoming in *CBQ*.
77. Kraus, *BK*, 201, 206.
78. Buttenwieser, *The Psalms*, 203.
79. Leslie, *The Psalms*, 186.
80. Koch, "Tempeleinlassliturgien und Dekaloge," 60.
81. H. H. Rowley, *Worship in Ancient Israel*, 1967, 113.
82. Cf. Kraus, *BK*, 114.
83. Davison, *CentB*, 130.
84. On this point, see the excellent essays by B. Gemser, "The Object of Moral Judgment in the Old Testament," *Adhuc Loquitur*, ed. by A. van Selms, *POS*, VII (1968), 78-95 (article first published in 1961); and "Gesinnungsethik im Psalter," *OTS*, 13 (1963), 1-20.

IS THERE A CLASS-ETHIC IN PROVERBS?

BRIAN W. KOVACS

Graduate Student at
Vanderbilt Divinity School

> Why, Faustus, hast thou not attained that end?
> Is not thy common talk sound aphorisms?
> —Marlowe, *Doctor Faustus*

The Egyptian scribal academies used instructions, collections of sayings called *sebayit,* to teach apprentices both the skill of writing and the scribal art of life. As part of his curriculum, the young scribe would copy and memorize a few lines each day. Among the sayings, the admonition-form (*Mahnspruch*) predominates over direct statement (*Aussage*) until the period of the later teachings. A brief *Rahmenerzählung* generally sets the scene, then a statement of purpose couched in co-ordinated infinitives precedes the maxims.[2] The Book of Proverbs commences with much the same apparent form: superscription, purpose stated in co-ordinated infinitives, motto. Chs. 1-9 present a series of admonitory discourses. The terms "father," "son" and "mother" may reflect the technical terminology of the school.[3] Christa Bauer-Kayatz has cast serious doubt on the late date customarily accorded these chs. Multilingual Hebrew scribes who had ready access to international literatures could easily have mediated Egyptian didactic writings and even hypostatic wisdom (*ma'at*) in the monarchic era; manifold Egyptian influences have been detected elsewhere in Hebrew literature.[4] Since Udo Skladny's content analysis of the four central mashal collections also argues a preexilic date,[5] attempts to locate Hebrew aphoristic wisdom in a royal academy or court school are soundly founded on Egyptian analogy. Certainly, the presence of a literarily-dependent parallel to the Teachings of Amenemope at Prov. 22:17-23:12 supports the inference.[6] Thus, on the basis of form and *Sitz im Leben,* one would expect to find some sort of class-ethic or professional code.[7] There are, however, some difficulties with this conclusion.

First, a few scholars find the origins of aphoristic wisdom within a folk milieu because of the direct expression of common experience, usually without theological reflection, that typifies the more frequent Hebrew *Aussage* form.[8] Others trace back certain forms of the proverb to an early clan wisdom (*Sippenweisheit*); the paternalism of the school originates in patriarchalism.[9] Both views confront important form-critical problems. It is hard to accept that Egyptian instructions, didactically-oriented school collections of *Mahnsprüche* and *Aussagen,* should so closely approximate in form and content either Hebrew folk (popular) or clan literature. More, folk sayings elsewhere in the Hebrew Bible seldom if ever show the balance or parallelism of the meshalim in the four collections, let alone display such remarkable consistency of style. They often lack the latter's two-line form. Isolated, they cannot present the catchword structure and paronomastic ordering of the collected maxims.[10] Unlike the discourse passages, these collections use *Mahnsprüche* quite sparingly; the vocative $b^e nî$ occurs only twice (19:27; 27:11).

Second, R. B. Y. Scott has recently joined those who hold that the four collections evidence redaction and revision and therefore do not present a single world-view nor arise from a common setting. He concludes that a secular sayings collection has been reworked by a theologising yahwistic editor, as supported by theological inconsistencies and the pattern of differences in parallel aphorisms.[11] An adequate response would require us to go far beyond the bounds of this study. In defense of a more unitary view of the collections, we appeal to Gustav Boström's analysis of the paronomastic structure that ties the sayings together.[12] Seamless redaction in poetry is quite difficult. The proverbs present a developed and sophisticated application of catchwords, synonym-sequences, assonances, word-plays, repeated forms and thematic units which we contend bespeak a cultivated aesthesis that editing might be expected to disorder.[13] Horst Preuss compares the theology of the maxims with that of comparable wisdom in the ancient Near East. Except for a specific cultic use of *yir'ath yhvh,* they are entirely consistent; and the absence of normative Hebrew theology has long been recognized (e.g., covenant, election, promise, Zion).[14] Joachim Conrad finds that the technical terms in the *Gegensätze* (righteous-wicked, wise-fool) comprehend comparable semantic fields in the collections.[15] Finally, we believe that analysis of wisdom rhetoric—its preference for the generality, technical language (especially in yhvh-statements), proprieties—would alternatively explain much of Scott's evidence.

Third, a number of scholars, including many influenced by the Germanist André Jolles,[16] attribute aphoristic wisdom to the attempt to articulate and explain common experience. While set in the academies, proverbs appeal to a universal audience; their internationalism reflects an inclusivism of thought and temperament. Though recent work on authority and world-ordering righteousness (*ma'at*) has caused them to retrench,[17] Gerhard von Rad and Walther Zimmerli still appeal to an experiential base that resists assertion of class-ethic.[18] On the other hand, Hermisson regards *Standesethik* as an "of-course."[19] Thus, the everyday common-sense character of proverbial wisdom requires explanation. The issue of *Standesethik* deserves to be examined in terms of the evidence.

We take for our investigation the four great mashal collections, which Skladny labels, for convenience' sake, A (chs. 10-5), B (16:1-22:16), C (chs. 25-7), and D (chs. 28-9). They almost certainly pre-date the discourses. They present adequate material for useful content-analysis, without complicated exegetical problems raised by some of the other collections. Most important, they have much in common. The vast majority of sayings are in two-line balanced form with parallelismus membrorum. Antithetic parallelism dominates in A and D; synthetic and synonymous, in B and C. Thematic groups of maxims occur, especially in C. Dislocations in the LXX along with added sayings at its seams suggest that these are indeed separate groups, although the term "collection" should here indicate only the relative thematic independence of the sayings and not some fact of composition. Common form plus the uniformities of content already mentioned make these four groups most appropriate for this short study.

We shall begin by clarifying the various meanings of class-ethic (*Standesethik*) which are not dependent on one another. Within each meaning, we shall note the possible range from openness to closure, toward the world of experience and toward their potential audience. We then shall consider the evidence in the sayings with respect to the alternative definitions, from the least rigorous to the most stringent. Two points should be emphasized. First, the proposed definitions are independent of one another. Hence, different kinds of evidence must be adduced for each, and one could respond to the problem posed by each meaning quite differently without involving himself in hopeless inconsistency. Second, many difficulties in deciding the issue of *Standesethik* and wisdom result from a failure to recognize that closure is not implicit in class-ethic per se. It represents a separate matter to be decided.

Class-ethic can mean three rather different things. At minimum, class-ethic is the ethos of a specific social group—a system of values and a corresponding perspective on the world founded in that group and common to it. Their view may be open to the world or closed, addressed universally or to a select few. The form-critical search for *Sitz im Leben* assumes that a literary work clearly reveals class-ethic in this basic and limited sense.[20] Second, *Standesethik* refers to a restricted ethic or in-group morality. Different standards of conduct are applied to outsiders as opposed to members of one's own social group. This type of class-ethic implies sharply varying values inward and outward. Patriarchal tribalism is often considered to display an in-group morality: outlawry constitutes an extreme case of restricted morality at work. A third definition of class-ethic construes it as a professional code. To assure its own security, to conduct its affairs reliably, a professional group requires set (stated) standards of conduct. Class-ethic means these professional standards. There is implicit a distinctive scale of values common to the profession, but the ethic and the audience can remain relatively open and the ethos is not necessarily regarded as all-encompassing. Over against in-group morality this sense is more demanding with respect to evidence and analysis, hence our use of the terms rigorous and stringent.

Each of these definitions admits of degrees of closure. Closure implies some rejection of the world and its interests in favor of a turning inward toward the values of one's own particular social group. One's audience then becomes limited to his own circle. Openness entails acceptance of the world and a broad, if not universal, audience. Class-ethic need not be closed, nor do its conditions need to be extremely narrow and rigid. These are, however, descriptive categories and we should not attempt to psychologize them.

We need not belabor the point that these collections are not closed. The evidence cited to support the experiential position of von Rad and the anthropocentric-optimistic stand of Zimmerli conclusively shows the openness of these wise toward their world, experience and learning.[21] They are not utterly inflexible. They did not polemicize by applying willy-nilly a pre-conceived abstract intellectual system through all of life, though they did possess a set of explanations and categories with which to organize and comprehend experience. The practice of collecting such diverse and heterogeneous proverbs as well as the artistic activity of coining them would contradict closure of content or attitude. As to audience, we shall argue that the wise were not universal; the fool appears unamenable to reflective instruction, and the wicked man rejects it. Still, the sages address the problems of instructing the ignorant, disciplining the young, and counseling those in authority; so, their audience is wide—thus, relatively open.

Equally, the first definition should require little further argument. The paranomastic structure, refinement of form, coherent and consistent terminology, and comparable view of the world among the collections oppose the notion that they originated in some generalized popular or folk setting. The social location of Hebrew aphoristic wisdom, while we may debate its details, must be among the literati and those with scribal education.[22] That their world-view has so much in common in form and content and even theology with other ancient Near Eastern wisdom, to the exclusion of otherwise normative Hebrew theology, bespeaks this definable social group at work as the one that had useful access to these international points of view. Finally, this group produced wisdom and didactic literature in Egypt and probably in Mesopotamia, so the inference is logical. The counter-inference is not plausible, that the sophisticated writings of the learned in one society should so closely resemble the popular wisdom of another (or that located in some quite different social group), especially when the two societies are closely affiliated socially and intellectually. The two stronger definitions, however, are more interesting.

Is there an in-group morality in Hebrew proverbial wisdom? Here again the extreme case involves closure: a morality which is observed only with respect to members of the group while no standards except perhaps enlightened self-interest apply toward outsiders. An in-group ethic need not be closed. Paternalism represents an extreme of openness which may still support a restricted morality. In this respect, the wisdom of these collections appears again to be somewhat open through sayings which we have chosen to call *noblesse oblige*. Throughout, we find concern continually expressed for the *déclassé* of society: the widow, the poor, the oppressed, the powerless. Servants and slaves are mentioned with a touch of irony (17:2; 29:19, 21). Others are implied by meshalim about weights and measures, false testimony, and even the victim of the practical joker (26:18-9). Domestic animals are even mentioned (12:10). Weinfeld classified these interests as humanism, regarding wisdom as the source of deuteronomic social ethics.[23] Certainly the comparison is no less impressive with the social and ethical imperatives of prophets like Amos and Micah.[24] One is struck by the repetition of many of these sayings and by their concentration on certain specific social transactions to the exclusion of others. Thus, while false testimony is roundly condemned, the meshalim display an oft-remarked ambivalence toward bribery that might well be termed grudging admiration (17:8; 18:16; 19:6; 21:14; 25:14?). Such concessions evoke the description of wisdom as pragmatic and worldly-wise. Fensham has examined such sayings elsewhere.[25] When used by kings, statements of social concern for the poor and oppressed expressed their devotion to duty and affirmed their discharge of social responsibility. The king has behaved properly in office, undertaking those tasks required of a dutiful king. Similarly, the social concern of the wise can plausibly be founded in the need to assert and uphold social responsibility. Thus, the specific situations they mention are less important for themselves than for what they express about the wise: they are responsible and dutiful citizens who act to uphold the proper social order. The ideological dimension of these proverbs probably exceeds their specific moral application. Two additional points support this interpretation.

First, the characteristic style of collection A, predominant in the others as well, remains the *Gegensätze* or antithetic pairs. Many of these sayings, especially about the righteous and the wicked, verge on the abstract to the point of banality. Clearly, unless these sayings are simply trivial, something is amiss in our interpretation of them. Scott argues that sayings concerning the wise and the fool show a concern with experience that makes them lively and vivid by comparison ("recognizable human beings in imaginable situations"),[26] but many of these maxims are no less abstract and routine than the dichotomies of the righteous and wicked man.[27] We miss the full impact of meaning that the Hebrew wise man understood in these terms and their equivalents, which suggests that the terms functioned ideologically. What filled the concepts was not some specifiable group of categories, else we should be able to discover how to expand them with meaning,[28] but the implication of an entire world-view, identification with a "way of life." Lacking these identifications, we do not experience the sayings in their depth, but superficially. That other aphorisms as well should have this ideological dimension, therefore, should not surprise us.

Second, the wise were quite concerned with the attitude of a person—his disposition toward life. We call this orientation somewhat prolixly a person's intentionality. The meaning of a deed, thus its ethical significance, not only cannot be separated from, but seems to rest upon, the way in which a man approaches life.[29] Hence, it again follows that the wise appeal to the accepted statements of social justice to validate their social responsibility (as intentionality).

Finally, we adopt the somewhat polemical term *noblesse oblige* specifically to counter those students of Max Weber or Emile Durkheim who wish to find here some incipient theory of *ressentiment*.[30] Like those in almost every society, the Hebrew intelligentsia were probably administrators and teachers, a group separate from the rich or the powerful—sometimes counselors whose power consisted solely in the adroitness of their speech, but not statesmen (Ahikar excepted). While they could plead for social justice, they had neither the wealth nor the power to bring it about themselves.

We should not underrate the significance of intentionality, because it demonstrates the two systems of values at work which verify in-group morality. Since Egyptian influences are clearly discernible in the meshalim, much recent wisdom scholarship has sought an order in Hebrew wisdom analogous to the Egyptian *ma'at*.[31] This world-ordering system is made the foundation of some kind of doctrine of retribution: (1) where right acts set in motion by their very nature good consequences, and evil acts entail evil outcomes;[32] (2) where every action consists of deed and consequence, the effect and the deed forming a unit with a common moral standing;[33] or (3) where the pattern of a person's behavior, not any particular act, brings about appropriate responses in the world.[34] Generally, this order is taken to govern all of creation; Würthwein does not exclude even Yahweh himself.[35] Where Yahweh is considered independent, he may be regarded as the guarantor of this system who alone has adequate knowledge of its totality in the face of human finitude, or else as the potential interposer in an almost-mechanical system who breaks the causal chain in accord with his wisdom and justice.[36] Skladny, for example, argues that these four collections can be placed in a historical sequence on the basis of marginal differences in both their implicit social worlds and, more important, their conception of the doctrine of retribution.[37] As wisdom develops, he contends, the relationship between act and consequence changes radically, as does the role of Yahweh. In A and D, the earliest collections, the wise made no more distinction between thought and act than they did between deed and consequence. While Yahweh appears, he is principally the guarantor of the system who justifies the order and empowers it to bring about its inexorable effects. In B, the sages have come to realize the inaccessibility of plans and attitudes; deeds alone determine outcomes. The naive optimism of A and D is gone. Yahweh, however, has become the creator and knower of all; no sphere of existence lies outside his ken. Also, one cannot comprehend the totality of the created order; Yahweh brings every deed to its consequence according to his judgment. He is non-mechanistic and active. In D, retributive justice has declined in favor of a personal and individualistic relationship to Yahweh. This position is reached partly by extrapolation from B; C is a later *Bauernethik* which centers on the tangible and practical, since Yahweh's order is utterly incomprehensible. Skladny also perceives changes in content. A and D bespeak a court setting, in the royal school; B is still administrative and academic but broader and more democratized; C reflects departure of wisdom from the court for a simpler, more rural, setting. We observe an important caveat: these distinctions are founded on statistical analyses, based in marginal differences of content and style.

Whether we accept the *ma'at*-like creative order with which man must harmonize himself (or accept the consequences of his refusal) postulated by Gese and Schmid, or the retributive justice of Skladny, based on what he ambiguously refers to as the "order" of creation,[38] we find a sharp division in the world of the wise. We remain unconvinced by Skladny's chronology, but his reference to *Haltung* when taken as "attitude" is central.[39] The overt act alone determines neither the outcome nor the ethical significance. People act. The person who acts and where he stands with respect to wisdom and righteousness are the important things. The meaning of an act depends on intentionality; the same act can evoke radically different responses. Fool's talk is so much jabber (26:7, 9); the wise give effective counsel (15:22-3). Fools should be beaten; wise men should be mildly rebuked when they stray, but not struck (17:10, 26; 19:25). Even the comprehending servant is better-off beaten (29:19). The wicked experiences his fears; the righteous, his hopes (10:28). Honor among thieves is its own condemnation (29:24). A man's associates determine his fate (14:7). While both the wise man and the fool are convinced of the rightness of their ways, wisdom brings honor and life, while folly is its own reward (16:22). Wisdom is increased by wise associations and apparently through collective judgments of the wise (11:14). "Hatred stirs up strife, but love covers all offenses" (10:12). "He who conceals hatred has lying lips, and he who utters slander is a fool" (10:18). On any other terms, this last statement is inconsistent.

The adversity sayings reinforce the importance of right disposition.

The wise recognized the dilemmas of life, that one is compelled to choose between seeming evils. The wise clearly would prefer to sacrifice wealth (19:22; 28:11), position (16:19), plenty (15:16-7) for wisdom, justice, quiet and restraint, not to mention the "fear of Yahweh." They do not assert naive retribution; wisdom is not valuable simply because of what it is supposed to bring in return, but for itself. Theirs would be an incomprehensible pragmatism that sacrificed ends for means. They see that Yahweh and the natural world sometimes bring unavoidable adversity from which wisdom cannot save them (e.g., 14:13; 21:30; 28:3). One's attitude, his intentionality, however, can make reward out of loss: "all the days of the afflicted are evil, but a cheerful heart has a continual feast" (15:15). Right relationship with Yahweh makes effective wisdom; "when a man's ways please the Lord, he makes even his enemies to be at peace with him" (16:7). So with all matters cultic and religious, right intentionality constitutes the *sine qua non* of prayer and sacrifice: "The sacrifice of the wicked is an abomination to the Lord, but the prayer of the upright is his delight" (15:8). The same passionate impetuosity which is the fool's nemesis in word and deed pursues him in the cult. Thus, "it is a snare for a man to say rashly, 'It is holy,' and to reflect only after making his vows" (20:25). Further, the rites of the wicked wickedly done are merely doubly abominable; "the sacrifice of the wicked is an abomination; how much more when he brings it with evil intent" (21:27). The pairs of antitheses set out these distinctions well. Certainly, righteousness is regularly set against wickedness, and wisdom against folly, without significant interchange—they delimit distinct semantic fields.[40] Still, righteousness seems to be a precondition of wisdom, with folly the precondition of wickedness. Only a righteous man can hope to seek wisdom successfully; the evil man is first of all a fool.

The wise do not slavishly support the status quo. Distinctively iconoclastic statements recur among the sayings, while others set out a different standard of values. The wise slave will rule the foolish son and share in inheritance (17:2). Rich and poor alike were created by Yahweh (29:13). Pride brings failure; humility leads to honor. To quest for success or favor means defeat; fidelity, trust in Yahweh, restraint bring what cannot be sought directly. Thus, even if the wise man is oriented toward the acknowledged Hebrew goods-of-life (long life, success, progeny, and recognition), he may not seek them directly nor by the path of his own planning. Only by pursuing wisdom for its own sake, so that it is good and valuable in its own right rather than instrumentally, by means of the discipline of restraint, can he succeed. It is only a slight exaggeration to say that the wise could seek success only by giving it up.

The distinct standards applied by the wise and their critical evaluation of folly and wickedness both ultimately imply a virtually unbridgeable gulf separating wise and fool, righteous and wicked, reminiscent of the ritual boundary between sacred and profane, profane and taboo. Thus, "why should a fool have a price in his hand to buy wisdom, when he has no mind?" (17:16). (1) Acts inevitably bring consequences that are all but irremediable. (2) One must develop not only the right action or wise pattern of behavior, but the entire orientation toward life, the intentionality, if he would be right or wise. Hence, the education of children to establish this disposition ranks high among wisdom concerns from the first. (3) Human planning is ineffectual against the determinations of Yahweh. These three elements justify our drawing a sharp line between the wise and others and our perceiving in their ethos an in-group morality.

The third definition is the most difficult to resolve, although much of what we have just said can be applied to establishing that the wise certainly had their own definite standards of conduct. In the Egyptian instructions, including notably the Teachings of Amenemope, references to the scribal profession and its life are routine. Indeed, the Teaching of Khety son of Duauf satirizes the trades to vaunt scribalism.[41] There are various scribal tools mentioned: pen, ink and palette. They praise the work of recording the heritage of the past and the perpetuation of oneself in transmitted knowledge. The same emphasis fills Sir. 38:24-39:11.[42] Yet we search in vain among these meshalim for similar clear references. Never do they unmistakably mention the ideal scribe. The comparison with Egypt, however, is otherwise tantalizing and apt, especially when we consider such phrases as "the Lord weighs hearts" (16:2; 17:3). We find considerable similarity between the patterns of life espoused by the Egyptian and Hebrew wise. Thus, the Hebrew aphorisms support an ethic of restraint. A man should be cool of passion, not precipitous and hasty. The intemperate man of passion commits himself too quickly, whether in matters secular or religious, and then becomes entangled in his words. The cool man does not waste speech (e.g., 16:20-30). There are many suggestions of courtly life—how to get along with the king, injunctions against incurring royal wrath, and warnings about kingly power (16:10-15; 25:2-7). Presumably the repeated references to speech have some sort of courtly setting, where the ability to deal in terms of court etiquette while presenting one's ideas in meticulous but attractive fashion would be essential to professional survival, let alone advancement. Thus, the wise man knows the virtues of competent speech as well as silence. The ethic of restraint, however, enables him to avoid incurring the wrath of the powerful unnecessarily (14:15-18, 29-30). Perhaps this situation also explains the somewhat cavalier attitude toward bribery already mentioned; it was a sort of given administration that could easily be assimilated intellectually. Again we have the implication that the wise were advisors and administrators but that fundamental power, and thus consequences, lay with others. We find several distinct groups of king and court sayings among these collections.

The instruction and discipline of youth play an important role among the wise, because of the fatefulness of one's decision for or against the life of wisdom (13:24; 19:18). If for no other reason than that the meshalim cover such diverse matters of life, we may infer that the wise man was expected to know at least something about many things, from trade to war, from the courts to the cult. We cannot exclude the possibility that references to family apply to the academic setting as the technical terms of academic respect instead of (or in addition to) simple filial devotion. The matter of instruction brings us to the crucial question of authority. What is the wise man's warrant? The prophet has *koh 'amar yhvh;* the priest has torah, tradition, and rite. Würthwein states the presuppositions of wisdom in basic terms: wisdom can be learned; wisdom can be taught; man can conform to wisdom's order; wisdom's order compasses everything, even the pattern of Yahweh's activity.[43] Scholars of *ma'at* have approached authority from the side of order. The wise man's warrant consists in his appeal to a cosmic order which interpenetrates the entire world and all of life and which joins behavior and consequences with the sanction of the creator's unsearchable wisdom.[44] Others approach the problem of authority through the effective word of counsel.[45] *'etsah* does not mean simply giving advice which can then be accepted or rejected according to the whims of the hearer. When given as counsel, it is the divine word no less than torah or oracle. Not surprisingly, then, 'mashal' can mean 'oracle' as well as 'proverb.'[46] The word of Ahithophel amounted to a divine oracle (2 Sam. 16:23). In the admonitions of the wise, the motivating clause is no more essential to the saying's authority than are such clauses for torah and oracle.[47] In this sense, wisdom is authoritative *dabhar,* the word of Yahweh. Whether one must then appeal to order per se as the validation of this word seems rather dubious. In any case, to speak of order in the ancient Near East quickly suggests the opposing myth of chaos.[48] If comparisons with *ma'at* and appeals to cosmic order are valid, then the basis of such a sharp division between the wise and the fool, the righteous and the wicked, becomes clear. The wicked and the foolish have not simply rejected good advice, choosing to follow their own misguided intellects. They are not merely ignorant or even obscurantist. Rather, they have repudiated the creative order of Yahweh in favor of the countervailing forces of chaos (*isf.t* for *ma'at*). While their decision may not be fateful for the cosmos in mythic terms, its social consequences could not lightly be dismissed. If so, we have tended to overemphasize in wisdom study the postulated differences between wisdom—and priestly—thought. The order-chaos motif would form the point of contact between knowledge and rite. Since both are founded in noetic traditions, such affinities do not want for plausibility. Such a mythic dimension would also support the ideological *Tendenz* which we earlier educed.

Finally, many of the aphorisms in these four collections reflect a concern with propriety, the appropriateness of time and place. One cannot study the meshalim without immediately recognizing that they display innumerable contradictions. If we reject the theory that no single world-view brought these sayings together or composed them, then we must cope with their contradictions, especially if wisdom is to be authoritative. Propriety helps provide that explanation.[49] It represents the sacral and profane characters of persons, places and times. Behavior appropriate to a wise man is improper in the fool. What is fitting at one time may bring a curse at another. "Like a gold ring in a swine's snout is a beautiful woman without discretion" (11:22). "To make an apt answer is a joy to a man, and a word in season, how good it is!" (15:23). "Fine speech is not becoming to a fool; still less is false speech to a prince" (17:7). "Like a lame man's legs, which hang useless, is a proverb in the mouth of fools" (26:7). "He who blesses his neighbor with a loud voice, rising early in the morning, will be counted as cursing" (27:14). "The partner of a thief hates his own life; he hears the curse, but discloses nothing" (29:24). Generally, the bounds of propriety coincide with the antitheses, although there are sayings which show that propriety is a virtue with its own distinct applications (e.g., 25:14; 28:3). To be wise, therefore, is to know both the right and the fitting occasions for given undertakings.

Court and king sayings, instruction and discipline, an ethic of restraint, observance of proprieties, and a system of authority suggest a professional ethic of administrators or officials. We assume from Sir., Egyptian analogies, and other ancient Near Eastern literatures that this ethic is scribal, but overt references to specific scribal activities are lacking.

We conclude that wisdom displays evidence of class-ethic, though wisdom tends to be open to experience, concerned for the *déclassé* and interested in the instruction of children and youth in general. The mashal collections come from a distinct social group and retain marks of that origin. More strictly, the wise perceived a gulf, crossed if at all only with the greatest difficulty, between themselves and fools, between the righteous and the wicked, and perhaps between world-order and chaos. They thus had their own realms of sacred and profane. They possessed a distinctive value-system which revalued the life and behavior of outsiders to such a degree that we regard it as an in-group morality, though by no means closed to the world. Finally, there are indications of a specifically scribal ethical code probably associated with their employment as administrators and officials in governmental chancellories and offices as well as the court. The situation of the schools is perhaps implied, though seldom; scribal tools and activities are never clearly identified as such. Since the literature seems to have a strong ideological cast, we suggest that it was not compiled as school text or instruction for intiates but rather as a stylized form of intellectual reflection. The wise man wrote meshalim and collected his colleagues' compositions because they so aptly expressed *in nuce* valued aspects of his life. His principal audience were his *confrères*. To write a mashal was to engage in a demanding but satisfying aesthetic and intellectual exercise. Though we lack the assumed elements of his existence which would give us full insight into their power and beauty, we are beginning to perceive their depth and the high art of their collection.

NOTES

1. An earlier version of this paper was read to the Old Testament Section of the Southeastern region of the *SBL* in Atlanta, March 1973.
2. Hellmut Brunner, *Altägyptische Erziehung,* 1957; R. N. Whybray, *Wisdom in Proverbs,* 1965, 33-71; Cf. H. Duesberg and I. Fransen, *Les Scribes Inspirés,* 1966, 15-95.
3. P. A. H. de Boer, "The Counsellor," *SVT*, III (1969), 62-71.
4. *Studien zu Proverbien 1-9,* 1966; *Einführung in die Alttestamentlichen Weisheit,* 1969, 36-92.
5. *Die Ältesten Spruchsammlungen in Israel,* 1962.
6. B. Couroyer, "L'Origine Egyptienne de la Sagesse d'Amenemopé," *RB* (1963), 208-224; Ronald J. Williams, "The Alleged Semitic Original of the *Wisdom of Amenemope,*" *JEA* (1961), 100-106.
7. Robert Gordis, *Poets, Prophets, and Sages,* 1971, 160-97.
8. Claus Westermann, "Weisheit im Sprichwort," *Schalom. Alfred Jepsen Festschrift,* 1971, 73-85.
9. Erhard Gerstenberger, *Wesen und Herkunft des "Apodiktischen Rechts",* 1965, 110-144; Kayatz, *Einführung,* 13-21.
10. Johannes Schmidt, *Studien zur Stilistik der Alttestamentlichen Spruchliteratur,* 1936, 17-25.
11. "Wise and Foolish, Righteous and Wicked," *SVT*, XXIII (1973), 146-165; cf. William McKane, *Proverbs,* 1970, 1-33; Michael V. Fox, "Aspects of the Religion of the Book of Proverbs," *HUCA* (1968), 55-69.
12. *Paronomasi i den Äldere Hebreiska Maschalliteraturen,* 1928. *Semitics* (1970) is largely devoted to style and rhetoric.
13. Schmidt, *Studien,* pp. 17ff. We need further research on the contributions of style to the structure of Proverbs.
14. "Das Gottesbild der Älteren Weisheit Israels," *SVT*, XXIII (1973), 117-145.
15. "Die Innere Gliederung der Proverbien," *ZAW*, (1967), 67-76.
16. *Einfache Formen,* 1956; Hans Jürgen Hermisson, *Studien zur Israelitischen Spruchweisheit,* 1968, 27-36.
17. Berend Gemser, *Adhuc Loquitur,* 1968, 138-149; Hans Heinrich Schmid, *Gerechtigkeit als Weltordnung,* 1968; *Wesen und Geschichte der Weisheit,* 1966.
18. von Rad, *Weisheit in Israel,* 1970, 13-101; *OT Theology* I, 1962, 418-441; Zimmerli, "Zur Struktur der Alttestamentlichen Weisheit," *ZAW*, (1933), 177-204; "Ort und Grenze der Weisheit im Rahmen der Alttestamentlichen Theologie," *Les Sagesses du Proche-Orient Ancien,* 1963, 121-137.
19. *Spruchweisheit,* 94-96.
20. Wolfgang Richter, *Exegese als Literaturwissenschaft,* 1971, 145-148. In this connection, he speaks of "Gattung."
21. von Rad, *Weisheit,* 39-148; Zimmerli, "Ort und Grenze," 121-137. Cf. Johannes Fichtner, *Die Altorientalische Weisheit in ihrer Israelitisch-Jüdischen Ausprägung,* 1933; Walter Baumgartner, *Israelitische und Altorientalische Weisheit,* 1933.
22. von Rad, *Weisheit,* 41-53; Hartmut Gese, *Lehre und Wirklichkeit in der alten Weisheit,* 1958, 33-45; William McKane, *Prophets and Wise Men,* 1965.
23. Moshe Weinfeld, *Deuteronomy and the Deuteronomic School,* 1972, 244-306; "The Origin of the Humanism in Deuteronomy," *JBL* (1961), 241-247.
24. Cf., Hans Walter Wolff, *Amos' Geistige Heimat,* 1964.
25. F. Charles Fensham, "Widow, Orphan, and the Poor in Ancient Near Eastern Legal and Wisdom Literature," *JNES* (1962), 129-139.

26. "Wise and Foolish," 161. Cf. Conrad, "Gliederung," 67-76.
27. Cf. 10:30 and 14:34 with 14:16 or 13:1.
28. Trevor Donald, "The Semantic Field of 'Folly' in Proverbs, Job, Psalms, and Ecclesiastes," *VT* (1963), 285-292; cf. Scott, "Wise and Foolish," 157-161.
29. Gemser, *Adhuc Loquitur*, 78-95; von Rad, *Weisheit*, 165-181.
30. Cf., von Rad, *Weisheit*, 115; Weber, *Economy and Society*, 1968; "Ressentment" can also be found in Nietzsche's thought.
31. Gese, *Lehre und Wirklichkeit*, 11-21, 33-45; Schmid, *Gerechtigkeit*.
32. Klaus Koch, "Gibt es ein Vergeltungsdogma im Alten Testament?" *ZThK* (1955), 1-42.
33. Schmid, *Weisheit*, 146-169; cf. Walther Eichrodt, "Vorsehungsglaube und Theodizee im Alten Testament," *Festschrift Otto Procksch*, 1934, 45-70.
34. K. H. Fahlgren, "Die Gegensätze von s^edaqa im Alten Testament," *Um das Prinzip der Vergeltung in Religion und Recht des Alten Testaments*, 1972, 126-129.
35. Ernst Würthwein, *Die Weisheit Ägyptens und das Alte Testament*, 1960.
36. Gese, *Lehre und Wirklichkeit*, 38-45; Schmid, *Gerechtigkeit*, 157-160, 175-177.
37. *Spruchsammlungen*, 71-82.
38. *Spruchsammlungen*, 22.
39. *Spruchsammlungen*, 40-46, 71-76.
40. Donald, "Semantic Field of 'Folly,'" pp. 285-92. Conrad, "Gliederung," pp. 67-76.
41. *ANET*, 432-434.
42. Cf. Ps. 45:2(1); Jer. 8:8.
43. Würthwein, *Weisheit Ägyptens*, 8.
44. Schmid, *Gerechtigkeit*, 159; von Rad, *Weisheit*, 13-20, 41-53; cf. Hermisson, *Spruchweisheit*, 97-136.
45. de Boer, "The Counsellor," pp. 42-71; James L. Crenshaw, *Prophetic Conflict* (1971), pp. 116-23; Gemser, *Loquitur*, pp. 138-49.
46. Allen H. Godbey, "The Hebrew *Masal*," *AJSL* (1922-3), pp. 89-108.
47. Gemser, *Loquitur*, pp. 96-115.
48. Schmid, *Gerechtigkeit*, pp. 46-52.
49. von Rad, *Weisheit*, 182-188.

THE HUMAN DEED IN A TIME OF DESPAIR: THE ETHICS OF APOCALYPTIC

LOU H. SILBERMAN

Hillel Professor
of Jewish Literature
and Thought at
Vanderbilt University

In memory of my friend and colleague of twenty years.
"Venifqadta ki yippaqed moshavekha"

Martin Buber, in his essay "Prophecy, Apocalyptic, and the Historical Hour,"[1] sets up, extrapolating from "two basic human attitudes set in polar opposition", a similar polarity between prophecy and apocalyptic. His intent, it would appear, is to refute in a radical fashion the widely accepted position, succinctly stated by Russell,[2] that apocalyptic is "in many respects a continuation, or at least a development of [prophecy], however different it may be at times in form, feeling and content." It is, according to his citation from B. W. Anderson, "prophecy in a new idiom."

Buber will have none of this. The disjunctive is radical beyond differences in "form, feeling and content," for it reflects two irreconcilable "human attitudes." In one instance, the individual is certain that he is "able to participate... in the real decision that will be made about the make-up of the next hour..." In the other, recognizing that he is but "a man come to grief... he may banish all such impulses [to participate] and surrender... to the turmoil..."[3]

Essentially the two attitudes may be defined as "affirmation of choice" and "denial of choice," but not as understood philosophically, "the old... quarrel between indeterministic and deterministic views of the world."[4] The question put is: "Do I dare the definitely impossible or do I adapt myself to the unavoidable? Do I dare to become other than I am... or do I take cognizance of a barrier in my present existence as something that will eternally be a barrier?" These are the two attitudes that Buber will transpose "from biography to history." "Does an historical hour ever experience its real limits otherwise than through undertaking to overstep those limits it is familiar with? Does the future establish itself ever anew, or is it inescapably destined?"[5]

Turning to Judaism, Buber finds in it the embodiment of "these two basic attitudes" in "the purity and unconditionality of the religious sphere." The former is expressed in "the prophets in the ages of the kings",[6] the latter in "the apocalyptic writings... in the age of late

Hellenism and its decline." But having set these in different periods, the relevance of historical circumstances is rejected. The faith of prophet and apocalyptic in "the one Lord of the past, present, and future" is the same as is the certainty that it is "His will to grant salvation to His creation." The dichotomy arises as to "how this will manifest itself in the pregnant moment in which the speaker speaks, what relation this moment bears to coming events, what share in this relation falls to men ..."

In order to make his case, Buber "disregard[s] all that is atypical, elementally significant though it may be." He "must disregard the question of what apocalyptic motifs are already, here and there, to be found among the classic prophets and what prophetic motifs are still, here and there, to be found among the late apocalyptics." He "must show the essential difference of the basic attitudes through the clearest examples.'[7]

The question of how legitimate this radical pruning of the material to provide "the clearest examples" is, cannot be so easily put aside, for it may be that what one ends with is not a polarity of human attitudes but with the confrontation of two singular "authors" whose particular positions may not be generalized beyond themselves.

For Buber, prophecy or what he understands to be the prophetic attitude, is embodied in Jeremiah, who offers as the divine message the possibility of "dialogical reciprocity between heaven and earth." Man may make the turning and God will respond. But there may come a point at which the alternative, the turning by man or unalterable doom, is no longer offered. "Yet even here in this threat the gate of grace still remains open for man when he turns his whole being back to God."[8] On the other hand, for the apocalyptic writer, in this case the Fourth Book of Ezra, "There exists ... no possibility of a change in the direction of historical destiny that could proceed from man, or be effected or coeffected by man. The prophetic principle of the turning on the part of the community is no longer even thought of."[9]

What must be noted at this point is the occurrence of the words "historical destiny", "individual form", "community", for it is exactly these words that point to the crucial relevance of historical circumstances so arbitrarily rejected by Buber. Jeremiah's message that interprets his visit to the potter's shed is directed immediately and unmistakably to the house of Israel, and in it divine sovereignty over kingdoms and nations is affirmed. Indeed, as Buber points out in the subsequent paragraph, "the young Jeremiah had received . . . his summons as announcer to the nations.' " [10] Thus the turning called for is that to be done by the whole people as a people, as an active participant in the historical nexus. It is not viewed as a moralistic calculus made up of the good deeds of individuals ever approaching an infinity. It is the *Wesenumkehr of 'am Yisra'el,* "the people of Israel."

But it is just this reality, this "person", *'am Yisra'el,* that is absent for the apocalyptist and which, therefore, limits his call. He can call only to individuals, setting before them limited and specific ethical tasks that can and will provide a way in the meaningless present until such time as the obedient people will reappear. The despair of the author of IV Ezra is engendered by the absence of Israel:

> "Why is Israel to the heathen given over for reproach,
>   Thy beloved people to godless tribes given up?
> The Law of our fathers has been brought to destruction
>   the written covenants exist no more;
> We vanish from the world as locusts,
>   our life is as a breath." [11]

Buber himself has made much of this. In his essay "Judaism and Mankind" he wrote: "Once we have grasped this fully, we can perceive the significance of what we call *galut,* exile. The great creative epoch was followed by the long span of years which one can truly call the Age of Exile, for it expelled us from the very core of our existence. It was the era of barren intellectuality, an intellectuality that, far removed from life and from a living striving for unity, fed on bookish words, on interpretations of interpretations . . ." [12] It is not my concern at this point to argue with Buber's judgment, but merely to indicate that he suggested the relevance of the historical circumstances for attitudes. More than that, in *The Prophetic Faith,* Buber argues that after the Babylonian captivity the effective decision-making of the people as a whole was never reconstituted.[13]

Without accepting Buber's stylized structure of Jewish history, it is nonetheless possible to recognize, against his insistence that prophecy and apocalyptic represent two basic human attitudes, that they are rather responses to the historical or non-historical hour, and that the ethical demands flowing from them are necessarily colored by the situations in which they are made. It is impossible to deny the presence of ethical demand in much apocalyptic writing, yet it is as evident that it is ethics in another key than that found in prophecy. In place of a call to community as community, there is the earnest call to the individual who must endure in a period devoid of a sense of history and thus of the possibility of an "effective decision".

"Blessed are they who come (into the world) and keep thy commandments" says the author of IV Ezra,[14] and of those who "have scorned and not kept the ways of the Most High/ that have despised his law/ and that hate those who fear God", he writes that one of the ways of their suffering after death is that "they are now unable to make a good repentance for life", which clearly indicates that such a possibility had existed.[15] Thus the last vision that Buber dismisses as "merely an ingredient of the literary fiction" is, whether original or not, true of the apocalyptic understanding of the situation: "Now, therefore, set in order thy house,/ and reprove thy people;/ Comfort the lowly among them,/ and instruct those that are wise./ Now do thou renounce the life that is corruptible,/ let go from thee the cares of mortality;/ cast from thee the burdens of man,/ put off now the weak nature;/ lay aside thy burdensome cares,/ and hasten to remove from these times!"[16] The only possibility in "these times" is life lived in accordance with the Torah whose "restoration" is "Ezra's" task, "for in them [the Scriptures] is the spring of understanding, the fountain of wisdom, and the stream of knowledge."[17] The past is irredeemable; the present, limited to the individual's response to the divine demand; the future—in God's hand—will see the restoration of the community: "Take courage, O Israel;/ be not sorrowful, O House of Jacob!/ For you are remembered before the Most High,/ the Mighty one hath not forgotten you for ever." [18]

By faithful obedience *as individuals* in the chaos of the present, the possibility of restoration in the future is disclosed. It is the same "who knows whether He will not return and be sorry" that Buber points to as belonging to the offering of alternatives that marks for him the "task of the genuine prophet." [19] Yet it is said in a muted way, for this turning in obedience is not "effective decision"; it is preparation or perhaps no more than anticipation that "effective decision" will again be possible. This is quite close to what Moshe Greenberg wrote of Ezekiel: "For the student of religion, Ezekiel's doctrines and their effect are a striking attestation to the power of faith to bring order into chaos, find meaning where it was not, and thus lay the basis for a people's survival and regeneration." [20]

The meaning of such a situation and the attitude it calls forth, as contrasted with Buber's immutable human attitude uneffected by the situation, is poignantly made clear by the contemporary German theologian, Helmut Gollwitzer in his report of his years spent as a prisoner of war in Russian labor camps. While admitting the discomfort for me of setting side by side members of Hitler's *Wehrmacht* and Jews of the first and second Christian centuries—even with the defensive phrase *mutatis mutandis* or even the Hebrew *l^ehavdil*, nonetheless the perception rings true. Writing of the "Plenni", *i.e.*, the slave, tempo in the camps, he illuminates that very situation Buber touches upon when, writing of the period of the Second Commonwealth, he notes: "Since the outlines of the temporal order are drawn by the Persian Empire, the leaders' tendency to build a society imbued with the spirit of the Divine is weakened . . ." [21]

Gollwitzer points out how "solidarity disappeared, envy and distrust poisoned the atmosphere, gossip played its part in this closely knit life; any community spirit, any appeal for a communal sharing of the burden or for the strong to stand-in for and be sacrificed to the interests of the weak were always illusory questions." [22] This was, of course, part of the intention of the Russians. What did this mean in the life of the individual prisoner? "The prisoner was not without any expectations in his life, he was in no wise condemned to hopeless slavery, indeed he expected a great deal and was the personification of expectancy; he expected everything from the future and not from the present, from a definite future time, a 'day' which was for him in biblical language 'the day of the Lord'; the day that made life in the present worthwhile . . . and gave meaning to life. . . . Joylessness was a characteristic of the present to an extent almost unknown in civilian life. . . . The present had lost its value. Only the eschatological relationship between the prisoner and time gave the present any value. . . . Life in the present had value only so far as it gained meaning from its eschatological[23] purpose, towards which it moved. In itself, apart from that purpose, life was meaningless, and only a few were tempted to deceive themselves about it, and to be content with a short-sighted policy of making the best of what was temporary.[24] Not until we were 'free', released from the domination of the foreign power could there be any sense in labour or good works again."[25]

While it is clear that Gollwitzer uses Christian eschatological language and ideas as a structure for his description, nonetheless they seem not to be imposed upon the substance, but are rather a response to the situation. The prison camp is indeed the world of the apocalyptist, a world under foreign domination and without community to respond as community to the divine demand called for by that domination. All that is available is the response of the individual, and that response was faithful obedience that transformed the meaningless task into something that could provide inner, if not outer, meaning. "Because the present had no value in our eyes, our life lacked any of those working objectives which are normally made necessary by one's profession or one's fellow men; this made us indifferent both to our work and our fellowmen and did not allow us to take things seriously."[26] It was only when something else was added to the situation that the prisoners were allowed their humanity. Writing of the passages in the Epistles addressed to slaves, Gollwitzer declares: ". . . they opened the door which enabled these men to preserve a human attitude toward tasks which according to reason could offer us no human relationship. These passages told them that they must conceive of their work as done 'to the Lord.' Every thrust of a spade could be transformed from a task undertaken with reluctance into a service done to the Lord . . . forced labour need not remain forced, it could be transformed from a meaningless drudgery into a service full of meaning (although all the external meaninglessness persisted!), into a service offered to the Lord." [27]

The portrait of the prison camp, it seems to me, provides a more cogent explanation of the world of the apocalyptist than does Buber's invariable "human attitude." More than that, it offers insight into the human deed in a world of despair. Ethics are reduced or at least limited in such a situation to the response of the singular individual as he allows the light of a meaningful future to shine over the chaos of the present. Under foreign domination, he knows himself to be absent in any effective sense from the scene of history, but he is certain that his present obedience will prepare him for his role in that scene whose renewal he thus affirms is imminent. If history, for him, seems to be holding its breath, it is not because he refuses to become embroiled in any decision "about the make-up of the next hour" but because he must wait until the *pneúma,* that great breathing out, has occurred. He, like "Ezra" finds himself calling to the obedient in hopeful waiting for the life-giving *rûaḥ* that shall allow bone and sinew and flesh and skin to stand up once again.

What is called for, then, is not an invidious distinction between prophecy and apocalyptic on the one hand or an over-eager insistence that they are somehow the same or that the latter is in a special way the heir of the former. Rather is a careful delineation of apocalptic called for, not in formalistic terms, but in terms appropriate to the apocalyptist's perception of his world and the deed that world calls for from him. If it turns out that the deed is done only for himself, if it makes him, in Gollwitzer's words, ". . . indifferent both to [his] work and [his] fellow men and does not allow [him] to take things seriously", then one must question whether indeed one is dealing with apocalyptic or a *tertium quid.*

Buber was right when he wrote: ". . . does an historical hour ever experience its real limits otherwise than through undertaking to overstep those limits that it is familiar with?"[28] What he failed to realize is that for the apocalyptist that overstepping cannot be taken until the "overstepper" exists within the historical realm. It is absence of that community that alone can "dare the definitely impossible" that gives rise to his despair. At the same time, within the more limited sphere of individual response, he holds his ground, performing that deed that, again in Gollwitzer's words: "transformed ... meaningless drudgery into a service full of meaning (although all the external meaninglessness persisted!) into a service offered to the Lord."[29]

NOTES

1. In *Pointing the Way*, tr. and ed. by Maurice Friedman, 1957, pp. 192-207. The German text has the title "Prophetie und Apokalyptik"; and was published in *Sehertum: Anfang und Ausgang*, 1955, pp. 49-74. There are some minor omissions in the English translation and, as indicated below, there are several places where I disagree with the translation offered.
2. D. S. Russell, *The Method and Message of Jewish Apocalyptic: 200 BC-AD 100*, 1964, pp. 92-96.
3. Buber, *op. cit.*, 192. The text there reads "factual decision" but the German (p. 49) has *faktischen Entscheidung*, meaning real or effective. On p. 198, the same translation of the German word (p. 59) occurs three times. In each case "effective" or "real" would be a better translation. See the previous paragraph at the top of p. 198 where the German (p. 58) *faktisch zu wählen* is translated "actually choosing".
4. *Ibid.*, p. 193 (German p. 50).
5. *Ibid.*, (German p. 51).
6. The German has *die Prophetie*, prophecy.
7. *Ibid.*, p. 194. (German, p. 53).
8. *Ibid.*, p. 196. (German, p. 56).
9. *Ibid.*, p. 202. (German, pp. 66-67). The word "simply" stands for the German *schlechthin* and distorts the meaning of the sentence that is better rendered: "The prophetic principle of the turning is not denied absolutely in its individual form, but a turning on the part of the community is no longer considered . . ." What Buber has done is to affirm individual turning as an apocalyptic possibility, while denying communal turning. This is, of course, crucial. See *The Prophetic Faith*, 1949, pp. 2-3. "I emphasize the word 'community', for even where he [the prophet] is mentioning individuals, the main purpose is the realization in the whole of public life."
10. *Ibid.*, p. 195 (German, p. 54).
11. Ch. 4, 23-24 (Charles, II, 566.)
12. In *On Judaism*, ed. N. N. Glatzer, 1967, p. 29. The German original "Das Judentum und die Menschheit", *Drei Reden über das Judentum*, 1911, p. 49.
13. *Op. cit.*, p. 234. See, too, "The Holy Way" in *On Judaism*, p. 120, "In the history of the Second Commonwealth, a distorted image of the idea of divine rule is realized . . . the so-called theocracy that develops in a community robbed of all the vitality of free communal life finds its ultimate embodiment in the caricature-like figure of the Hellenistic high priest."
14. 7:45 (Charles, II, 584).
15. 7:79, 82 (Charles, II, 588).
16. 14:13-14 (Charles, II, 621).
17. 14:47 (Charles, II, 624).
18. 12:46-47 (Charles, II, 615). See, too, 9:38-10:24, "The Vision of the Disconslate Woman" (Charles, II, 603-608).
19. *Op. cit.*, p. 197 (German, pp. 57-58).
20. Moshe Greenberg, "Prolegomenon" to *Pseudo-Ezekiel and the Original Prophecy*, by Charles Cutler Torrey, etc., 1970, p. xxix.
21. "The Holy Way", *op. cit.*, p. 120. If Buber's comment is correct (and I think it is), then, by the time the period in which apocalyptic emerged arrived, the possibility of "effective decision" had long since departed the scene.
22. Helmut Gollwitzer, *Unwilling Journey: A Diary from Russia*, 1953, pp. 95-96.
23. It is important to note that "eschatological" in this context meant "going home".

24. Contrast this with Buber's description of the human attitude he equates with apocalyptic, "surrender . . . to the turmoil". Again, Buber cancels the historicity of the future rather than emphasizing the non-historicity of the present for the apocalypticist. See *op. cit.*, p. 203.
25. *Op. cit.*, pp. 87-88.
26. *Op. cit.*, p. 92.
27. *Op. cit.*, pp. 92-93.
28. *Op. cit.*, p. 193.
29. See note 26.

THE SIGNIFICANCE OF "LAST WORDS" FOR INTERTESTAMENTAL ETHICS

WALTER HARRELSON

Dean and Professor
of Old Testament at
Vanderbilt Divinity School

During the period 200 B.C.—A.D. 100, a large number of Jewish, Jewish-Christian, and Christian works were produced which have the character of "last words," or "testaments." Copies of a number of these, fragmentary or complete, have been preserved. Paul Riessler's collection of non-biblical Jewish documents contains seven writings to which the title "testament" has been assigned.[1] The most important of these for intertestamental ethics is clearly the Testaments of the Twelve Patriarchs, to which we shall turn shortly.

I.

This body of literature has a very long history in ancient Israel and is not without parallels in other ancient literatures. The Hebrew Bible contains many such "last words," found in a variety of literary forms and contexts, and providing the background for the testaments of intertestamental and early Christian times. Genesis 49 and Deuteronomy 33 are the clearest examples of the background for the Testaments of the Twelve Patriarchs.

These "last words" have been studied by a number of scholars. Ethelbert Stauffer published (in an appendix to his book on New Testament theology)[2] a list of "Abschiedsreden und Abschiedszenen" in Old Testament, intertestamental, and New Testament literature, with the references grouped under twenty-five different headings. This is an extremely useful table, but Stauffer did not elaborate its significance for New Testament theology. Johannes Munck published an essay titled "Discourse d'adieu dans le Nouveau Testament et dans la littérature biblique" in the Festschrift for Maurice Goguel,[3] in which considerable attention is given to the form and general significance of the "last words," especially in reference to New Testament literature and thought. No treatment, to my knowledge, focuses attention on the significance of "last words" or "testaments" for biblical or intertestamental ethics.

II.

The portrayal of such last words varies considerably in the Old Testament occurrences. In Gen. 24:1-9 and 47:29-31, we have deathbed oaths, sworn to by the survivors at the urging of the one about to die. In Gen. 27:18-40 and 48:1-22, the emphasis falls upon the power of the word of blessing spoken by the dying patriarch, a word that cannot be recalled once it is spoken and which, by the power inherent in the blessing, accomplishes what is declared. The last words of Joshua (Josh. 23-24) and Samuel (1 Sam. 12) appear in scenes of covenant reaffirmation. Here, weight is placed upon the necessity for obedience to the covenant law, the avoidance of idolatry, and on the quality of leadership of the spokesmen. In 1 Kgs. 2:1-9, David charges Solomon to be faithful to God's requirements and gives his son certain specific charges to fulfill (see the fuller, edited account in 1 Ch. 28-29).

The expression "last words" appears for the first time, to my knowledge, in 2 Sam. 23:1, where the editor of the Books of Samuel has placed a poem titled "the last words of David."[4] This poem promises blessing upon those who rule justly and in God's fear. Its special purpose, however, is to affirm the enduring kingship of David, through his descendants, in line with Nathan's prophecy (2 Sam. 7:1-17).

The Book of Deuteronomy contains farewell words of Moses in several places (31:1-8, 24-29; 32:1-47; 34:1-12). Indeed, the entire book may have been understood in ancient times as Moses' summary of the Torah near the time of his death.

In the Apocrypha, various "last words" have been recorded. Tobit gives charge to his son to leave Nineveh for Media and promises prosperity for him there (Tob. 14). The dying martyrs whose last words are recorded in 2 Macc. 6-7, address the tormenters and comfort one another. Mattathias gave very specific counsel to his sons on the occasion of his death (1 Macc. 2:49-70), with illustrations from the history of Israel, charging them to hold to their zeal for the law, depending upon God to support them. Other passages could be cited. The most interesting of these "last words," however, appear in the literature bearing the title "Testament." To these we now turn.

III.

The list of testaments in apocryphal and pseudepigraphical literature is impressive. The seven testaments in the Riessler collection are those attributed to Abraham, Adam, Job, Isaac, Moses, Solomon, and the Twelve Patriarchs. Some of these bear heavy marks of Christian additions and interpolations, as is well known. Some, indeed, are believed by many interpreters to be of Christian authorship. The Testaments of Abraham, Adam, Job, Isaac, and Solomon are not published in Charles' edition of the Old Testament Pseudepigrapha. None of these appears to be as old as the testament of Moses and of the Twelve Patriarchs. We shall deal only with the latter two, with emphasis given to the Testaments of the Twelve Patriarchs.

A word should be said about the term "testament." In the Greek manuscripts the term regularly found is *diatheke*. The Hebrew term presumably was *savva'ah*. In Moses Gaster's edition of the medieval fragment of the Testament of Naphtali, the text reads *svv't nptly*.[5] Charles proposes that behind the Greek text lay the Hebrew *savva'ah;* he reconstructs the title of the Testament of Reuben, for example, as follows: *svv't r'vbn bn y^cqb*.[6]

IV.

The Testament of Moses, commonly referred to as the Assumption of Moses, consists largely of an apocalyptic portrayal of the history that lies before God's people, presented to Joshua by Moses near the time of the latter's death. Chapters 2-10 contain this sketch of Israelite history up to the time of the author—at some time within the first half of the first Christian century—and forecast the imminent coming of God's kingdom. Chapters 11 and 12 relate Joshua's response, his grief and dismay at the thought of Israel's not having Moses as leader, followed by Moses' words of comfort to Joshua. The story, preserved only in one Latin manuscript, breaks off at this point. Presumably, the original writing, and perhaps the Latin translation, once continued with the story of Moses' assumption into heaven and related his visions of what he saw at the moment of his death.

Although the content of the various testaments varies greatly, several elements recur in many of them. As in the Old Testament "last words," we sometimes have rehearsals of the history of the people of God as the dying one has experienced it. More frequently, there are forecasts of the coming history of his descendants. Gen. 49 and Dt. 33, as is well known, contain certain elements of the later history of the twelve tribes. In the apocalyptic testaments, however, the forecast has the familiar apocalyptic features. In none of the "last words," however, is there found the ethical emphasis that appears in the several Testaments of the Twelve Patriarchs.

V.

The Testaments of the Twelve Patriarchs have been preserved, wholly or in part, in a number of translations. The Greek manuscripts contain the full set of testaments of the twelve sons of Jacob in the form most nearly complete. Discovery of portions of the testaments of Levi and Naphtali among the Qumran documents has led scholars to believe that the full testament of the twelve patriarchs may be a Christian, perhaps a Jewish-Christian, composition. I find it difficult to account for the existence of a fragment of the Testament of Naphtali akin to the medieval Testament of Naphtali on that premise, since the tribe of Naphtali has no special reason for having been singled out. We can well understand the appearance of a Testament of Levi; indeed, it is easily conceivable that the Testament of Levi may be the oldest of the testaments and may have been produced prior to the conception of a Testament of the Twelve Patriarchs. The discovery of a Testament of Naphtali at Qumran, however, leads me to believe that the conception of a set of twelve testaments, one for each of the twelve sons of Jacob, dates to pre-Christian Jewish times. Thus, I shall treat the Testaments as a set of Jewish writings, much influenced by Christian tradition, but not a Christian or Jewish-Christian writing. The Testaments in their present form may come from the first or second Christian century, but the idea of a set of twelve testaments, not just of individual testaments later placed together, is a Jewish one antedating Christianity.

Now, it is precisely this idea of a set of testaments of this scope that seems to me so important for an understanding of the Testaments' contribution to intertestamental ethics. I shall try, in the remainder of this paper, to indicate why this is the case.

We have testaments in number that offer counsel to descendants but whose contents clearly are dominated by the future that awaits those living near the end of the age. In the Twelve Patriarchs, the weight of emphasis falls upon ethics, although the place of the future rule of God, and of the agents of that rule, is of course important. Other "last words" in the biblical literature also stress the need for commitment to God's requirements. It is, however, the character of the ethical teaching in the Twelve Patriarchs that sets this document apart from almost all other writings of the period.

R. H. Charles held and made popular the view that apocalyptic writers chose to issue their writings under pseudonyms of ancient Israelite worthies because otherwise such writings would not be able to find acceptance over against the authority and autocracy of the Torah.[7] Such a view of the dominance of intertestamental Jewish life by the Torah, eliminating the creation of other works save under pseudonyms, is of course untenable today. We have many writings produced at Qumran which are anonymous and required no such authorization.

Rather, it was the fact that the structures of the Jewish community were so gravely imperiled by the political, cultural and economic developments of the period which contributed to the search for traditions, teachings, visions, and authorities from Israel's past. This search rested upon the conviction (a) that these existing traditions were in fact sound and that the apocalyptic authors were bringing ancient visions up to date through revelations to themselves, that gave God's guidance to their contemporaries,[8] and (b) that the counsel augmented and supplemented the Torah which was by no means set aside by the apocalyptists.

Moreover, the fact that the apocalyptists turned to individual ethics and emphasized the motives of human conduct and the attitudes of persons is to be traced to the same set of historic and cultural conditions. Jewish life was enormously precarious during the period. The people were under the dominance of foreign political powers, and were subject to great cultural pressures to conform with the dominant customs and ethical practices. The Maccabaean liberation, vastly important as it was, did not change the fact that God's people could dispose over its life only to a very limited extent. The rise of communities like that at Qumran is unmistakable evidence that many Jews found it almost impossible to live as a people of God in the midst of Syrian, Egyptian, or Roman political domination. Thus, the message of apocalyptic ethics necessarily tended more and more to be addressed to the individual.[9]

The Testaments of the Twelve Patriarchs, more than any other intertestamental document, reveal this emphasis upon individual conduct. Even so, the author (or authors) was able to find a framework and setting within which to overcome the tendency to an over-individualized ethic. His choice of the twelve sons of Jacob as spokesmen for his ethical views was brilliant—even if he had at hand an earlier apocalyptic testament of Levi or of Judah, as well he might. He selected ancient worthies whose sins had been enshrined in the Torah. Starting with these sins, he elaborated them, filled out the stories in midrashic style, using such material in order vividly to state the sins of hatred, envy, jealousy, intemperance, lying, and the like. This manner of presenting vices and commending the corresponding virtues is thoroughly Hebraic. The prototypes of envy, hatred, or jealousy are men of Israel's past, on whom the life of God's people has depended. Despite their failings, they were used by God to fulfill his purposes. And more—though they were given opportunity to repent and mend their ways, and did so, the stories clearly indicate that their change of heart did not come about easily. Their repentance was no easy thing, and they were recipients of no cheap grace.

Of equal or greater importance is the author's use of the device of having the descendants gather around the dying patriarch and hear his counsel to the entire living family. His ethical admonitions were addressed to the individual family members, calling for individual response. He spoke not to the whole of Israel but to the whole of his family, his tribe. His counsel thus had the effect upon readers, we may believe, of filling the gap between a prophetic or priestly ethic addressed to all Israel God's people, on the one hand, and the individual Israelite on the other. Hellenistic ethics, clearly a great influence at the time within Judaism and also a great influence in early Christianity, was not the model for our author. He set his message in individual terms but within a communal or family setting. The counsel to the patriarchs' descendants, with its vivid reminders of sin and its consequences, comes through as an enormously valuable piece of Jewish ethics for a community that had the greatest difficulty discerning where God's people could be found, then and there, to be.

I see, then, the Testaments of the Twelve Patriarchs as an example, almost unique in intertestamental writings, of an approach to Jewish ethics that seeks, with very considerable success, to provide a path for the individual in a time in which Jewish theology and ethics were in grave difficulty. God's Torah had been given to a community with a distinctive mission in the world and to the nations. Obedience to Torah required a structure of communal existence which historical realities had very nearly brought to an end. Could the individual Israelite not keep Torah? Of course he could, but the individualizing tendencies were clearly a threat to the sense of peoplehood that was a cardinal element in Jewish faith. We can see in the apocalypse of 4 Esdras with what seriousness and pathos the question of obedience to God's Law was faced. The ethics of the Testaments of the Twelve Patriarchs served well to place a communal frame around the remarkably penetrating individual ethic commended by the author.

The writing would have served equally well in early Christianity to prevent a too radical individualizing of Christian ethics. This dimension of the writing may have been as important a factor in its finding a large place in the early church as was its eschatology.

VI.

A closing word may be said about the relation of eschatology and ethics in the Testaments. I believe that the Testaments of the Twelve Patriarchs offers a distinctive insight in this connection as well. The author writes as an apocalyptist. His picture of the near End of the age and of the agents of God representing the tribes of Levi and Judah who shortly will arise offers a bridge between the prophecies of Zechariah and some of the documents of the Qumran community. His ethical counsel to those who await the coming End is much fuller, much less an "interim ethic," and much less capable of being understood as a passive waiting for God to act than is the case with any other intertestamental apocalypses. The author commends a quality of life within the particular community of which he is a part that can be realized as one awaits the End. As an explication of the demands of Torah that deal with human motivation and attitude, his ethics well fits an expectant community that lives in the world but is not fully a part of the world. The document may have affinities with Qumran, but it bears few "sectarian" marks. It offers hope in the Last Day for the Gentiles as well as for Israel, and in the meantime it enjoins a quality of life suitable for and expressive of the life God will have in the Kingdom.

This flowering of a "last words" tradition in Israelite literature is entitled to occupy a significant place in biblical ethics. One who ponders its contents can hardly continue to see in apocalyptic ethics either an ethics of despair or a counsel of perfection.

FOOTNOTES

1. Paul Riessler, *Altjüdisches Schrifttum ausserhalb der Bibel*, 2nd ed., 1966.
2. Ethelbert Stauffer, *Die Theologie des Neuen Testaments*, 4th ed., 1948, 312-315.
3. *Aux Sources de la Tradition Chrétienne*, 1950, 155-170.
4. *Ve'eleh dibhre davîdh ha'ah^{a}ronîm.*
5. *Studies and Texts*, III, 1971, 22.
6. *Apocrypha and Pseudepigrapha of the Old Testament*, II, 1913, 283.
7. *A Critical History of the Doctrine of a Future Life*, 2nd ed., 1913, 203. See D. S. Russell, *The Method and Message of Jewish Apocalyptic*, 1964, 130-131, who denies the position of Charles.
8. See Russell's fine treatment of this point: *Method and Message*, 158-173.
9. See the treatment of this point in Professor Silberman's essay in this volume.

VIRTUE AND REWARD IN PHILO

Samuel Sandmel

Distinguished Service Professor
of Bible and Hellenistic
Literature at Hebrew Union
College—Jewish Institute
of Religion

I.

In simplest terms, in a usual religious system, a man whose deeds are good reaps some reward and one whose deeds are evil reaps some punishment. Inquiring minds have naturally discovered shadings and qualifications and expressed definitions and redefinitions and even reservations in various forms. The matter raised in this paper is a very narrow one: does Philo regard ethics (good deeds) as a precondition to salvation (reward), or how does the matter seem to be to him? I stress narrow, for limitations of space preclude a broad discussion.[1] I deliberately omit related items such as grace and theodicy.

The way to begin, so it seems to me, is not with the deeds but rather with the harvest reaped, and to move back from there to the question of the effect of deeds. For a reason which will emerge below, I present the Philonic material in two parts. First: In Philo's treatment of Abraham, he tells us that Abraham, once having attained perfection, achieved the highest kind of spiritual joy, equivalent to a steadfast apprehension of the wisdom of God; he experienced *ecstasis*, prophecy, thereby passing beyond the bounds of human happiness. Abraham sojourned among the divine *logoi*, angels, traveling along with them. After Abraham's death, his immaterial, immortal soul being incorruptible went "to his fathers", a biblical phrase which could mean, says Philo, the domain of the astral bodies, or the (Platonic) world of ideas, or the ether, the fifth essence.[2]

This attainment by Abraham was matched by those of Isaac and Jacob, whose comparable perfections, however, arose from methods other than Abraham's. The attainment in each case represents man's highest achievement and, hence, is not susceptible of being surpassed by any other humans.

To what extent does Philo hold that Abraham earned that high state, earned as distinct from his being a recipient of God's grace, and how does he understand the role of "good deeds"? And from what source did Abraham (or Philo) draw valid criteria for terming some deeds good and others bad? And was the opportunity which was afforded the patriarchs available to their descendants and also to worthy people not their descendants? The issue of the criteria is posed by the Bible in that Abraham lived before Moses and the promulgation of Moses' laws. A Jew inheriting Moses' laws could conceivably define good deeds in terms of obedience to both the affirmative and negative commandments; for Philo this option was not available respecting Abraham.

Philo's solution of the problem of Abraham's preceding Moses in time was to suppose that Abraham was self-taught, in the Law of Nature.[3] The Law of Nature was by definition unwritten, for its locale was in the "intelligible world" (*cosmos noetos*) where all (Platonic) ideas were to be found. On the other hand, the laws of Moses, being written, required a spirited defense by Philo on the supposition that since their locale was in the sensible world (*cosmos aesthetikos*), they were possibly subject to imperfections; Philo's defense took the form of a contention that the Mosaic laws are consistent with the law of nature, and, indeed, the best possible imitation of it.[4]

But if the unwritten Law of Nature is ideal, not a series of particulars, how does Philo bridge the possible gap between whatever might be the definition of good deeds and the absence from the Law of Nature of these particulars? He does this through various statements, some crystal clear, some not, on virtue and the virtues. One needs to speak of both virtue (singular) and also the virtues (plural) because Philo speaks of generic virtue, the (Platonic) idea of virtue, which, like the Law of Nature, is found in the intelligible world, and of the specific virtues, imitations of, or substitutes for, generic virtue which are found in the perceptible world. If a man possesses the particular virtues (that is, if he is just, brave, self-controlled, and moderate in his actions), the possibility exists for him to move from possessing these specific virtues of the perceptible world into possessing generic virtue itself in the intelligible world.

Philo is not so much concerned with deeds as deeds, as he is with deeds as reflective of, or as embodying, virtues; the deeds, indeed, only exemplify the perceptible virtues. The commandments in the

Law are susceptible of being allegorized, and normally in Philo such allegorization turns a specific commandment (a deed to be done) into a facet of the specific virtues.[5]

In Philo's treatises, *De Abrahamo* and *De Decalogo*, he uses a two-fold division, of which the first part of each treatise deals with virtue towards God (piety), and the second with virtues towards fellowmen. He presents these latter as the four Stoic cardinal virtues: justice, bravery, self-control, moderation.[6] The treatises illustrate the piety and the four cardinal virtues through citing the actions depicted in Scripture; the emphasis, to repeat, is not so much on what Abraham actually did, but on what it was that Abraham did that exemplified the virtues he possessed.

The progression from virtues to virtue, I have said, involves a progression from the perceptible world to the intelligible world. Such a progression entails the capacity of the mind to free itself from bondage to the body, which bondage is a consequence of the dual nature of man's being, as a mixture of the material and immaterial. The progression can occur if the mind is able to control and regiment the senses and passions whose residence is in the body. One might say (as Philo would not) that the instrument by which the mind progresses is reason;[7] in Philo's context, reason is that facet of the higher mind which is able to draw concepts from mere perceptions, a capacity denied the lower mind; the lower (which even a dog can possess) is limited to assembling and sorting out the perceptions of the senses. A person whose higher mind properly utilizes reason, particularly right reason,[8] moves on and arrives at wisdom, which, if it is true wisdom, lies in the conceptual world.

Wisdom and generic virtue for Philo are synonymous to the point of being one and the same. Thus Sarah is allegorically both wisdom and generic virtue; Eden is also generic virtue, and its four rivers, Gen. 3:10-14, are the four cardinal virtues of the perceptible world.

Generic virtue, then, is an attainment. The specific virtues are at most only descriptions of the qualities of a given man, and they do not necessarily lead to generic virtue, for that way is possible only by means of reason.

Generic virtue is, therefore, not a means of qualifying for reward, but is rather the reward itself. It has synonyms in addition to wisdom: spiritual joy, the vision of God, prophecy, and the immortality of the soul.

Reason, not deeds, leads to virtue. Misdeeds are acts against reason, especially those acts in which the body dominates the mind, rather than being controlled and regimented by it.

II.

Second, since Philo is a legatee of Scripture, and rewards and punishment figure with some prominence, especially in passages such as Lev. 20 and Dt. 28, one must reasonably expect a reflection in Philo of these scriptural motifs. Even before turning now to the matters set forth in his treatises, "On the Virtues" and "Rewards and Punishments", we can reasonably expect Philo to give only formal assent to material rewards and punishments, and to put his emphasis instead on the spiritual. It is exactly this which he does in those treatises.

"On the Virtues"[9] deviates somewhat from Philo's usual manner, namely, his usual use of the four cardinal virtues of the Stoics cited above. Instead, his first section (vv. 1-50) is on bravery. The second is on *philanthropia,* a "sister and twin" to piety (51-174). The third is on repentance, especially that of converts from idolatry (175-186). The fourth (187-227) is on *eugenia,* usually translated "nobility", which is defined (189) as "the peculiar lot of a mind purged clean of every blemish". Colson, the translator in the Loeb edition of Philo, notes that here Philo is utilizing a Stoic doctrine similar to usual Stoic paradoxes in which the literal sense of nobility is scorned in favor of wisdom (and the like) as the "true" nobility. That is to say, Philo's deviation in this treatise is only formal and not substantial. Rather, like a homilist, Philo is varying his manner, but does not perceptibly alter his usual content. Very little in the treatise relates to our topic, despite its suggestive title.

As to the treatise, "On Rewards and Punishments", Philo turns first to the rewards which came to Enos, who symbolizes hope; his name in Hebrew means "man". Enos has "a special distinction implying that no one should be thought a man at all who does not set his hope on God" (8-14). The reward to Enoch (15-21) who symbolizes repentance, is two-fold: one, a new home away from pleasures and desires; and two, solitude, the shunning of crowds and their innate evil. The reward to Noah (22-23) is also two-fold: one, "his salvation amid the general destruction", and two, "his appointment to take into his charge and protection the specimens of each kind of living creatures, mated in couples to produce a second creation to make good the annihilation of the first."

The treatise then turns to Patriarchs. Abraham's reward was his faith (28-30); Isaac's was spiritual joy (31-35), and Jacob's was the vision of God (36-46). Next in order comes Moses, who possessed the virtue of piety in a special degree, and through it gained four special rewards: the offices of king, legislator, prophet, and high priest (52-56).

As to punishment, it can suffice here to cite Philo's treatment of Cain, the first murderer. Cain was not executed, for such a punishment is a human aberration; rather, Cain was sentenced to "live forever in a state of dying and so to speak suffer a death which is deathless and unending", a ceaseless groaning and trembling, deprived of hope (72-73).

As to the blessings (based on Dt. 27), first comes victory over enemies (wild beasts and men); when man tames the wild beast within him, he can thereafter tame the wildest of beasts, and proceed to end war forever (85-97). The second blessing is wealth; in simple form, wealth means food and shelter, and beyond these, an abundance of produce; yet a store of wisdom in heaven will accompany material wealth as a reward (98-107). Beyond wealth is health, and beyond health are "the perfection and completeness of every part" of the body (118-126). Curses, the last section of the treatise, are the expected opposite (127-161).[10]

It does not seem to me that in the "blessings and curses" materials Philo adds to what is to be found in Scripture in the manner in which rabbinic literature or Christianity embellished these with heaven and hell and the like. One can get the impression that Philo would have been happier had Scripture not explicitly specified material rewards, for his acceptance of them seems unenthusiastic. To him true rewards are spiritual, not material.[11]

Perhaps the Philonic view is well expressed in two frequently encountered aphorisms: "Virtue is its own reward" (attributed to Claudianus) and "The only reward of virtue is virtue", a statement by Ralph Waldo Emerson in his essay, "Friendship". Reason, not deed, is the crux of virtue, for deed is the consequence of reason, and deed appears to be a reflection of virtue, not a means of attaining it.

III.

There is no doubt in my mind that the above is not only what Philo says, but he says it repeatedly throughout his writings. Hence, one can gain the impression that deeds (the particulars) are of no profound or paramount concern to Philo. Yet I wonder if this is really the case. Is it not possible that one needs to distinguish between the rationale which a "philosopher" offers, and that which he is rationalizing? I incline to think that only philosophically does Philo regard virtues as their own reward; practically I have seen nothing in Philo to obstruct a quite opposite conclusion that a man achieves virtue by his deeds. It would be wrong, I feel, to conclude that because Philo is so explicit in regarding reason alone as the instrument by which to attain salvation, that for him deeds are of no relevance. Rather, though, virtue may indeed be its own reward, still a man can apparently earn it.

NOTES

1. Such is provided, for example, by Harry Wolfson in *Philo,* II, Chapter XII, "Ethical Theory", pp. 164-321.
2. The references include *Abr.* 204; *Questiones ad Genesin* IV, 11; *Deter.* 5-70; *Heres* 249-263; 313-315; *LA* III, 40-44, 203, *Mat.* 152; *Virt.* 207, 216; *Somn,* II, 244; cf. my *Philo's Place in Judaism,* pp. 175-185.
3. The rabbis, on the other hand, "solved" this same problem by holding that Abraham observed the Mosaic requirements in advance of their promulgation. See *Philo's Place,* pp. 86-87; 191; 201.
4. See *Philo's Place,* pp. 190-191, 198.
5. See, for example, *Special Laws,* IV, 132-135.
6. A comparable structure is found in 4 Maccabees.
7. See *Philo's Place,* pp. 160-165.
8. *Philo's Place,* 165-166. In brief, right reason (*orthos logos*) is impeccably correct reasoning, rare in a man, but able to get its fortunate possessor to salvation. To help frail men who do not possess it, Moses' laws were devised, for they embody right reason and serve that man whose possession of right reason is insufficient. A *gôy* with right reason can come to salvation; Judaism, though, brings salvation to humans of even small gifts of reason.
9. A number of problems arise about "On the Virtues"; cf. Colson, Loeb edition, VIII, pp. xii-xviii. These problems are not directly related to our discussion.
10. "Blessings and Curses" are possibly to be differentiated in the context of the treatise from simple rewards and punishments in that these materials, constituting sections at its end of the treatise, were possibly once separate treatises accidentally joined to it.
11. See Colson, VIII, p. 449.

OLD TESTAMENT ETHICS AND THE ETHICS OF JESUS

MILLAR BURROWS

Emeritus Professor,
Yale Divinity School

The opportunity to contribute to this volume affords me the privilege of honoring a man who was my student in three institutions. As a student, Philip Hyatt already showed the qualities of mind and character that marked his scholarship and his life to the end. What impressed me most of all when I first knew him was his determination to get to the bottom of every question that confronted him and to find his own answers.

The purpose of this essay is less ambitious than its title, chosen *brevitatis causa,* may suggest. It is only to compare Old Testament ethics and the ethics of Jesus on a few major points. Neither the Old Testament nor the teaching of Jesus contains a philosophical system of moral values and principles or a comprehensive code of moral behavior. Both, however, are concerned with human conduct; both teach a way of life based on fundamental assumptions concerning the meaning and ends of life; and of course they are historically connected.

As the basis of comparison we must take the Old Testament as Jesus knew it.[1] The Scriptural quotations and allusions in his sayings are drawn widely from the law, the prophets, and at least the Psalms among the *Kethubhim,* with the addition of Daniel, unless we attribute the parousia sayings (as I do not) to later tradition. Therefore, questions of historical and literary criticism within the Old Testament are irrelevant for our inquiry.

The teaching of Jesus, however, cannot be treated historically without taking into account the problem of authenticity in the sayings and parables attributed to him. A matter concerning which specialists are so far from being agreed obviously cannot be discussed here in detail. In these few pages I can only compare the Old Testament and Jesus' teaching as I understand them. A brief indication of the presuppositions of this essay must therefore suffice.

Only what is recorded in the synoptic gospels will be used, and of that only what, with varying degrees of confidence, I regard as probably authentic.[2] Sayings which fit the situation of Jesus' ministry, and are consistent with what is most certain about his teaching, are accepted, whether or not they agree with what other Jewish teachers of the time said or might have said. If they also fit later situations in the church, that fact may often explain their preservation rather than their origin, though the possibility of modification or even creation cannot be dogmatically excluded.

Jesus' ministry did not immediately follow the completion of the Old Testament, and Judaism had not stood still in the meantime. We cannot assume, therefore, that anything in his teaching which did not come from the Old Testament was necessarily new. If it was not new, however, it was not for that reason less important. What he himself considered most essential was probably largely what he shared with the other Jews.

Between the ethics of the Old Testament, Judaism, and Jesus on the one side and classical or modern philosophical ethics on the other, there is a fundamental difference. The philosophical systems are secular and anthropocentric; Israelite and Jewish ethics and the ethics of Jesus are religious and theocentric. The philosopher's *summum bonum* is what man considers best for man; the Old Testament, Judaism, and Jesus are concerned with human welfare also, but in strict subordination to the will of God. What God wills is what is best for man, but it is not to be found by human reason; it is revealed.

The Old Testament, Judaism, and Jesus agree that man is free to choose, and is responsible for his choices. Philosophical discussions of freedom and determination or predestination have no place, though there is some speculation on the porblem in post-biblical literature. The tragic attractions of evil and the existence of sinful tendencies in man are recognized, but they can be resisted. If a Jeremiah says something to the contrary (e.g., Jer. 17:9), he is relieving his feelings, not formulating a doctrine; and what a psalmist says about his enemies (e.g., Ps. 14:2f.) is not a generalization about human nature. The men of Qumran and their two spirits and the rabbis with their good impulse and evil impulse agreed on this. Jesus said that the things which defile a man come from within, from the heart (Mt. 15:18f.; Mk. 7:21f.); he said also, "Blessed are the pure in heart" (Mt. 5:8).

Vestiges of a primitive conception of collective responsibility remain in the Old Testament. There were doubts, however, about the morality of collective punishment even at the hands of God (Gen. 18:23-25). The nearest approach to such ideas in Jesus' sayings is the bitter denunciation of the Galilean cities, with no distinction among individuals or groups (Mt. 11:20-24; Lk. 10:13-15). Doubtless all that is meant here is that each of these cities as a whole, like the nation as a whole, had not responded to Jesus' proclamation of the kingdom of God. Much the same may be said of his condemning "this generation" as evil (e.g., Mt. 12:38-45; 16:4; 17:17 par.).

By contrast with the teaching of Jesus, the Old Testament on the whole seems this-wordly, prudential, and (individually or nationally) self-centered. Israel did not, like its eponymous ancestor, strike a bargain with God, saying in effect, "If Yahweh takes care of me, I will worship him and return ten per cent of what he gives me" (Gen. 28:20-22); but the Torah says, "If you obey the commandments ... Blessed shall you be in the city, and blessed shall you be in the field. Blessed shall be the fruit of your body, and the fruit of your ground, and the fruit of your beasts. ... Yahweh will cause your enemies ... to be delivered before you" (Dt. 30:16; 28:3f., 7).

Jesus told his disciples to seek the kingdom of God, and not to worry about food and clothing; but he said also, "And all these things will be added to you" (Mt. 6:31-33; Lk. 12:29-31). He did not deny or ignore human needs and values. The Son of Man himself came eating and drinking; he was even called "a glutton and a drunkard" (Mt. 11:19; Lk. 7:34), though the difference between him and his critics at this point was a matter of social respectability rather than ethics. Judaism, by and large, was never an ascetic religion, and John the Baptist was condemned for his austerity (Mt. 11:18; Lk. 7:33).

Thus Jesus recognized the legitimacy of a secondary motivation for right conduct. His promise of "houses and brothers and sisters and mothers and children and lands" in this age, "with persecutions" (Mk. 10:30; cf. Lk. 18:30), was of course not meant to be taken literally, yet it does represent substantial compensation in human fellowship. The Beatitudes afford other examples (Mt. 5:3-12; Lk. 6:20-22), and the Woes which follow in Luke (6:24-26) show the other side of the picture. Certainly Jesus did not intend that his disciples should deliberately mourn or court persecution in order to gain the kingdom of heaven, or be merciful merely for the sake of obtaining mercy. Secondary aims and needs, however, were not to be allowed to come first. Jesus compared the kingdom of God with a treasure or a pearl for which a man would gladly sacrifice everything he had (Mt. 13:44-6).

In contemporary Judaism the thought of retribution was prominent, yet many sages, from Antigonus of Socho on, said that one should not be like a servant who serves for the sake of a reward. The Old Testament itself, for that matter, in spite of first appearances, is not limited to this world's goods in its promises of rewards for obedience. In late Old Testament times, when the faithful remnant was suffering more and more at the hands of foreign oppressors, there came a change of emphasis in this regard.

The rich man who came to Jesus asked not for the way of life in this world but for the way to eternal life (Mt. 19:16 par.). Only a glimpse of this idea appears in the Old Testament (Dan. 12:2), but in Jesus' day Judaism was much concerned with it. A favorite expression of the rabbis for the final reward of the righteous was "a share in the life of the coming age". So Jesus, promising "a hundredfold now in this time" to those who had forsaken all to follow him, continued "and in the coming age eternal life" (Mk. 10:30; Lk. 18:30). He spoke of entering life as he spoke of entering the kingdom of God; according to Mark he used the two expressions interchangeably (Mk. 9:43, 45, 47 par.).

For Jesus the *summum bonum* was the kingdom of God. Both Greek *basileía* and Aramaic *malkhûth* mean primarily kingship, royal authority and power, sovereignty. The thought of God as King runs through the Old Testament from Jgs. 8:23 to Zec. 14:17. It is especially conspicuous in the Psalms and in the Aramaic part of Daniel. God's kingship is "established from of old" (Ps. 93:2), an "everlasting kingship" that "endures throughout all generations" (Ps. 145:13; Dan. 3:33; 4:31 [4:3, 34]; 6:27 [26]). Extending over all the earth, it is exercised mainly for the benefit of Israel (Pss. 10:16; 44:5 [4]; 47:2-10 [1-9]). It has pronounced ethical implications (Pss. 24; 97:2, 10), and an eschatological aspect in connection with the idea of divine judgement (Pss. 96:10, 13; 98:9; Ob. 1:15-21).

In the sense of God's eternal, universal sovereignty the term 'kingdom of God' (in its more characteristic Jewish form, 'kingdom of heaven') occurs frequently in the rabbinic literature. Jesus usually associates it with the coming age, but such a saying as the one about receiving the kingdom like a child (Mk. 10:15; Lk. 18:17; cf. Mt. 18:3) reflects the basic meaning of the expression. The rabbis spoke of receiving or taking the yoke of the kingdom of heaven as a higher kind of service than taking the yoke of the commandments. It was probably in this sense that Jesus said, "Seek first the kingdom of heaven" (Mt. 6:33; Lk. 12:31). Praying that on earth as in heaven God's name may be hallowed, his kingdom come, his will be done (Mt. 6:9f.; cf. Lk. 11:2), is a threefold expression of essentially one and the same desire.

What God wills is revealed in his law. "He has showed you, O man, what is good" (Mic. 6:8). For Jesus, as for the Old Testament and its Jewish interpreters, the revelation of God's will in the Torah is to be understood in the framework of the covenant between God and Israel. This was a gift of love (Dt. 7:6-12; Hos. 11:1). It could have been rejected; but Israel had accepted it (Ex. 19:8; 24:3, 7), thereby adding to the Creator's natural right to obedience the obligation of free choice and commitment, solemnly reaffirmed on stated occasions (Dt. 27:11-26; Josh. 24:1-28).

Jesus was accused of breaking the law, or allowing his disciples to do so (e.g., Mt. 12:2 par.). The points on which this charge was brought were not strictly in the realm of ethics, but they acquired ethical significance through being associated with meeting human needs (providing for parents; healing disease or satisfying hunger on the Sabbath). Jesus exhibited a notable independence in the interpretation and application of the law (Mt. 7:28 par.). According to

Matthew, however, he denied that he wished to destroy the law or the prophets, declaring that, as we might put it, every dotting of an *i* and crossing of a *t* must be fulfilled (Mt. 5:17-19).

Although he apparently retained some traditional practices, he regarded the oral law as inferior or even opposed to the will of God revealed in the Torah. There were other Jews, of course, who revered the Scriptures but rejected the traditions of the elders. The word 'tradition' (*parádosis*) appears in only one passage in the gospels, where all that the evangelists report on this subject is brought together with a threefold application (Mt. 15:1-20; Mk. 7:1-23). Criticism of the disciples for eating without having washed their hands is met by the rejoinder, quoting Isa. 29:13, that the Pharisees and scribes follow precepts of men. Abuse of the *qorban* tradition is cited as an example; and the whole dietary law is rejected in principle on the ground that what comes out of the mouth, not what goes into it, defiles a man.

Matthew's presentation of Jesus' teaching suggests the figure of a new Moses with the laws of a new covenant, but the parallel is not developed or emphasized. (The reference to the new covenant in Mt. 26:28 is dubious textually.) Matthew also displays a casuistic interest in giving specific directions for dealing with an offender (Mt. 18:15-17); and the exception which he alone gives to Jesus' condemnation of divorce and remarriage shows a moral ideal being hardened into a regulation (Mt. 5:32; 19:9; cf. Mk. 10:11f.; Lk. 16:18). Even in Matthew, however, Jesus' ethical teaching is not given as a code of rules. It is not stated in legal terms, but in varied literary forms. Jesus did not promulgate laws; he set moral standards.

The Torah itself, for that matter, does not consist entirely or mainly of laws to be enforced by civil authorities. Portions of legal codes, with lists of offenses and penalties, are incorporated; but many, if not most, of the laws rely upon divine sanctions and appeal to the free choice of the people. It has been said that the book of Deuteronomy belongs to the literature of persuasion. This is almost equally true of the whole Torah.

Post-biblical Jewish ethics sometimes seems more legalistic than the law itself, perhaps because it is chiefly known from legal sources.

The *haggadah* and the apocrypha and pseudepigrapha make no such impression. The scribes, eager to make the revealed will of God effective in every detail of life, sought the exact meaning from the law by deductive reasoning, with necessary adjustments to changed situations and circumstances. Jesus offered no such elaborate footnotes to the Torah. He looked for the basic purpose of the law, according to the known nature and will of God.

He also looked beyond the overt act to the inner intention and desire. The most familiar expression of this criterion is the series of antitheses in the Sermon on the Mount (Mt. 5:21-48; cf. Lk. 6:27-36). The Old Testament puts more stress on acts than on intentions, yet the demands of law and prophets alike for just, humane, and faithful dealing with others presuppose basic attitudes. The Decalogue forbids not only stealing, but even coveting anything that belongs to one's neighbor (Ex. 20:17; cf. Dt. 5:21), and the Holiness Code says, "You shall not hate your brother in your heart . . . or bear any grudge against the sons of your people, but you shall love your neighbor as yourself" (Lev. 19:17f.).

The rabbis distinguished intentions from acts. Although they differed among themselves concerning the extent to which merit was determined by intention, they agreed that one should live "beyond the line of justice". At heart, however, they were lawyers. Their fine distinctions and exact definitions evince an essentially casuistic frame of mind.

Jesus' saying about fulfilling the law refers also to the prophets (Mt. 5:17). Usually in the gospels the fulfillment of prophecy has to do with events which had been, or were believed to have been, predicted; but that is not what is meant here. The prophets as well as the lawgivers were concerned with Israel's recognized obligations under the covenant. They did not lay down new rules or principles of conduct, but denounced violations of the known will of God and urged Israel to return to God and his ways (e.g., Isa. 55:7; Jer. 6:16; 18:11; Hos. 12:7 [6]; Zec. 1:2-6; Mal. 3:7). So Jesus appeared in Galilee, calling not for a new morality, but for repentance (Mt. 4:17; Mk. 1:15).

Recent stress on the cultic connections and functions of the prophets has somewhat obscured an important difference between the law and the prophets at this point. The priests and Levites, as teachers of the law, were involved with both ethical and cultic practices. Their concern for holiness embraced both moral and ritual purity. Unfortunately this very fact encouraged an assumption that God could be satisfied with formal worship regardless of human relations. Against this the prophets fulminated, voicing the wrath of God himself. In spite of the prominence of ritual in the law, they pronounced sacrifice and festivals futile without justice and mercy, or even as not desired by God at all (e.g., Am. 5:21-24; Hos. 6:6; Isa. 1:12ff.; Mic. 6:6-8; Jer. 7:22f.). The same subordination of the ritual to the moral law found expression also in some of the Psalms (e.g., Pss. 40:7-9 [6-8]; 50:9-15; 51:18f. [16f.]).

Jesus stood in the prophetic tradition. He did not reject the whole cultus on principle, but according to Matthew he twice quoted Hos. 6:6, "I desire steadfast love (Greek, mercy) and not sacrifice" (Mt. 9:13; 12:7). He is reported to have told lepers to go to the priests for ritual cleansing (Mt. 8:4 par.; Lk. 17:14). He observed and cherished the Passover (Lk. 22:15). He revered the temple and altar (Mt. 23:16-22), but spoke of the temple in prophetic language as a house of prayer and used another prophet's words for what the money-changers had made of it (Mt. 21:13 par.; Isa. 56:7; Jer. 7:11). He did not say, "Do not tithe mint, anise, and cummin"; he called justice, mercy and faith "the weightier matters of the law", saying, "You should have practised these, and not omitted those" (Mt. 23:23; cf. Lk. 11:42).

The commandments he cited in reply to the rich man's question (Mt. 19:18f. par.) include only ethical ones, omitting such purely religious precepts as those against polytheism, idolatry, misuse of the divine name, and working on the Sabbath. Matthew mentions also love of the neighbor here (Lev. 19:18), and Mark adds "Do not defraud", presumably from the same chapter in Leviticus (19:13; cf. Dt. 24:14). Even if the selection of these particular commandments should be attributed to redaction or tradition, it is clear that while Jesus did not repudiate the established forms of worship, he explicitly put human relationships ahead of ritual observances (Mt. 5:23f.).

The very expression, "weightier matters of the law", implies a freedom of selection and subordination inconsistent with strict legalism. Logically all the laws, being divine commandments, carried an absolute obligation, with no room for grades of importance. As a matter of fact, however, not even the strictest of the scribes went that far. A distinction between more and less weighty is implicit in the scribe's question about the first of the commandments and his agreement with Jesus' reply (Mt. 22:34-40 par.). The same desire to organize the law, so to speak, is evident in the story of Hillel giving the Golden Rule as the whole law ("the rest is commentary"), and later in Akiba's designation of Lev. 19:18 as its fundamental principle.

Already in the Old Testament this interest appears. The prophets' insistence on justice as more important than cultic observances separates what is essential from what is not. Micah boils down what the Lord requires to doing justice, loving loyal devotion, and humbly walking with God (Mic. 6:8). There is a striking parallel, if not a direct allusion, to this verse in Jesus' choice of justice, mercy, and faith as the weightier matters of the law.

In addition to the distinction between more and less weighty, there is in Jesus' teaching a tacit elimination of the lower levels of Old Testament ethics—if one may argue from silence in such a fragmentary record. Vestiges of primitive attitudes and customs, already outgrown or being outgrown within the Old Testament itself, are simply ignored. An example already noted is collective responsibility. Another is Jesus' teaching concerning personal resentment and vengeance.

Against a primitive background of blood revenge and unlimited retaliation (Gen. 4:15, 24), Hebrew law had sought to regulate the age-old customs, providing cities of refuge for those guilty of unintentional manslaughter (Nu. 35; Dt. 19:1-13; Josh. 20), and restricting the execution of the *lex talionis* to the established civil authorities (Ex. 21:23ff.; Lev. 24:19f.; Dt. 19:15-21).

Resentment and the desire for revenge were not condemned; but apparently quite early it came to be felt that a man must not avenge himself; he must leave vengeance to God and be content to enjoy the discomfiture of his foes (I Sam. 24:12; 25:26ff.; Ps. 58:11 [10]; Prov. 20:22; 25:21f.; Jer. 11:20). The same verse in Leviticus that demands love for one's neighbor forbids taking vengeance upon him (Lev. 19:18). Jesus refused to put any limit on the duty to forgive (Mt. 18:22; cf. Lk. 17:4).

In this connection we have perhaps the most extreme instance of the way Jesus "fulfilled" the law. Not only must his followers forego vengeance; they must allow themselves to be exploited and injured, must turn the other cheek, do more than is demanded, love their enemies (Mt. 5:38-44; Lk. 6:28-30). When asked what was the first of the commandments, Jesus named not one, but two (Mt. 22:34-40 par.): first, the religious root of a life pleasing to God, the commandment to love God (Dt. 6:4f.); and second, the ethical root, the commandment to love one's neighbor as oneself (Lev. 19:18).

In the Old Testament the neighbor means a fellow Israelite, not by explicit contrast with non-Israelites but by virtue of the fact that the laws are addressed to Israel. This was naturally the understanding of the word in post-biblical Judaism. The parable of the Good Samaritan extends the application of the commandment to include at least Samaritans, and by implication any persons in the relationship of need and service (Lk. 10:29-37).

It should not be necessary to say that neither in Leviticus nor in the gospels does love mean a diffuse, sentimental, complacent benevolence. It is an active relationship of genuine concern for individuals in personal contacts. The phrase "as yourself" neither commends nor condemns self-love, but assumes it and uses it as a measure of the right love for others.

Compared with the sensible, down-to-earth ethics of the Old Testament and the detailed moral precepts of Judaism, realistically adjusted to the exigencies of actual living, Jesus' ethical teaching often seems visionary, idealistic, out of touch with the limitations and demands of human existence. The characteristic Hebrew concern for the unfortunate and the disoriented is reflected in Jesus' sayings (Mk.

12:40-44; Lk. 20:47 and 21:1-4; Lk. 10:36f.; 16:19-31), as well as in his acts of mercy. But was he really interested in the problems of individuals and society in this world? Must the ghost of the "interim ethic" still haunt us?—was his ethical teaching meant only for a short interval before the coming of the kingdom?

Old Testament ethics did not contemplate an end of the cosmic order in the foreseeable future, though a psalmist saw it as coming eventually (Ps. 102:27[26]), and a prophet said, "For behold, I create new heavens and a new earth" (Isa. 65:17). When the prophets threatened the imminent destruction of the nation, it was because of disobedience to the will of God; and the warning was often given in the hope that repentance might still avert his wrath (e.g., Jer. 26:3; Joel 2:12-14). After the blow fell, restoration and exaltation were promised. Persecution under foreign conquerors produced special stress on fidelity and courage, but the substance of the moral code was not modified.

Is it otherwise with the ethics of Jesus? That he expected the kingdom to come soon seems to me practically certain. That he saw this as involving a transformation of the world-order is not certain, but probable. It does not follow, however, that the way of life he taught was only for the intervening years or days. Love for God and one's neighbor, readiness to do more than is required, concentration on the weightier matters of the law, humility, purity, single-minded devotion to the service of God and renunciation of the service of Mammon—these are necessary for entering the kingdom of God precisely because they are the qualities that will characterize life in the kingdom. "To such belongs the kingdom of heaven" (Mt. 19:14 par.); "theirs is the kingdom of heaven" (Mt. 5:3, 10; cf. Lk. 6:20).

As has already been observed, the scribes and rabbis agreed with Jesus in making the commandment of love primary. It has also been noted that he did not, as they did, go on to work out the implications and ramifications of that commitment. Luke reports that he said to a man who asked for help in getting his rightful inheritance, "Man, who made me a judge or a divider over you?" (Lk. 12:14). In the same chapter Luke also quotes a question addressed to the people:

"And why do you not judge for yourselves what is right?" (v. 57). Jesus' teaching leaves the responsibility for decisions to the individual, and requires constantly new decisions in new situations. In that sense it may fairly be called a situation ethic; but it is a situation ethic under God, judging every issue by the standard of love for God and man.

There are, of course, some specific instructions among Jesus' sayings. They illustrate the implications of the law of love; they also present difficult problems. Scholars have long been perplexed by the existence of two quite different kinds of sayings side by side in the gospels. Some apparently contemplate an indefinite continuation of the present cosmic and social order; others stress the imminence of the end of the age. There is also another contrast, more immediately pertinent for our purpose. Some sayings have the calm, pedagogical tone of wisdom literature, inculcating a righteous life in the normal relationships of home and community; others demand a radical sacrifice of good and kindred. This disparity calls for explanation no less than the other.

The two sets of contrasting sayings are related, but not identical. It might be expected that the non-eschatological sayings and the wisdom sayings would be the same, and for the most part this is so. There are sometimes eschatological references in the wisdom sayings, but with no suggestion of imminence (e.g., Lk. 14:13f.). The sayings which demand the renunciation of human ties and earthly security, however, are not at all the same as those which stress the nearness of the end. On the contrary, the former make little or no allusion to the future, though this is not always true of their present context; and the sayings which proclaim the imminence of the end, or warn that it may come at any time, make no such radical demands.

Only a few sayings of this last type contain any ethical teaching at all; but what these few require is the same righteous daily living taught by the non-eschatological wisdom sayings, with special stress on fidelity. Thus, for example, what have been perhaps the most cherished texts of the social gospel, the "inasmuch" verses, occur in the midst of the decidedly eschatological account of the final judgment by the

Son of Man (Mt. 25:31-46). Here social awareness and helpfulness, not a flight from domestic and economic involvements, are exalted. Again, the "faithful and wise servant" is characterized as the opposite of the one who thinks his lord's coming is delayed, "and begins to beat his fellow servants, and eats and drinks with the drunken" (Mt. 24:45ff.; Lk. 12:42ff.). So in Luke's form of the apocalyptic discourse, Jesus warns against "dissipation and drunkenness and cares of this life" (Lk. 21:34).

No doubt the tradition of these and similar sayings was affected by the delay of the parousia, but just how much and exactly in what ways is a matter of guesswork. The important point here is that the demand to sell all or to hate one's nearest and dearest is not found in such eschatological connections. Only by a conjectural and questionable reconstruction of what Jesus expected to happen at Jerusalem can this demand be associated with the parousia or the coming of the kingdom of God.

How then can we account for the combination of sayings concerned with the common life of society and others requiring the sacrifice of normal relationships? The easiest way would be to deny the authenticity of one group or the other. In dealing with the presence of both non-eschatological and "apocalyptic" sayings, it used to be said that the disciples misunderstood Jesus, reading into his teaching their inherited Jewish apocalyptic notions. Thus Jesus was made a consistent teacher of social ethics. Others held that the disciples read into his teaching their inherited Jewish moral ideas; and he became a consistent apocalyptic seer. Undoubtedly some sayings must be regarded as secondary on other grounds, but we cannot dispose of a whole category of sayings by such an arbitrary and subjective procedure.

More worthy of respect is the hypothesis that the wisdom sayings and the radical demands were addressed to different audiences. Those of the former type would be for all who accepted the gospel of the kingdom of God and endeavored to do God's will; the demands for renunciation would be addressed to an inner circle consisting of those who accompanied Jesus in his itinerant ministry and on the final, fatal journey to the holy city.

On this hypothesis, when Jesus said, as Luke reports, that to be his disciple a man must hate his father and mother and the rest of his family (Lk. 14:26f., 33: cf. Mt. 10:37f.), what he meant must have been that any who did not meet this test could not belong to the band of dedicated followers who would face peril and death with him. So when he told the rich man to sell his possessions and give to the poor (Mt. 19:21 par.), he might have meant, "You will have eternal life if you keep the commandments, but if you want to devote yourself wholly to God's kingdom, get rid of your property and come with us." Yet when the man turned away, Jesus said that it would be hard for the rich man to enter the kingdom of heaven (Mt. 19:23 par.), apparently implying that to keep the commandments was not enough to gain admission.

Jesus adopted voluntary poverty for himself (Mt. 8:20; Lk. 9:58), and told his "little flock" to sell their possessions and acquire heavenly treasures (Lk. 12:33; cf. Mt. 6:19f.). At the same time he allowed some well-to-do women to provide for him and his disciples out of their private means (Mk. 15:41; Lk. 8:2), which they could not have done if they had already given all they had to the poor. He also commended Zacchaeus, says Luke (not the most conservative of the evangelists), for giving half of his goods to the poor (Lk. 19:8f.)— presumably *after* restoring four-fold what he had gained by fraud.

The impression of special requirements for an inner circle is strengthened by Matthew by the use of the word 'perfect' in two places: "You therefore must be perfect, as your heavenly Father is perfect" (Mt. 5:48); and "If you would be perfect" (19:21). In the former instance Luke reads "Be merciful as your Father is merciful" (Lk. 6:36); in the latter neither Mark nor Luke has the expression (Mk. 10:21; Lk. 18:22). The word occurs nowhere else in the gospels. That Jesus himself used any of the possible Aramaic equivalents in either connection is improbable.

He is more likely to have said "merciful" than "perfect". In either form, the saying about being like the Father recalls a verse in the same chapter of Leviticus that contains the commandment to love one's neighbor: "You shall be holy; for I the LORD your God am holy" (Lev. 19:2; cf. 11:44; 20:26). The conception of holiness was associated in the Old Testament with the separation of Israel from the nations and their defilements. A few echoes of such an idea are heard in Jesus' sayings (Mt. 5:47; 6:7, 32; 20:25 par.). Holiness as *imitatio Dei* is much stressed in the rabbinic literature, with special reference to compassion and mercy.

It is unlikely that Jesus propounded a double standard, with strict rules for a closed inner group and an easier yoke for others who sought the kingdom of God. He demanded radical renunciation by any who chose to accompany him, because the fact of accompanying him made such renunciation necessary. The sayings in question are actually not so much demands as warnings. Following him who had no place to lay his head (Mt. 8:20; Lk. 9:58), and who went, as was written of him, to rejection and suffering (Mt. 26:24 par.), was not to be undertaken without counting the cost (Lk. 14:28ff.). To that extent and in that sense the wisdom sayings and the radical demands were addressed to different audiences.

But this suggests a further possibility: the two groups of sayings come from different periods in Jesus' ministry. Any reconstruction involving development or change in his teaching is necessarily hypothetical. It seems reasonable, however, to suppose that the sayings of the wisdom type came early in his ministry, and the radical demands were made after it became clear that a crisis, possibly fatal, was inevitable. From the time when Peter and the rest left their nets (Mt. 4:20 par.), warnings that discipleship meant sacrifice might have been given; but they would become sharper and more emphatic when a direct confrontation was deliberately sought. Perhaps the significance of Caesarea Philippi as a turning point is not a theological construction after all.

Regardless of what Jesus may or may not have expected to happen, the question remains whether his ethical teaching is actually applicable to normal life in society in an indefinitely continued succession of generations and centuries. Where he gave specific instructions, every item can not be equally relevant for all situations. Jesus' attitude to the state, for example, is more relevant for a country ruled by a hostile occupying power than for an independent democracy.

Essentially, aside from the special demand for renunciation in view of the immediately impending crisis, what Jesus taught was the ethics of the Old Testament, with some shift of emphasis, but with no change of substance. Even his most radical demands may be applicable in a crisis or an "apocalyptic situation"; indeed, it is fair to ask whether anything that presupposes normal social life can be relevant for the state of the world today. In any case, readiness to make any necessary sacrifice for God's kingdom is always imperative.

So far as we know, Jesus never explicitly condemned war or slavery or inequality of race or sex. He reaffirmed and broadened a basic principle which eventually and inescapably demands putting an end to such evils. He did not specify in advance solutions for the moral and social problems of mankind. He indicated the direction in which solutions must be sought. To say that his way is the right way is a confession of faith, which can hardly be better expressed than in the words of Peter in John 6:68: "Lord, to whom shall we go? You have the words of eternal life."

FOOTNOTES

1. Old Testament citations are made by chapter and verse according to the English versions.

2. To avoid involvement in any theory of source or priority, material found in three gospels is cited in the form, "Mt. 8:3 par.". When a passage occurs in any two gospels, both are cited.

NOTE ON BIBLIOGRAPHY

The literature on these subjects is enormous. In the preparation of this essay I have found the following works especially helpful for review, clarification, and fresh insights:

Belkin, Samuel, *In His Image. The Jewish Philosophy of Man as Expressed in Rabbinic Tradition,* 1960.

Hempel, J. *Das Ethos des Alten Testaments BZAW,* 67, 2nd ed., 1964.

Hiers, R. H. *Jesus and Ethics,* 1968.

Jeremias, J. *Neutestamentliche Theologie,* Erster Teil, Die Verkündigung Jesu, 1971.

Schnackenburg, R. *The Moral Teaching of the New Testament,* tr. from 2nd German ed., 1962, by J. Holland-Smith and W. J. O'Hara, 1967.

van Oyen, H. *Ethik des Alten Testaments,* Geschichte der Ethik, Band 2, 1967.

THE ETHIC OF ELECTION IN LUKE'S GREAT BANQUET PARABLE

J. A. Sanders

Auburn Professor of Biblical Studies
at Union Theological Seminary,
New York

It may seem strange, to those familiar with J. M. D. Derrett's probing essay on the parable of the Great Supper, that further work would be indicated so soon thereafter.[1] One learns much indeed from Derrett's treatment of the parable, especially in its Matthean guise; and one is cheered to see a study such as his pursuing lines of inquiry long neglected. But agreeing in the main with Derrett's vision of the problems posed, I am disappointed that some aspects of the parable in Luke were left untouched.

My own work on the parable began some ten years ago while reflecting on the apparatus to Dominique Barthélemy's edition of The Qumran Rule of the Congregation. In the apparatus to 1QSa ii 6 Barthélemy has a one-line simple reference to Lk. 14:21, but does not suggest the direction of his own thinking about it.[2] Yigael Yadin, in his masterful edition of the Qumran War Scroll, made no reference at all to the Lukan material despite the obvious similarities between battles, banquets and guests appearing in the two.[3] A year later, 1963, saw the publication of the English translation of J. Jeremias' *Parables,* but there had clearly been no attempt to make improvements over the German edition and there was still nothing there even close to my vision of the sorts of problems presented by the parable.[4]

In 1966 Robert Funk published *Language, Hermeneutic and Word of God.* Central to Funk's effort to make direct application of the so-called New Hermeneutic, or *Sprachereignis* (language-event) hermeneutic of Ernst Fuchs and Gerhard Ebeling, is a long section in two chapters on the parable of the Great Supper. These chapters, in the design of the book, bear a great deal of the burden of Funk's argument concerning the validity of the New Hermeneutic. I have no quarrel with the New Hermeneutic as such. On the contrary, such an approach in its proper place, combined with the even newer emphasis called the Sociology of Knowledge,[5] can be an extremely valuable tool in exegesis and in the new efforts being launched to recover a valid sense of "canon" for our day.[6] But Funk had gleaned through the finest of New Testament scholarship on the parable and still did not see the parable in the way I see it.

I consider the first obligation of the exegete to be that of attempting to recover the point originally scored, to use James M. Robinson's very apt phrase. And the point originally scored cannot be recovered until the words preserved in the text before us are understood in terms as nearly as possible like those of the original context in which they were spoken or read. This is what any professional interpreter should mean by full context. Literary criticism, from form-criticism through redaction-criticism rightly insists on context in the sense of perceiving a text in the light of its primary and then full literary units. But that is only a part of the meaning of "full context." To deal with such units apart from the context into which they were spoken in antiquity is to deal with truncated, isolated units, disconnected from the focus of their meaning.

I

One of the extremely valuable emphases in the relatively new field of comparative midrash is that of seeing the contemporization of an ancient tradition in the light of the need of the community which recalled, and reflected upon, the tradition.[7] Comparative midrash, Rhetorical criticism, and Audience criticism are emerging, I am convinced, as the keys to much of what is going on in biblical work today.[8] This underscores the need for the sort of historical exegesis associated with the name of J. Philip Hyatt.

The exegete (of any ancient literature) must view the text before him as only one of two foci necessary to understand what it says. The more one works on ancient rhetoric, the more one is convinced of this observation. The second focus was the actual situation into which the textual material was first interjected. This focus is often extremely difficult to reconstruct, but the effort must be made. For here is where one must seek the complement to what the speaker in the preserved text presupposed. The better the rhetoric, or the more "occasional" the writing, the more apt the presuppositions the rhetor made. Rhetorical criticism, of any literature of any period, clearly shows that the speaker makes his best and most striking points, not when he belabors the obvious, but when he presupposes in his audience the concerns he knows they have, their knowledge of recent events which affect their lives, etc.

Such an observation can be depressing for the exegete of ancient literature. For clearly we shall never recover anywhere near the amount of material necessary for reconstructing the situational foci of biblical texts. But it does mean that we are all the more obligated to try to do so. The language-event school is clearly open to the criticism that their excitement in other areas has led them very nearly to ignore historical context.[9] The point originally scored, or the concept (*Begriff*) the original speaker or writer intended to convey, depends directly on the extent to which the second focus is available.

But simply locating the place and date of original writing hardly reconstructs the situational focus. Answers to "introductory" questions are hardly sufficient. It is necessary to attempt to recover, as nearly as possible, the mentality, the concerns, the hopes and fears of those to whom the textual material was first addressed. In work on any given text, one may have to test several different such "original" contexts. Redactional criticism, very much in vogue these days, can be effective only as one seeks to know the concerns and desires of the redactor's congregation. In order to see fully what the ideas of the biblical redactor were, one needs to know the concerns and needs of his congregation, to what in them he was addressing himself. In order to probe back of that moment in history to an earlier one, form-criticism becomes quite important. But once an early unit has been defined one still has to be careful about the stage of development with which he is dealing. If one probes too far back one may simply be left with an ancient hellenistic or Near Eastern proverb (or other small unit); and proverbs are notoriously flexible, always needing full historical context to know how the user was bending its meaning, according to the point he wanted to score with his hearers. Sometimes knowledge of how a proverb or legend was understood outside the Bible is a deterrent in reconstructing what it meant when spoken in the first "biblical orbit" situation so that it ended up in our canon. To import meanings from one context to another without regard to the second full context can be disastrous. The exegete must be aware of all the possible questions pertinent to *fully contextual exegesis*.[10]

How a text was understood by an audience is the crucial question. Was the biblical speaker or writer comforting his congregation or audience, or was he, perhaps, challenging them? How did he wish to move his constituency? If he was "only instructing" them, what was his goal in forming/informing their thinking? The basic hermeneutics of the speaker or writer becomes extremely important at this stage of work. And here precisely is the crucial locus of current work in comparative midrash. When one has recovered what Old Testament authoritative tradition lies at the base of an Early Jewish (including New Testament) text, then he is in a position to move to another level of work: to compare the various ways that the same Old Testament tradition was being contemporized in that same period of Judaism in order to see what the going emphases were and how they were being used elsewhere. Then he can look for clues in the text at hand to see if the hermeneutics can be determined. In the case of the New Testament, of course, the matter is complicated by the ever-present (and frequent) possibility that the redactor, on the one hand, and Jesus, on the other, may have used the very tradition at hand in opposite ways, i.e., with different hermeneutics and convictions.[11] This observation becomes especially impressive when one thinks that by the methods of comparative midrash he has possibly recovered a use of an Old Testament tradition by Jesus; he must always entertain the possibility that while the evangelist may indeed have received the tradition from Jesus, he may have understood and used it in a way diametrically opposed to the way Jesus had used it. Or, he may discover, that by reporting what Jesus said exactly as he said it, the redactor or evangelist may have produced the opposite effect in *his* audience from that which Jesus had produced in *his,* precisely because the audiences were asking different questions. In fact, the more one works on the gospels, the more he suspects this was the case: where Jesus may have been issuing a prophetic challenge in *his* day, what he said, in the later context, could be taken in the opposite way. For instance, if a prophetic critique of Jesus aimed at the co-religionists of his day is repeated, even verbatim, to an early Christian congregation in A.D. 70, it was probably received in the later situation not as a prophetic critique of themselves but statically as a condemnation of Jews.

These observations again emphasize the need, in exegesis, to understand *full context* to mean the two foci, text and audience. Statically transmitted material from the situation of Jesus to the situation of Matthew can score a point diametrically opposite to what it had scored in the earlier situation. In the case of Jesus traditions, if we understand Jesus to be employing prophetic-critique hermeneutics in his situation, i.e., conveying a challenge from the Old Testament to his own Jewish in-group, unless Matthew converts what Jesus did so that it also conveys a challenge to *his own* Christian in-group, then the message of Jesus is subverted. I have come to the point in my own work on the gospels that one of the reasons they do indeed appear to be so anti-Jewish is that Jesus' own hermeneutics, as the gospels largely want to insist, were often prophetic. Any prophetic-critique hermeneutic in the Bible (Old Testament or New) statically conveyed to a non-Jewish audience is automatically anti-Jewish, if not anti-Semitic. This observation may be used with the force of a rule of exegesis. Therefore, if New Testament scholarship is confident that at the Redaction critical level much in the gospels is anti-Jewish (in the struggle of nascent Christianity to affirm its identity as the New Israel), then conversely, that same material in Jesus' situation in Palestine in the First Century may have been prophetic in hermeneutics. If, to put it another way, the evangelists after 70 A.D., for their own reasons and needs, intended to put the Jews down, and Jesus had actually conducted in large part a prophetic ministry in his life, then such Jesus traditions accurately (i.e., statically) received, provided the very anti-Jewish material the early church needed without much further ado. Conceivably all they had to do in such cases was record, as closely as possible, his ipsissima verba. The fact that contemporization by static analogy completely subverted what Jesus said in the sense of the point *he* originally scored would perhaps have hardly occurred to them. In other words I hardly think the evangelists were consciously subverting Jesus' intent; I think, on the contrary, they thought they were being faithful to him. Faithful, in the sense that some historians in modern times think they have been faithful, when they have failed to breathe the ambiguity of reality into their work by failing to seek out always the two foci (textual and contextual) necessary for understanding any text.[12]

Part of what is necessary, in attempting to reconstruct the New Testament point originally scored, is to seek the First Century foil in the second focus.[13] We must assume that *both* Jesus *and* the evangelists had reasons for saying what they said. They had points to make. This means, methodologically, that one cannot assume that they were attempting to phrase an eternal verity received by revelation applicable to all time. It means that one must assume they had something to say a) that would have been understood by contemporaries, and b) that would have been to some extent different from what the contemporaries already were thinking. By informing them, they were attempting to form their thinking. They had a reason for saying what they said. They were being relevant to their situation. By this method one sets aside the quest for what was "unique" or "original" as genuinely dominical, and instead looks for an aspect of "overagainstness" in what Jesus is reported to have taught.[14] And this would particularly be the case if, in testing out the method, one assumes (until proved otherwise) that the hermeneutic employed was that of prophetic critique.[15]

It is often pointed out that integral to the comparative midrash method of work on early Jewish literature is the assumption that what is in the text studied is there because it met a need of the community to whom it was addressed. But it must be remembered that the need of the community may have been a challenge to their thinking about themselves and their life-style. In the case of the Old Testament prophets, this point is utterly clear.[16] But we have to leave open the possibility that the New Testament also exhibits Jesus' use of such a prophetic-critique hermeneutic. Current efforts to develop sound method in comparative midrash must not exclude this possibility. On the contrary, it seems to me at this juncture of work, that we need to test out the possibility of prophetic-critique hermeneutic before moving on to other possibilities.

II

For some years now, my students and I have been diligently searching the available (and in some cases unpublished) Qumran literature to find evidence of the use of prophetic-critique hermeneutic there. So far we have been significantly unsuccessful. In no instance have we found a case at Qumran of contemporizing of an Old Testament tradition as a challenge to the in-group. Such an observation in no way mitigates the fact that the faithful at Qumran had a high doctrine of man and of sin. On the contrary, they apparently daily confessed their manifold sins and wickedness and unworthiness, in general confession, collectively and individually.[17] But, interestingly, every instance of interpretation of the Old Testament is favorable to the sect. Every blessing is seen as flowing toward themselves in the End Time and every possible curse on their enemies—whether the Hasmonaeans, the Romans or the cosmic forces of evil. In other words, they were a normal denomination!

By contrast, following the above outlined method, it is abundantly and overwhelmingly possible that, whereas the early Christians often followed just such in-group exegesis also, Jesus himself may have employed prophetic-critique hermeneutics in what he had to say to his in-group Jewish contemporaries. In fact, it is highly possible, in the realm of canonical criticism, that one reason the teachings of Jesus were so popular in the period after his death, and especially following the fall of Jerusalem in A.D. 69, is that reviewed in light of the needs of the struggling Christian community of that time, Jesus' prophetic strictures against his fellow Jews looked like the comfort and support they thought they needed for their own views of themselves as the New Israel. As noted above, this false transfer of the Jesus traditions was effected by static analogy to their situation.

Obviously what is needed in any attempt to reconstruct the second focus in the time of Jesus (as contrasted with the time of the evangelists) is extrabiblical material from Palestine of the earlier time period. And, in contrast to rabbinic literature which is notoriously difficult to date and control, Qumran provides just such material.[18] It is precisely all pre-A.D. 70 material which, like the New Testament, accepts as its acknowledged base of authority the Old Testament. Sound methodic procedure would then be to find passages in both Qumran literature and the New Testament which treat of the same Old Testament material in order to compare the hermeneutics used in each. Fortunately there is a plethora of such cases. One of these is provided by the Great Banquet parable in Lk. 14 and several passages in Qumran Cave 1 literature.

III

The Central Section of Luke's Gospel has been an enigma of New Testament scholarship. Until Canon Streeter's *Four Gospels* this section was variously called the Travel Document, the Peraean Section, the Samaritan Document, etc.[19] Since Streeter it has almost universally been designated by the term, Central Section. Even so, little headway has been made into probing its significance, why Luke arranged his material in this way, and what he was attempting to convey by so doing. An immense breakthrough was signaled in 1955 by C. F. Evans in a little-heralded article in which he showed, beyond all doubt, that Luke had arranged his material parallel to Dt. 1-26. Evans' article has received precious little attention, however; and the reason for this, I think, is that he failed to probe Luke's major purpose in doing what he had done.[20]

Evans stresses, rightly, the point that Luke presents Jesus in this section as the "prophet like Moses" fulfilling Dt. 18:15. The substance of Evans' work is the observation that in Lk. 9:51-18:43 the evangelist follows the order of Deuteronomy by using catch-words easily traced in the LXX of that Old Testament book. Though Evans does not make it explicit, what he has seen very clearly is the midrashic technique of calling the reader's attention to a well-known Old Testament authority. Luke, in excellent midrashic fashion, insists that to understand what Jesus said and did, to perceive the real truth about him, one must draw down, as a backdrop to his report of his words and deeds, the one authority needed to test the accuracy of its claims concerning Christ, the Old Testament. We modern historians, in quest of answers to our needs, pull down a map or a chronological chart, as a backdrop to test the truth of such claims.[21] To do so, however, is not to meet Luke where he himself indicated we should; and we pass judgment against him that he did not know what he was talking about in these matters. He, therefore, a) did not know Palestine at the time of Jesus, and b) did not know Jesus very well. My point is not that Luke knew Jesus very well, but that the backdrops we often insist on using do not constitute a true control factor in making historical judgments about biblical materials.

If Evans is right that Dt. 18:15, the promise of the prophet like Moses,[22] is at the heart of what Luke wants to say about Jesus in this section, and if he is right that the sequential pattern of Dt. 1-26 lies back of this section, then special attention is drawn, I think, to what can readily be seen, in the light of Evans' work, as the heart of this central section of Luke's Gospel—the Great Banquet parable in Lk. 14. The fact that this parable is at the heart of the whole section becomes clear when one realizes that the principal reason Luke arranged his material in this fashion was that Luke understood Jesus' teaching for the most part as a prophetic critique of current inversions of the Deuteronomic ethic of election.

In order to test this hypothesis I set aside a day in which to do a vertical reading of the *Gospel*. Using the Greek *Synopsis* edited by Kurt Aland (1964), I read Luke at one sitting, always with the question in mind: Is it possible that Luke was presenting Jesus as delivering a prophetic critique against false assumptions about election? And, *mirabile dictu*, while much in the sections of Luke preceding 9:51, but not much after ch. 18 can be so construed, everything in the Central Section *can* be so understood. It seems that, if one takes Evans' brilliant lead, the purpose of this famous section becomes evident. It will be the purpose of another study to attempt to establish that point.[23]

Certainly the work I had already done on the Great Banquet parable indicated very clearly that such was precisely the motive of this parable. The balance of this paper has as its purpose to establish this point.

IV

One of the first observations one makes about the Great Banquet parable is that the three excuses submitted by the *keklemenoi,* who are unable to attend, are based on the four causes for deferment from serving in the army of the Holy War of Yahweh given in Dt. 20:5-8. Evans correctly sets Dt. 20 parallel to Lk. 14:15-35 in his schema.[24]

The four acceptable reasons for exemption from service in the army of the faithful, according to Dt. 20, are: 1) having built a house as yet not dedicated; 2) having planted a vineyard the fruit of which had yet to be enjoyed; 3) having married and not yet consummated the marriage; and 4) being fainthearted. In the parable only three reasons are given: 1) having bought a field not yet inspected; 2) having bought five yoke of oxen not yet examined; and 3) having married recently.

Dt. 20	Lk. 14
Built house not yet dedicated	Bought field not yet inspected
Planted vineyard not yet enjoyed	Bought oxen not yet examined
Marriage not yet consummated	Recent marriage
Fainthearted	. . .

The parable follows the first three stipulations in Deuteronomy rather closely. Or, to put it another way, the distance between the first three stipulations in Deuteronomy and the three in Lk. 14 is no more or less than might be expected in a midrash of this sort from this period. The important point is that the parable follows the

Deuteronomic Holy War legislation in enumerating both economic and social reasons as base for exemption from participation.

Important is the fact that the fourth stipulation in Dt. 20 is omitted from the parable. Interestingly enough it is the converse in 1QM x 5-6. Only the fourth reason for exemption occurs in the War Scroll. But Yigael Yadin, the editor of the scroll in its definitive edition, explains that elimination of the first three groups would have taken place on going forth from Jerusalem, so that they could simply remain at home.[25] The fourth, however, according to General Yadin, could be determined only at the battle front where 1QM x 5-6 sets the process. Yadin has no doubt whatever that this was the procedure. Faintheartedness can be determined only when the army has come face to face with the enemy; the other exemptions can and should be determined back home before starting out to the field of battle.[26]

By calling to the attention of the hearer or reader the Holy War legislation of Dt. 20, Jesus or Luke's Jesus, in excellent midrashic fashion, says one must have Dt. 20 in mind in order to understand the point of the parable. This, as Evans has demonstrated, would have been no surprise to Theophilos or to any knowledgeable reader after him, since Lk. 14 but takes its place in the Deuteronomic sequence being pursued in the Central Section of the Gospel, a sequence already established as necessary to perceiving the theme being pursued.

That Dt. 20 is concerned with a battle and Lk. 14 with a banquet occasion is no surprise either. Lk. 14:14-15 has already established the parable as describing or dealing effectively with the great eschatological banquet. That the legislation of Dt. 20 should then be rung into the substance of the parable in 14:18-20 would be what an astute hearer or reader would have expected at that point. The Holy War legislation is eschatologized at Qumran, as Yadin has shown from the War Scroll; and certainly the messianic banquet as anticipated in the Rule of the Congregation (1QSa) is eschatological.

Following the shift of emphasis, from the this-worldly questions of life-style in the teaching on humility in Lk. 14:7-14 (which occurs precisely at the end of that teaching [14:14] and in the transition comment from a guest at table [14:15]), the parable of the Great

Banquet speaks directly of the guest list of the kingdom table in the Eschaton. The relation of battle to banquet in the eschaton is amply discussed by J. Derret and need not detain us here.[27]

Of greater interest than such matters (where no real surprises lurk) is the fact that it is only in Lk. 14 and 15 and in 16:25 that we find forms of *kaleo* (and *parakaleo*) having other than the very neutral meanings of "named" or "designated" or "called" and the like. The reason such a restricted use of *kaleo* is so interesting is that which we have already pointed out: a vertical reading of the Central Section of this Gospel with Dt. 1-26 as backdrop clearly indicates that Luke's great concern is with abuses of Deuteronomy's theology and ethic of election.[28] The surprise is that Luke does not use this all-important word elsewhere (save in such phrases as "You shall call his name John" 1:13, etc.) to signify election, not even in Acts. Clearly he wants to underscore its use, then, in this core material of the Central Section of his Gospel. That *kaleo* (with *parakaleo*) serves Luke, in both the Great Banquet and Prodigal Son parables, with the ambiguity of both meanings, "invite" and "elect", is emphasized by the one exception, in 16:26, where it can only mean comforted or entreated in the sense of "elect": Lazarus is elect while the rich man at whose gate on earth he ate scraps is cursed or in pain. Lazarus is in heaven, the rich man in Hades—the final proof of election.

Such is the theme of the whole Central Section: the Deuteronomic ethic of election has been subverted. Whereas Deuteronomy stressed that obedience brings blessings and disobedience curses, one cannot go on to assume (as many ever since Deuteronomy did assume—see the book of Job) that suffering indicates one is not elect while riches or ease on earth indicates that one is elect. As I shall attempt to demonstrate in another study, it is my contention that every pericope in Luke's Central Section pursues this theme.[29] But clearly the theme reaches a sort of climax in the parables of the Great Banquet, the Prodigal Son and the Rich Man and Lazarus. It is for this reason that most discussions to date (nearly all negative) of whether *kaleo* in Lk. 14-16 has to do with election are now seen as irrelevant and impertinent.³⁰ The interest now shifts to the question of why Luke limited his use of them to these three chapters. And the answer is not difficult to secure. In the two parables in chs. 14 and 15, the center of attention is a banquet. *Kaleo* clearly means "invite" in the context of dinners and banquets, and it is only in such a context that Luke can stress his major point that those who are confident that they shall be at the eschatological banquet in all likelihood will not be. This literary concept of double entendre serves his purposes admirably indeed, and it is introduced by the apparently mundane discussion in 14:7-14 of a wisdom teaching on earthly practices of inviters and invitees. Luke thereby insists that we understand the meaning "invite" so that we do not think only of "elect" as we might otherwise do. It is an excellent rhetorical device and well executed. Also, as Larrimore Clyde Crockett has admirably shown, Luke is intensely interested in table fellowship and centers his discussions of election and the relation of Jews and Gentiles in pictures of table fellowship.³¹ *Keklemenoi* in Luke means "apparently elect" or "those who consider themselves elected."

V

There are a number of links forging the intimate relation between the teaching of humility in 14:7-14 and the parable in 14:16-24. Among these the principal ones are as follows: 1. The formulary introduction to the parable itself appears in v. 7 along with the introductory matter leading into the didache material of vv. 8-14, just as the mise-en-scène for both the teaching and the parable is provided at the head of the report of the deed (and challenge) of healing on the Sabbath which begins ch. 14. These are Lukan redactional techniques which cannot be overlooked. 2. The key word *keklemenoi* (invited and "apparently elect") appears four times, twice in the teaching pericope (vv. 7-8) and twice in the parable itself (vv. 14 and 24). 3. The four-word listing "poor, maimed, lame, and blind" appears precisely in the two pericopes, at 14:13 and 14:21. 4. The exhortation which closes the pericope on humility ends on the same eschatological note which introduces the parable (vv. 14 and 15). Thus the "resurrection of the just" in v. 14 and "shall eat bread in the kingdom of God" in v. 15 both fix the focus of the parable upon the question of who is truly elect. It would indeed appear as though the ethical lesson of the parable is given before the parable itself is told; that is, the challenge to the life-style of those who consider themselves *keklemenoi* is levied before the picture is painted of how it will actually be when the herald goes forth to proclaim that the kingdom table is prepared to receive those who have been "called" (*keklemenoi*). The one is a challenge to the life-style of the *keklemenoi* and the other a challenge to their very identity.

The parable itself is presented in three parts: 1. Vv. 16-17 describe the "invitation" and despatch of the herald. 2. Vv. 18-20 present the excuses or the reasons the *keklemenoi* "beg off" (*paraiteisthai*). 3. Vv. 21-24 describe the reaction of the host and his utter freedom to alter the guest list at will, by which he has the herald "bring in" (v. 21) and "compel" (v. 23) others to come.

The herald is despatched to call in the "many" (*kai ekalesen pollous*). Clearly *pollous* here means not crowds, or the like, but an in-group. As has been established on other bases, *polloi* is often the equivalent of the frequent use of *ha-rabbim* at Qumran, a synonym of the elect.[32] The message of the herald is simple, "Come, for now all is ready."[33] The banquet table is prepared to receive those who are to eat bread in the kingdom of God.

At this point, as might have been expected in the Deuteronomy sequence, the *keklemenoi* begin to send in their reasons for not heeding the call. But we must not imagine that Luke has simply transferred the Deuteronomic material here out of context. The same excuses applicable to the eschatological war are pertinent to the eschatological banquet. In such a context, as already stressed, battle and banquet should be seen in the same light. And the fact that the fourth reason for exemption from the eschatological scene, faintheartedness, is omitted from the parable underscores the reasoning developed by Yadin for the omission of the first three from 1QM x 5-6.[34] The first three excuses listed in Deuteronomy would fit the banquet aspect of the eschaton while the fourth would fit the battle aspect.

Matthew's use of the banquet tradition is quite a different matter from that of Luke's.[35] Matthew does not follow Deuteronomy at all, but rather develops a midrash on Zeph. 1. Hence, Matthew's presentation of the supper as a *gamos* (wedding banquet) given by a king for his son relates to the battle (because of Zeph. 1) in quite a different manner from Luke's *deipnon* (banquet); Matthew cryptically summarizes the excuses as concern for farm and business; Matthew pictures an army in the place of Luke's servant or herald; Matthew describes the newly called guests as "all you can find" or simply as "both bad and good"; Matthew brings in the murder theme by picturing the *keklemenoi* as unworthy and finally rejected by the king.[36] By contrast, central to the parable in Luke is the new list of guests specifically named as the poor, maimed, blind, and lame (as in 14:13). First, it must be noted that no form of *kaleo* is used by Luke at this point. The new guests are simply brought in or compelled to come in. It is as though Luke wants to be very careful indeed in his use of this key word. He reserves it here to designate those who would have considered themselves elect. Thus does he emphasize the freedom of the host to alter the guest list at will. "Blessed is he who shall eat bread in the kingdom of God" indeed! God can indeed be angry at the "elect" (Lk. 14:21) and execute his power and freedom in favor of whom he wishes.[37]

In order to understand the list of new guests one must once more turn to the Old Testament and to Qumran. The Rule of the Congregation, which specifically deals with a) those who may be admitted to the Qumran community and b) those who will sit at table when Messiah comes, establishes an index of those who are forbidden access to either (1QSa ii 5-22). And the War Scroll establishes an index of those who are forbidden to approach the field of battle of the last great Holy War when the holy angels will fight on the side of the faithful against their enemies (1QM vii 4-6).

Both lists of the forbidden are manifestly drawn from the category of the sons of Aaron in Lev. 21:17-23, who are proscribed from approaching the veil or altar to offer the *leḥem 'ᵃᵉlohîm* (bread of God).

Lev 21:17-23	1QSa ii 5-22	1QM vii 4-6
blind	afflicted in flesh	(women and boys)
lame	crushed in feet or	lame
mutilated face	hands	blind
limb too long	lame	halt
injured foot	blind	permanent defect in
injured hand	deaf	flesh
hunchback	dumb	afflicted with impurity
dwarf	defective eyesight	of flesh
defect in sight	senility	impure sexual organs
itching disease	(the simple—i 19-20)	
scabs		
crushed testicles		
any blemish		

Though there are differences of terminology in the three lists, clearly Lev. 21 lies back of both proscriptions in the Qumran documents.[38] And there can be little question that the twice-recorded "poor, maimed, blind and lame" in Lk. 14 reflect in part such proscriptions. Qumran drew on the list in Lev. 21 to clarify both who should not approach the field of eschatological battle and who should not be present at the messianic table. The Lukan list, however, seems to reflect the levitical only as refracted through such legislation as that of Qumran; and it is used with the opposite intention. It is as though the Great Banquet parable was specifically constructed to contradict the sort of membership or guest lists now known from the Qumran literature.

The Rule of the Congregation, just before and after the list of those forbidden access to the core of the community, gives two quite different kinds of lists. The first specifies those who are "invited" to the Community Council, and the second specifies those who are "invited" to the Community Council at that time when God will bring the Messiah for the messianic meal. The word "invited" occurs three times in this document (once as *niqra'im* and twice as *qeru'im*). (And, *mirabile dictu,* the other two occurrences of *qeru'im* in the Qumran literature are precisely in 1QM iii 2 and iv 10—the other document from Qumran so important for understanding the Great Banquet parable!)[39]

> These are the men who will be invited (*niqra'im*) to the Community Council (from the age of twenty): all the wise men of the congregation, the understanding and the knowledgeable, the pure in piety, the men of great virtue with the leaders of the tribes, together with their judges and captains, commanders of thousands and commanders of hundreds, of fifties and of tens, and the Levites—each in his assigned place of duty. These are the men of renown called by the Assembly (*qeri'ê mo'ed*), appointed to the Community Council in Israel in the presence of the Priests, Sons of Zadoq. (1QSa i 27-ii 3).

At this point comes the list of those forbidden to have membership in the Community Council. Then ensues one of the most interesting passages in the document for understanding the Great Banquet parable.

> This is the seating order of the men of renown, called (or, invited) by the Assembly to the Community Council whenever God will bring the Messiah to be with them. The High Priest will come at the head of all of the Congregation of Israel. As for all the elders (fathers?) of the priests, sons of Aaron, called (or, invited) by the Assembly, men of renown, they shall take their place under his primacy, each according to his status (or, dignity). Thereafter shall the Messiah of Israel take his place. And then shall the heads of the thousands of Israel take their place under his primacy, each according to his status (or, dignity) and according to the post that he occupies in their camps and on their marches. Thereafter shall all the heads of the elders (fathers?) of the Congregation as well as all the wise men of the Holy Congregation take their places under their primacy, each according to his status. When they shall be gathered about the

table of the Community, or for drinking the wine, and when the table of the Community shall be ready (prepared) and the wine mixed so that it can be drunk, let no one touch the first bite of bread or touch the wine before the priest. For it is he who shall bless the first bite of bread and the wine; and he shall be first to touch the bread and then bless all the members of the united Congregation, each according to his status. (IQSa ii 11-21)

Thereafter it is provided that this messianic meal may be celebrated proleptically whenever a minimum of ten men are gathered to do so.

VI

It would be difficult indeed to imagine more appropriate foils than these to what Luke reports Jesus to have said, in both the teaching on humility and in the parable. He has completely inverted both the guest list and the seating arrangement as stipulated in the Qumran documents. One should assume neither where at table he should sit nor indeed that he will even have a place at the table. And by focusing attention on the time of the "resurrection of the just" and on who "will eat bread in the kingdom of God," Luke makes it clear that Jesus is challenging the very identity of those who consider themselves *keklemenoi*. Like the classical prophets of the Old Testament Jesus precisely raises the question of the identity of Israel and challenges assumptions concerning election.[40] "I tell you, none of the *keklemenoi* shall taste my banquet" (14:24).

A final word is in order concerning the presence of the word *ptochoi* in the two lists of substitute guests in Luke. This word, poor, does not appear either in Lev. 21 or in the two Qumran lists of those forbidden. And it would be very difficult to imagine that it would, for in both the Old Testament and the Qumran literature all such words which might be rendered *ptochoi,* the poor, the afflicted and the humble, frequently appear as appelatives of Israel or the elect. At Qumran such words are used as self-designations of the sect: they considered themselves God's Poor Ones.[41] And throughout the Old Testament such terms often appear in covenant formulations of the self-understanding of Israel. Israel in the Old Testament is constantly reminded that she herself was a slave people and must always be conscious of the poor and powerless in order to continue to be God's people in the full sense of the meaning of the covenant people.[42] In a very real sense Luke's construction of these two pericopes constitutes a call of Jesus to harken back to this basic biblical concept. It is for this reason that what is here proposed is an understanding of the parable, and of the teaching on humility, as a prophetic critique of a common *inversion* of the Deuteronomic ethic of election. Deuteronomy may well say that God blesses the obedient and judges the disobedient. But it does *not* say that poverty and affliction and lack of bodily wholeness are proof of God's disfavor.[43] On the contrary, these Lukan constructions appear to insist on a common Old Testament theme that God has a kind of bias for those in apparent disfavor.

But that common theme can seem at times to run counter to another Old Testament theme, precisely the pious desire of the faithful to practice purity out of reverence for God. In Lev. 21 the afflicted are forbidden access to the veil and to the altar because of the deep concern in the Holiness Code for purity in the community's cultic relations with God. And at Qumran it is stated several times that the afflicted and impure are forbidden access to the Council or to the eschatological battlefield or to the messianic table, because of the *mal'akhê qodhesh* (the holy angels) who, it is feared, might have been offended by such impurity.[44]

To recognize the possibility of conflict between two such prominent biblical themes is to engage in the necessary canons of historical research; for such conflict demonstrates the historical principle of ambiguity of reality without recognition of which no student can claim to be a historian. The historian cannot assume "good guys" and "bad guys." He must scrupulously describe what his sources lead him to perceive. This same principle must be recognized as well in working on the *Disputationswörter* of the false prophets in the Old Testament. One cannot claim to have understood the so-called true prophets until he has made every effort to understand the best arguments of the so-called false prophets.[45] This is precisely what was meant above by the two foci of full context. The text before us can be understood only to that extent that we are aware of the context into which it was spoken or written. Only in this manner can the point originally scored be recovered. We need not always assume a debate as such; but we must assume there was a reason for speaking or writing.

Is Luke alone responsible for such material which so vividly comes alive when viewed as a prophetic critique of the in-group thinking of those who in the first century were confident they would be at the kingdom table? Any valid judgment of that question must finally depend on how crucial one views the Qumran materials for reconstructing the second focus, the foil to the parable; for surely they would indicate a Palestinian setting before A.D. 70.

Was Luke, in structuring this parabolic tradition in the way he did, attempting to say, "The Jews opted out and Gentiles must be urged to come in"? It is quite possible, indeed, that such was his purpose. Matthew seems clearly to intend such. Even so, a crucial question is in order. Is this not a working example of how a prophetic in-group critique of the earlier period (Jesus) can without malice aforethought be subverted by redactor (Luke) to say the opposite when contemporized by static transfer to fit the *later* second focus (Luke's congregation)? In such a case little need be changed of the substance of what was originally said when the later focus was so utterly different, and when the intent of the traditionist was so utterly different.

Is it not possible that recognition of such dynamics of focus may lead to a bit more optimism about recovering the teaching of the historical Jesus? The historian deals in probabilities, not certainties. Perhaps Luke's older reputation as a "historian" (reporting what was done and said by Jesus) should be as seriously entertained as his newer reputation as a "theologian" (making Jesus traditions relevant to his day). One does not have to make Luke out to be an antiquarian to appreciate him as a historian in the biblical sense. *His* hermeneutics and *his* second focus (*his* concerns in *his* time) need not be viewed as insurmountable hurdles when materials for reconstructing a second focus closer to Jesus' time and place are available—as they are indeed available for this parable.

NOTES

1. *Law in the New Testament,* 1970, 126-55. The present paper, in another form, constituted a portion of the Shafer Lectures given at Yale Divinity School in April, 1972.

2. *Discoveries in the Judaean Desert,* I, 1956, 177. See J. A. Sanders, "Banquet of the Dispossessed," *USQR,* 20 (1965), 355-63.

3. Y. Yadin, *The Scroll of the War of the Sons of Light Against the Sons of Darkness,* 1962, 63-86, 290-293, 304-305.

4. J. Jeremias, *The Parables of Jesus,* 1963, based on the sixth edition of *Die Gleichnisse Jesu,* 1962, 175-80; cf. pp. 63-69. Norman Perrin's *Rediscovering the Teaching of Jesus,* 1967, 110-16, follows Jeremias in all important particulars in interpreting this parable. Other studies in the same time period which treat the parable are: Eta Linneman, "Überlegungen zur Parabol vom grossen Abendmahl," *ZNW,* 51 (1960), 246-55 (cf. her *Parables of Jesus,* 1966, 89-91, 160ff.); O. Glombitza, "Das Grosse Abendmahl," *NT,* 5 (1962), 10-16; Ernst Haenchen, "Das Gleichnis vom grossen Mahl," *Die Bibel und Wir,* 1968, 135-55; and Dan O. Via, Jr., "The Relationship of Form to Content in the Parables: the Wedding Feast," *In,* 25 (1971), 171-84. However, Glombitza and Via are purely form-critical studies and they all ignore the Old Testament and Qumran materials.

5. Peter Berger, *The Social Construction of Reality: a Treatise in the Sociology of Knowledge,* 1966.

6. Cf. Brevard Childs, *Biblical Theology in Crisis,* 1970; J. A. Sanders. *Torah and Canon,* 1972; and a study entitled "Adaptable for Life: the Nature and Function of Canon" to appear in the G. Ernest Wright Festschrift (especially nn. 1-4 and 42-45 for bibliography). See also Morton Smith, *Palestinian Parties and Politics that Shaped the Old Testament,* 1971.

7. Cf. Renée Bloch's article on midrash in the *DBS,* V, 1957, cols. 1263-81.

8. James Muilenburg made a significant start in the area of rhetorical criticism of the OT in his "Form Criticism and Beyond" in *JBL,* 88 (1969), 1-18. In the field of Early Judaism rhetorical criticism is as important as "midrash criticism": cf. Henry A. Fischel, "Story and History: Observations on Greco-Roman Rhetoric and Pharisaism," *American Oriental Society, Middle West Branch, Semi-Centennial Volume,* ed. by Denis Sinor, Asian Studies Research Institute, Oriental Series, No. 3 (1969), 58-88 (and watch for anything Fischel might yet do in this area). The area of comparative midrash has been critically reviewed by my student Merrill Miller in *JSJ,* 2 (1971), 29-82; cf. now the bibliographies in *The Study of Judaism,* ed. by Jacob Neusner, 1972, 7-80. In the New Testament, *in sensu stricto,* see J. Arthur Baird, *Audience Criticism and the Historical Jesus,* 1969, and now Paul S. Minear, "Audience Criticism and Markan Ecclesiology," H. Baltensweiler and B. Reicke, eds., *Neues Testament und Geschichte. Cullmann Festschrift,* 1972, 79-90. E. Haenchen, *op. cit.* (above n. 4) engages in Audience Criticism with regard to Lk. 14 in comparing it to Mt. 22 and Thomas 64 and is quite right as far as he goes.

9. See especially Robert W. Funk, *Language, etc.,* 124-99.

10. Gen. 22 may serve as an illustration. At the earliest stage of the history of a story of child sacrifice in which a) the priest who must sacrifice is the boy's father and b) the boy is his only-begotten son, one in effect has probed back to a pre-Israelitic, probably Canaanitic provenance; and one must be careful not to confuse what such a story might have meant there with what it was intended to mean when it was adapted by Israel for her own uses. The archaeological and philological school of interpreters (such as E. A. Speiser and Nelson Glueck) in their suggestion that the

story was understood in Israel as an argument against human sacrifice probably did perceive one use Israel made of the story, but surely not the only one. G. von Rad, in his *Genesis*, 1961, was surely right also when he saw what it meant in terms of redaction-criticism and its place in the Abraham cycle of stories: it spoke to the question of whether God could keep a promise despite all evidence to the contrary. [See his more recent *Das Opfer des Abraham*, 1971, also—eds.]. And then at the canonical critical level I am quite convinced that the story had immense meaning in the exilic and postexilic period (after so many disasters and dashed hopes) because what it in effect said to those generations (precisely those who preserved it for us in canonical process) was that the God who had given Isaac in Sarah's barren womb gave Isaac a second time from off the altar; i.e., Judaism's very existence often got to the stage of contingency represented by the knife over the boy's body—and yet there was hope. Comparative midrash picks up at this point and studies the understandings of the same story into Early Judaism and New Testament times. See S. Spiegel, *The Last Trial*, 1967, especially pp. 33ff.; and cf. a forthcoming doctoral dissertation, "A Midrashic Approach to a Study of Paul's 'en Christo'," by my student David Bossman. Because the "second focus" is always changing, the message is always changing. This is a cardinal observation and is simply the base of *all* exegesis, all the way from earliest form-criticism and tradition-criticism down through canonical criticism and into midrash criticism, and the history of Jewish and Christian interpretation: and the New Testament is located at one stage in that long history. The expression "contextual exegesis" must not be limited to its literary critical aspect, the question of smaller and larger units: contextual must include what is here called the "second focus," the situation into which the text spoke *at whatever period indicated*.

11. See my "Adaptable for Life" cited above in n. 6.

12. This is an extremely important point that is overlooked by many otherwise responsible historians. Robert A. Lively, formerly of Princeton, now of Buffalo, calls it New History. Actually, of course, it is good history. Lively does not publish, but his ideas are incorporated in my "The New History: Joseph, Our Brother" (1968—available through the Baptist Ministers and Missionaries Benefit Board at 475 Riverside Drive, New York 10027). The need for historical context varies, more or less, with the form and content of the literary unit. At one end of the spectrum would be the political diatribe and the occasional homily, and at the other essays in pure mathematics, such as Euclid's Geometry or Einstein's theories of relativity. But even so, the supporting arguments in such essays are best understood (and in some paragraphs only become clear) when read in the context of where science was at the time—what questions were being put when the argumentation concerning the formulae was composed.

13. Cf. J. A. Sanders, "Dissenting Deities and Philippians 2:1-11," *JBL*, 88 (1969), 279-90.

14. The three criteria, often associated with the name of Norman Perrin (*Rediscovering*, see above n. 4), by which one may test a New Testament tradition as to whether it derived from the so-called "pre-resurrection mission," i.e., from Jesus, are gradually folding under persistent criticism. The linguistic criterion is clearly not valid; distinctiveness can unfortunately cut two ways; and coherence, in the sense meant, is hardly a first-century category.

15. This means that the authoritative tradition, from the Old Testament, was contemporized as a challenge to in-group thinking. One must, however, remember that by tradition we mean not only an Old Testament passage, but also images, patterns, etc. Cf. Roger le Déaut, "Apropos a Definition of Midrash," *In*, 25 (1971), 259-82. (This article was translated by my student Mary Howard Calloway.)

16. Cf. Sanders, *Torah and Canon*, 54-96; "Adaptable for Life . . ." sections VII-IX; and "Jeremiah and the Future of Theological Scholarship," *AndNQ*, 22 (1972), 133-45.

17. As is quite clear in 1QH and CD; see now Pss. 154 and 155 in 11QPs[a].

18. Cf. Jacob Neusner, *The Rabbinic Traditions about the Pharisees before 70*, 1971, in three volumes; but see especially Part III, 301-19. The Bar Ma'yan story in the Palestinian Talmud (Jeremias, *Parables*, 178-79; Perrin, *Rediscovering*, 114ff.) is not only impossible to date, but also impertinent.

19. B. H. Streeter, *The Four Gospels*, 1924. See also Arthur Wright, *The Gospel of St. Luke in Greek*, 1900, xix.

20. C. F. Evans, "The Central Section of St. Luke's Gospel," *Studies in the Gospels*, ed. by D. E. Nineham, 1955, 37-53. Evans' thesis has been pursued in Acts by M. D. Gouldner, *Type and History in Acts*, 1964. And a student has called to my attention a very popular, devotional type presentation of the Evans' thesis by John Bligh, S.J., *Christian Deuteronomy* (*Luke 9-18*), 1970. Months after the manuscript of this paper had gone to the editors, P. H. Ballard's excellent paper, "Reasons for Refusing the Great Supper," *JTS*, 23 (1972), 341-50, appeared. It is very encouraging to see this increasing recognition of the importance of Deuteronomy in Luke.

21. One of the values of the sociology of knowledge is its ability to help us understand ourselves precisely at those points we consider ourselves "objective." We are about seven generations into biblical scholarship and are now able to see that each generation in that noble procession was in basic ways responding to the *Zeitgeist* of its own time. Qoheleth's observations, especially in 3:1-11, emerge as keenly pertinent after studying Berger and Luckman.

22. Cf. Lk. 7:16; 9:8; and especially Acts 3:22; cf. now Richard Zehnlee, *Peter's Pentecost Discourse*, 1971, especially pp. 71-94.

23. Forthcoming in the Nils Dahl Festschrift.

24. By contrast note the recent judgments about the excuses by scholars who are unaware of the midrashic nature of the Lukan material and hence of the Old Testament rootage: K. H. Rengstorf, "unrealistic"; G. V. Jones, "unrealistic"; Eta Linnemann, "apologies for coming late"; G. Bornkamm, "fatuous"; J. Jeremias, "flimsy"! My own work on the parable had indicated the pertinence of Dt. 20:5-8, cf. Sanders, "Banquet of the Dispossessed," *USQR*, 20 (1965), 355-63; and, of course, Derrett, *Law in the NT*, 1970, 135ff., perceives its relevance. Actually I have found myself at several junctures in work on Luke reverting to Deuteronomy despite the standard New Testament works on Luke. I called this to the attention of my colleague, Reginald Fuller, and it was he who directed my attention to Evans. It was a felicitous confirmation in the sense that Evans was approaching the material along entirely different lines.

25. Yadin, *Scroll of the War*, 65 ff.

26. *Ibid.*, 69.

27. Derrett, *Law*, 135 n. 2 and 136 n. 1. To his references add Ps. 23:5.

28. Among the recent studies by the Georg Fohrer school on Deuteronomy as theology of the ethic of election, see Lothar Perlitt, *Bundestheologie im AT*, 1969.

29. See above, n. 23.

30. K. L. Schmidt, in the *TDNT, ad loc.*, is more nearly right in this regard than his critics; but even he did not, in my opinion, go far enough. Note, however, that his comment on Dt. 20:10 and the use there of *ekkalein* for *qara'* is not pertinent to our discussion.

31. Larrimore Clyde Crockett, *The OT in the Gospel of Luke with Emphasis on the Interpretation of Isa 61:1-2*, Brown University dissertation, June, 1966. See the

thesis of X. de Meeûs, *ETL,* 37 (1961), 847-70, to the effect that all of Lk. 14 is a literary unit like the symposia of Plato, Xenophon, and Plutarch (*apud* J. Martin, *Symposium. Die Geschichte einer literarischen Form,* 1931, 33-148).

32. Cf. J. T. Milik, *Ten Years of Discovery,* 1959, 101, and F. M. Cross, Jr., *The Ancient Library of Qumran,* 1961, 231; and see now the comprehensive study by J. Carmignac, *RevQ,* 28 (1971), 575-86.

33. Discussion of double invitations and the like, as by Jeremias followed by Perrin, are impertinent; hence the relevance of Midrash Lamentations 4,2 to our passage is obviated.

34. Yadin, *Scroll of the War,* 69 ff.

35. Derrett, *Law,* 126-55, fails at crucial junctures to distinguish between Matthew and Luke in their treatments of this material. This is a general criticism, I fear, one must entertain of Derrett's work; he pays insufficient attention to either tradition-criticism or redaction-criticism in his work on the New Testament. I, for one, admire his confidence in the manner in which he attempts to reconstruct what Jesus himself said and did, for I find it a corrective to other treatments which in my mind are too sceptical; but he is less than convincing when he pays little or no attention to the process intervening between Jesus and the Gospels. Derrett's astute observations about the importance of the targum to Zeph. 1 are actually limited to the Matthean guise of the parable.

36. The judgment of Perrin, and others, that the Gospel of Thomas "version is nearer to the teaching of Jesus than either of the others" (112f.) is in my analysis of Thomas incorrect. The first observation one must make in a synoptic study of Mt. 22, Lk. 14, and Thomas 64 is that Thomas, as well as Matthew, is totally unaware of the Dt. 20 base of the excuses. The only serious question is whether Luke molded the tradition he received to the Deuteronomic midrashic base or if he received it in a form approximate to the way in which he reports it. My own judgment is that Dt. 20 is so integral to the parable that the possibility must be entertained that it was this parable (which is at the heart of Luke's Central Section) received in a form close to what we have in Luke, which led Luke to construct his chs. 9-18 in the manner he did.

37. Much of the material in Luke stresses God's freedom to elect whom he wills: cf. his use of *dektos* in Lk. 4:19,24, and the meaning of *eudokia* in 2:14. The Sermon at Nazareth pericope will constitute another study soon to appear.

38. The midrashic relation between 2 Sam. 5:8 and 6:19 and the Great Banquet tradition in the New Testament needs to be studied now in the light of the developing methods here indicated. Note that the unpublished texts, 4QM[a] and 4QD[b], reflect the same proscriptions as those in the 1Q documents here cited. Cf. Mishnah Hagigah ii 7; M. Abot ii 6; M. Bekorot vii; and Tohorot vii; but cf. M. Abot i 5 and Abot de R. Nathan A vii. A related problem is that presented by 4QFlor 4 (the exclusion of the *mamzer, ben nekar* and *ger*), but this stems from Dt. 23:2-4(1-3): cf. Ezk. 44:6-9 as well as M. Yebamot ii 4, vi 1, viii 3; M. Kiddushin iii 12, iv 1; M. Ketubot iii 1, xi 6; M. Makkot iii 1; M. Sanhedrin iv 2; M. Horayot i 4; Ps. Sol. 17:28. And see now J. M. Baumgarten's excellent treatment of the *ger* at Qumran in *RevQ,* 29 (1972), 87-96.

39. These expressions for the "elect" in 1QSa and 1QM are undoubtedly drawn from Nu. 1:16; 16:2; and 26:9.

40. Cf. Sanders, *Torah and Canon,* 85-90.

41. Cf. 1QH ii 34, v 13-14, CD vi 16-21, xiv 14; and Ps. 154:18 (11QPs[a] xviii 15) and the notes thereto in Sanders *DJD,* 4 (1965), 66-67, and the ensuing discussion.

42. Deuteronomy designates Israel's concern for the poor and dispossessed, or

powerless, by the terms sojourners, fatherless and widows (cf. 14:29, 16:11-14 and 26:11ff.).

43. There is a sense in which the books of Job and Eccl. address themselves, in their time and way, to earlier inversions of the Deuteronomic ethic of election. Cf. Isa. 56:3-7. And, in a broad sense, it was precisely such a popular understanding of Deuteronomy's theology of election which turned Jeremiah into its most insistent antagonist. No biblical scholar of our day has seen this more clearly or demonstrated it more forcefully than J. Philip Hyatt.

44. Most clearly in 4QFlor 4, 1QSa ii 8 and 1QM vii 6 and x 11; but see also 11QMelch.

45. As brilliantly demonstrated by A. S. van der Woude, *VT*, 19 (1969) 244-60; see also Sanders, *Torah and Canon*, 85ff., and "Jeremiah and the Future of Theological Scholarship," *op. cit.* Precisely such a positive approach based on "discussion literature" underlies the recent study of false prophecy by an editor of this volume, J. L. Crenshaw, *Prophetic Conflict. BZAW*, 124, 1971. See also now F. Hossfeld and I. Mayer, *Prophet gegen Prophet*, 1973.

A. INDEX OF AUTHORS

Ahlstrom, G. W., 72, 75
Aland, K., 255
Alt, A., 22
Altmann, A., 167
Anderson, B. W., 74, 76, 193
Anderson, G. W., 166, 169
Ap-Thomas, D. R., 59, 72-74, 164

Baird, J. A., 267
Ballard, P. H., 269
Baltensweiler, H., 267
Barthélemy, D., 247
Barthelemy, D., 247
Barton, G. A., 54
Batten, L. W., 144
Bauer-Kayatz, C., 173, 188
Baumgartner, W., 188
Begrich, J., 22, 156, 168
Belkin, S., 243
Berger, P., 267, 269
Bernhardt, K. H., 74
Berridge, M., 121-122, 130
Bin-Nun, S. R., 109
Black, M., 73
Blank, S., 72-73, 129-130
Bligh, J., 269
Bloch, R., 267
Boccaccio, P., 50
Boecker, H. J., 109
Böhl, F. M. Th.L., 164-169
Bornkamm, G., 269
Boström, G., 174
Boylan, P. C., 164
Brekelmans, H. W., 73
Briggs, C. A. & E. G., 154, 166
Bright, J., 73, 121

Bruce, F. F., 166
Brunner, H., 188
Buber, M., 122, 193-7, 199, 201-202
Burrows, M., 59-60
Buswell, G., 72
Buttenwieser, M., 117, 129, 161, 165, 169

Calloway, M. H., 268
Carmignac, J., 270
Charles, R. H., 201, 209
Cheyne, T. K., 165-167, 169
Childs, B., 267
Conrad, J., 95, 174, 189
Couroyer, B., 188
Craigie, P. C., 74
Crenshaw, J. L., 51-53, 189, 271
Crockett, L. C., 259, 269
Cross, F. M., 74, 108, 167, 270
Cullmann, O., 267

Dahl, N., 269
Dahood, M., 53, 68, 75, 166, 168
Davies, G. H., 130, 166
Davison, W. T., 165-169
de Boer, P. A. H., 72, 188-189
Deissler, A., 153, 164-167, 169
Delakat, L., 167
Delitzsch, F., 53
de Meeus, X., 270
Derrett, J. M. D., 247, 258, 269-270
de Vaux, R., 76
Donald, T., 189
Driver, S. R., 130
Duhm, B., 117, 129, 164, 166-167
Duesberg, H., 188

INDEX

Dumortier, J. B., 74
Durham, J., 130
Durkheim, E., 179

Eaton, J. H., 164-167
Ebeling, G., 247
Eichrodt, W., 137, 189
Eissfeldt, O., 51, 70, 76, 130, 166-167
Ellermeier, F., 53
Elliger, K., 22, 95
Enslin, M. S., 72
Evans, C. F., 254-256, 269
Ewald, H., 144

Fahlgren, K. H., 189
Farbridge, M. H., 75
Fensham, G., 178, 188
Feuillet, A., 62, 72-73
Fichtner, J., 50, 53, 188
Fischel, H. A., 267
Fisher, L., 64, 74
Fitzmyer, J., 74-75
Fohrer, G., 22, 73-75, 108, 130, 269
Fox, M. V., 188
Frank, H. T., 72
Fransen, I., 188
Friedman, M., 201
Fuchs, E., 247
Fuller, R., 269
Funk, R., 247, 267

Galling, K., 22, 41, 50-51, 55, 95, 147-148, 164-167
Garcia de la Fuente, O., 164-169
Gemser, B., 169, 188-189
Gerstenberger, E., 121-122, 125, 130, 188
Gese, H., 50-51, 53-55, 181, 188-189
Ginsberg, H. L., 50
Glatzer, N., 201
Glombitza, O., 267
Glueck, N., 267
Goguel, M., 205
Gollwitzer, H., 197-201
Gordis, R., 50, 52-53, 144, 188
Gordon, C., 74
Gottwald, N. K., 73
Gouldner, M. D., 269
Graetz, H., 51
Graf, K. H., 117, 129
Gray, J., 74-75
Green, D. E., 73-74

Greenberg, M., 167, 197, 201
Gross, H., 73
Gunkel, H., 22, 116-117, 119, 129, 147, 154, 164-168

Habel N., 74
Haenchen, E., 267
Harper, W. R., 142
Harrelson, W., 76
Hartwell, H., 74
Haupt, P., 144
Hayes, J. H., 51
Hempel, J., 53, 243
Hermann, W., 54
Hermisson, H. J., 52, 175, 188-189
Herder, J. G., 47, 54
Hertzberg, H. W., 51, 53-55
Heschel, A., 72
Hesse, H., 47
Hiers, R. H., 243
Hölscher, G., 22, 116-117, 120, 125, 129
Horst, F., 22
Horton, E., 54
Humbert, P., 22, 51
Hyatt, J. P., 72-73, 118, 133, 143-144, 147, 164, 168, 227, 248, 271

Jahnow, H., 22
James, F., 164
Jenni, E., 95
Jepsen, A., 51-52, 95, 188
Jeremias, J., 243, 247, 267, 269
Jirku, A., 22
Johnson, A. R., 74-75
Jones, G. W. H., 76
Jones, G. V., 269
Jolles, A., 175
Jung, C. G., 25, 50

Kapelrud, A. S., 154, 164, 166-167, 169
Keil, C. F., 117, 129
King, E. G., 169
Kissane, E. J., 164
Knight, G. A. F., 137
Knitson, F. B., 74
Knobel, A., 117, 129
Koch, K., 53, 151, 162, 164-166, 168-169, 189
Köhler, L., 95
Koole, J. L., 159, 164-165, 168-169

INDEX

Kraus, H. J., 72, 74, 151-152, 164-169
Kroeber, R., 50-51, 53-54

Lambert, W. G., 51, 53
Lamparter, H., 164, 169
Lauha, A., 54-55
le Déaut, R., 268
Lescow, T., 165, 168
Leslie, E. A., 164-169
Lindblom, J., 134, 142
Linneman, E., 267, 269
Lively, R. A., 268
Loew, C., 75
Lohfink, N., 109
Loretz, O., 53

Marböck, J., 52, 54
Martin, J., 270
Martin, L. A., 129
Martin-Achard, R., 72-73
May, H. G., 73-75, 144
Mays, J. L., 140-141
McCarthy, D. J., 108
McCullough, W. S., 154, 164-169
McKane, W., 188
McKenzie, J. L., 69, 72, 74-76
McLeish, A., 55
Metzger, M., 167
Milik, J. T., 270
Miller, M., 267
Minear, P. S., 267
Miskotte, K., 49, 55
Mowinckel, S., 22, 73-74, 147, 164-167, 169
Müller, J. G., 54
Muilenburg, J., 76, 109, 118, 267
Munck, J., 205
Murphy, R. E., 72-75, 164, 166, 169

Neubauer, A., 130
Neusner, J., 267, 269
Nineham, D. E., 269
North, C. R., 75
Noth, M., 73, 95, 108

Orlinsky, H. M., 59-60, 72, 76
Osswald, E., 22

Pálfy, M., 54
Pedersen, J., 50, 54
Perlitt, L., 54, 269
Perrin, N., 267-270

Peters, J. P., 164
Pfeiffer, R., 50
Pidoux, G., 167
Pope, M. H., 74
Porter, J. R., 130, 166
Press, R., 22
Preuss, H. D., 52-53, 174
Prussner, F. C., 72

Rad, G. von, 22, 30, 50-54, 72, 74, 95, 103, 108, 130, 175, 177, 188-189, 268
Reed, W. L., 72
Reicke, B., 267
Rendtorff, R., 166
Rengstorf, K. H., 269
Reumann, J., 72
Reventlow, H. G., 120-121, 125, 129
Richter, H., 22
Richter, W., 188
Riessler, P., 205-206, 213
Ritschl, D., 137
Robinson, H. W., 76
Robinson, J. M., 248
Robinson, T. H., 144
Rowley, H. H., 73, 136, 169
Rudolph, W., 139-140
Russell, D. S., 201, 213
Rylaarsdam, J. C., 52, 72

Sanders, J. A., 267-271
Sandmel, S., 60, 72, 223
Schmid, H. H., 52, 181, 188-189
Schmidt, H., 117, 129, 164-166
Schmidt, J., 188
Schmidt, K. L., 269
Schmöckel, H., 73
Schnackenburg, R., 243
Schneider, J., 22
Scott, R. B. Y., 54, 73-74, 174, 179, 189
Seidl, E., 22
Silberman, L. H., 213
Sinor, D., 267
Skladny, U., 173, 175, 180-181
Slotki, I. W., 167-168
Smart, J. D., 138-139, 166, 168
Smend, R., 109
Smith, G. A., 117
Smith, J. P., 72
Smith, M., 72, 267
Snaith, N. H., 72, 135-136

Soggin, J. A., 164
Solovietchek, J. B., 55
Speiser, E. A., 267
Spiegel, S., 268
Stade, B., 169
Stalker, D. M. C., 72
Stauffer, E., 205, 213
Stoebe, H. J., 130
Streeter, B. H., 269

Terrien, S., 75, 164, 167
Thomas, D. W., 165
Thompson, H. C., 165, 169
Toombs, L., 164, 166
Torrey, C. C., 201
Toy, C. H., 144
Treves, M., 165, 167-168
Tsevat, M., 109, 129

van der Woude, A. S., 271
van Oyen, H., 243
van Selms, A., 169
Via, D., 267
Vischer, W., 73, 137, 167
Volz, P., 22, 118, 129

Ward, J. M., 74, 140-141
Weber, M., 179
Weinfeld, M., 178, 188
Weippert, H., 109
Weiser, A., 22, 74, 164-165, 167
Wellhausen, J., 151
Wessetzki, V., 95
Westermann, C., 22, 51-52, 95, 188
Whybray, R. N., 51, 188
Wildeboer, D. G., 52
Williams, R. J., 188
Willis, J. T., 165, 169
Wolfe, R. E., 144
Wolff, H. W., 52, 107-108, 137-138, 188
Wolfson, H., 223
Wright, A., 50, 269
Wright, G. E., 267
Würthwein, E., 189

Yadin, Y., 257, 260, 267, 269-270

Zehnlee, R., 269
Zimmerli, W., 46, 50-53, 73, 76, 95, 175, 177, 188
Zimmern, H., 22

B. INDEX OF SCRIPTURE

Gen.
1 28
1:1-2:4b 74
1:7 42
1:26 .... 40, 53
2:4b-25 74
3:6 17
4:15 235
4:24 235
5 80
12:1-3 75
14 74
14:19 64
18:23-25 229
19:21 61
19:25 61
19:29 61
22 267
28:20-22 229
49 .... 205, 208

Ex.
5 80
12:24-27 92
15 65
15:3 161
19:5 74
19:8 231
20:1-7 9
20:1-17 162
20:5-6 90
20:12 93
20:17 233
21:23 ff. 235
22:7, 9-10
  (6, 8-9), 10 10

22:8 (9) 10
22:21 (22) 93
23:10-19 9
24:3, 7 231
30:14 81
34:6-7 90
34:10-26 9

Lev.
5:4 154
11:44 241
17 264
18:6-18 9
19:2 241
19:3-12 9
19:13 234
19:13-18 9
19:17-18 233
19:18 .... 19, 234-236
19:34 233
20:9, 11, 12, 14 12
20:26 241
21 .... 262, 265
21:17-23 261-262
24:19-20 235
27:1-8 81
27:7 81

Nu.
1:3, 18 81
1:16 270
4:3 81
5:5 ff. 10
8:24-26 81
14:29 81
16:2 270

20:3 81
26:9 270
32:11 81
35 235

Dt.
1-26 .... 254-255, 258
4:2 48
4:21 109
4:25 108
5:6-21 162
5:9-10 90
5:21 233
6:4-5 236
6:12-14 108
6:15 109
6:20-25 92-93
7:1 .... 63, 65
7:4 108-109
7:6-12 231
9:7-8, 18 108
9:7-21 108
9:8, 14, 19, 20 109
11:16 108
11:16-17 109
11:24 63
11:24-25 65
13:1(12:32) 48
14:29 271
16:11 93
16:11-14 271
17:2-7 16
18:15 254-255
18:21-22 62
19:1-13, 15-21 235
20 .... 256-257, 270

INDEX

20:5-8 256
20:10 269
21:18-21 91
21:21 91
23:2-5(1-4) 150
23:20(19) 154
24:14 234
26:1-15 149
26:11 ff. 271
26:13-14 149
27 221
27:11-26 231
27:15-26 9
27:19 93
28:3-4, 7 229
29:19(20) 109
29:19, 23, 26-27
  (20, 24, 27-28) 109
29:22(23) 61
29:24(25) 108
29:24-26(25-27) 108
29:24-27(25-28) 109
29:27(28) 109
30:16 229
31:1 16
31:1-8, 24-29 206
31:16-17 108
31:16-19 .... 101, 109
31:17 109
31:29 108
32:1-47 206
32:35 15
33 .... 205, 208
34:1-12 206
34:7 .... 80, 89

Josh.
4:20-24 92
20 235
23-24 206
23:16 .... 101, 108-109
24:1-28 231

Jgs.
2:11-14 108
2:14, 20 .... 102, 109
2:19-20 .... 102, 108
2:20 108
3:7-8 108
3:8 .... 102, 109
6:7-10 104

6:13 92
6:68 242
8:22-23 161
10:6-7 108

Ruth
1:16 61

1 Sam.
1:3 .... 155, 161
1:11 81
1:12 164
1:21 155
1:24 ff. 81
2:12-14 91
2:12-17, 22-25 160
2:19 155
2:27-36 160
3:11-14 160
4:4 .... 151, 161
4:18 164
4:21-22 151
7:1-16 104
8:1-3 91
10:3 150
12 .... 102, 206
12:8-15, 22 102
24:12 236
25:26 ff. 236

2 Sam.
5:4 80
5:8 .... 150, 270
6:2 151
6:3-4, 13 160
6:12, 15 151
6:17 160
6:19 270
7 108
7:1-17 206
7:2, 6 160
7:11 68
11:2 17
12:14 109
12:16 151
16:23 185
19:32-38(31-37) 86
19:33(32) 80
19:35 ff. (34 ff.) 86
21:1 151
23:1 206

1 Kgs.
1:1-4 83
1:4 83
8:4, 9-11 151
12 84
12:8, 10, 11, 14 84
12:33 151
14:15 109
14:21 84
22:1-28 144

2 Kgs.
17:18 109
22:17 109
23:26-27 109
24:19-20 109

1 Ch.
6:22-23 10
15:2, 15 160
23:24, 27 81
28:29 206

2 Ch.
23:19 149
25:5 81

Ezr.
3:8 81
4:2-3 154

Neh.
10:31-40(30-39) 9

Job
4:17 32
5:9 42
8:14 15
9:8 32
9:30-31 10
10:8-11 32
10:12 39
11:6 39
11:7-12 42
12:4 39
13:13 ff. 5
14 206
16:18 ff. 5
19:25 ff. 5
21:6-34 5
23:10-12 .... 5, 11
26:7-14 32

INDEX

27:2-6 .... 5, 11
28:20-23 42
29 .... 5, 156
29-30 3
29-31 4-6
29:2 .... 4, 11
30 5
31 .... 3-22, 156
31:1-4 .... 8, 11, 163
31:1-34,
  38-40a 5, 7, 14
31:2 17
31:5-6 .... 8, 11, 14
31:5-8 .... 12, 17
31:5-23 .... 8, 11, 31
31:8, 12, 15 8
31:9-12 .... 12, 14, 18
31:10-11 18
31:13-14 11
31:13-15 14
31:15 32
31:16-23 .... 15, 18, 31
31:20-22 18
31:24-25 .... 15, 18
31:24-28 12
31:24-34 11
31:26-28 16
31:29-30 .... 15, 18
31:29-32 12
36:30b 163
38-41 .... 5, 27
38:4-11 32
40:2-5 21
40:8-14 20
40:11 ff. 20
40:15-24 32
42:2-3, 5-6 21

Ps.
2 .... 65, 67-68, 75
2:6 150
2:10 67
4:2 3
5 11
5:5-8(4-7) 163
7 11
7:16-17(15-16) 129
8 53
9:17(16) 129
10 75
10:16 231
14:2-3 228

14:31 32
15 .... 9, 147-151,
  153-154, 156-159, 169
15:1 .... 147-148, 150,
  154-155, 158-160, 163
15:2 .... 157, 162
15:2b 154
15:2 ff. 156-157
15:2-5 148
15:2-5b 147-148, 159
16:4, 11 32
17 11
17:5 32
18:21-25(20-24) 163
20:12 32
21:5(4) 66
21:8(7) 159
22:2 32
23:5 269
24 .... 74, 147, 150-154,
  156-163, 169, 231
24:1 153
24:1-2 .... 147, 150
  161, 163
24:2 153
24:2-3 157
24:3 .... 147-148, 150,
  154, 158-160
24:3-6 .... 9, 147-148, 150,
  156, 158, 163
24:4 .... 147, 154, 157, 163
24:4-5 156
24:5 147-148
24:6 .... 147, 151, 157-158
24:7 .... 150, 153
24:7-10 .... 147, 150-154,
  158, 161, 163
24:8 .... 150, 152-153
24:9 .... 150, 153
24:10 .... 150-151, 161
25:12 ff. 156
25:36-37 154
26 11
27:5 155
27:5-6 150
28:4-5 129
29:9-10 152
29:10 64
33:13-15 17
34:13 ff. (12 ff.) 156
34:13-15(12-14) 9
35:1, 4-8 129

40:5(4) 18
40:7-9(6-8) 234
44:2 ff. (1 ff.) 92
44:5(4) 231
47:2-10(1-9) 231
47:6, 9 151
48:2 150
48:3 66
49:7(6) 18
50:9-15 233
50:16-20 163
51:18-19(16-18) 233
52:9(7) 18
58 15
58:11 236
58:12(11) 129
61:5 .... 150, 155
61:7-8(6-7) 66, 150
62:11(10) 18
69:6(5) 17
69:23-29(22-28) 129
71:5 18
72 .... 59, 65-66, 68
72:1-4 66
72:3 69
72:8 67
72:8-11 67-68
72:9 67
72:12-14 66
72:14 67
72:17b 67, 75
72:19(18) 75
74 64
74:12 65
75:9-11 66
78:3 ff. 92
78:7 18
78:59-64 160
82 75
82:1 67
86:1 3
89 .... 59, 65-67,
  69-70, 74
89:4(3), 5(4),
  6-9(5-8) 69
89:6-19 64
89:10(9), 11 (10),
  15(14), 19(18) 69
89:22-28(21-27) 68
89:24(23), 25(24) 75
89:26(25) 68, 75
89:27(26) 68

INDEX

89:30-38(29-37)	69
89:37(36)	69
89:51-52(50-51)	75
90:10	80
90:12	269
92	88
92:14-15	88
93	74, 152
93:2	230
94:2	129
94:11	17
94:16 ff.	156
95	74
95:1-2	150
95:1-7	150
95:3-6	150
95:7-10	150
96	74
96-99	152
96:10, 13	231
97:2, 10	231
98:9	231
101	17, 66, 159, 163
102:3	3
102:27(26)	237
104:3	64
109	15
109:7(6)	129
109:7-20(6-19)	129
110	68
115	74
115:15	74
118:19 ff.	150
119:11	41
119:51	18
119:59	17
119:101-102	163
119:145, 149	3
119:168	17
121:2	74
124:8	74
132:6-9	167
134:1-2	163
134:3	74
137	15
137:8, 9	61
139	17
143:1	3
145:13	231
154	269
155	269

Prov.

1-9	173
1:15-16	17
3:26	18
4:5, 27	18
4:26	17
5	18
5:15-19	29
5:21	17
5:21-23	18
6:17-18	17
6:24-25	18
7:5-23	18
7:6-27	28
10:10	17
10:12, 18, 28	181
10:30	189
10-15	175
11:14	181
11:22	186
11:24	95
11:28	18
12:10	178
12:22	17
13:1	189
13:24	184
14:7	181
14:13	182
14:15-18, 19-20	184
14:26	93
14:16, 34	189
15:5, 32	91
15:22-23	181
15:23	186
16:1, 9	42
16:1-22:16	175
16:2	17, 184
16:14	51
16:7, 19	182
16:10-15	184
16:20-30	184
16:22	181
16:31	83
17:2	178, 182
17:3	184
17:5	19
17:7	17, 186
17:8	178
17:10, 26	181
17:16	183
17:25	91
18:16	178

19:6	178
19:18	184
19:21	42
19:22	17, 182
19:25	181
19:27	174
20:22	19, 37, 53, 236
20:24	42
20:25	182
20:29	83
21-26	53
21:2	17
21:14	178
21:27	182
21:30	42, 182
21:31	46
23:21	95
24:12	17
24:17-18	19, 53
24:19	19
24:29	37, 53
24:30-34	28
25:2	41
25:2-7	184
25:14	178, 186
25:21-22	19, 53, 236
25-27	175
26:7	181, 186
26:9	181
27:1	42
27:11	174
27:14	186
28:3	182, 186
28:11	182
28:13	39
28:24	93
28-29	175
29:12	17
29:13	182
29:19	178, 181
29:21	178
29:24	181, 186
30:2-4	42
30:13	17
30:17	17, 93

Eccl.

1:3-11	25
1:4	26
1:4-7	34
1:4, 10	40

1:9 .... 26, 50	6:2, 9-10 50	33:14-16 .... 9, 149, 156, 169
1:13 .... 29, 50	6:12 49	
1:13b 25, 28	7:1-10 26	33:15 17
1:14 50	7:6 50	33:20 150
2:11, 14, 15, 17, 19, 21, 23, 26 50	7:10 37	34-35 62
	7:13-14 .... 26, 31	40 69
2:16 40	7:14 29	40-66 158
2:17a 47	7:23b-24 42	40:8 26
2:24 .... 25, 50	7:24 40	40:9 .... 75, 125
2:26 25	7:29 .... 26, 31	40:9-11, 12, 21-23, 28 70
3:1 .... 27, 34	8:5-6, 9 25	
3:1-8 50	8:10, 12, 14 50	40:30-31 89
3:1-9 .... 25, 27, 34	8:13 44	41 75
3:1-11 269	8:15, 17 26	41:2-3, 14, 16, 20-21 69
3:1-15 ...... 25-27, 50-51, 55	9:1 30	
3:2a 50	9:6 40	41:15-16, 27 75
3:2-8, 3b, 4a 34	9:7-10 26	42:6 69
3:2-11 27	9:11-12 42	42:10 70
3:5a b 51	9:12 35	42:10-12 69
3:8 34	11:5 .... 26, 31-32	42:13 158
3:8b 50	11:7 49-50	43:6 70
3:9 26	12:1 29	43:15 69
3:9-11 50	12:1-7 85	44:3 158
3:10 .... 25, 28-29, 34, 41, 50, 53		44:6 69
	Isa.	44:23 70
3:10-15 27	1-12 62	44:24 .... 68-70, 74
3:11 .... 23-55, 26, 28, 31, 41, 45, 47, 51	1:10-17 157	44:24-45:17 68
	1:10-20 165	44:28 .... 68, 71
3:12-13, 14-15 27	1:12 ff. 233	45:1 68
3:12 28	1:17 93	45:1-3, 6 69
3:12-13 .... 25, 50	2:2-3 158	45:7 68
3:12-15 .... 28-29, 47	2:3 150	45:8 .... 69, 158
3:13 50	3:4-5 89	45:11 68
3:13, 22 26	5:2a 51	45:12 .... 68, 70
3:14 .... 40, 44, 50, 53	6 116	45:14 .... 67, 69, 73
3:14-15 50	7:12-14 63	45:14-17 72
3:15 .... 26, 38	8:18 130	45:15 69
3:16 25	9:2-7(1-6) 65	45:17 72
3:16-4:3 .... 25, 42-43	11:1-9 65	45:18 .... 70, 72
3:17 .... 25-26, 35	13-23 62	45:22 .... 69, 70
3:18-21 35	13:1-23 .... 61, 62	45:22-23 69
3:18-22 40	13:16, 18 61	45:22-25 60-61
3:19 50	14:1-23 62	45:25 72
3:21 40	14:21 61	46:13 75
4:4, 16 50	15 158	47 125
4:8 50	19:18 73	49:8 69-70
4:10 49	24 158	49:14-26 75
4:13 89	24-27 63	49:19 70
5:7(6) 43	26:19 138	49:22-23 70
5:10(9) 50	29:13 232	49:23 67
5:18(17) 26, 29	30:29 150	50:2 69
5:19(18) 47	33:10-16 158	51:1-23 75

INDEX

51:6-7 ... 158	11:21, 23 ... 119	25:15-38 ... 62, 73
51:9 ... 69, 158	11:21-23 ... 114, 117, 129	26:2 ... 48
51:9-11 ... 70	11, 12 ... 114, 125	26:3 ... 237
51:9-16 ... 65	12:1-4 ... 114	26:4-6, 9 ... 160
51:10, 15 ... 69	12:1-5, 6 ... 120, 129	26:12 ... 122
51:13 ... 74	12:3b ... 117	28:1 ... 119
52:1-12 ... 75	12:5 ... 114-15	28:1-17 ... 144
52:1, 11 ... 60	14:11 ... 120	28:5-9 ... 62
52:10 ... 69	15 ... 114, 121, 130	31:29 ... 90
52:11 ... 61	15:10 ... 129	31:31-34 ... 143
54:1-17 ... 75	15:10-11 ... 115, 129	31:33 ... 41
54:3b, c ... 75	15:11 ... 119	42:2-3 ... 120
54:9-10 ... 69, 71	15:11b ... 120	45 ... 125
55:3 ... 69	15:10-21 ... 120-121, 130	46:1-49:33 ... 62
55:7 ... 233	15:15 ... 115, 117	46:1-51:64 ... 61
56:1-7 ... 165	15:15-20 ... 129	46-51 ... 62
56:3-7 ... 271	15:16, 17, 19 ... 119	46:25-28 ... 62
56:6-8 ... 61	15:17-18 ... 115	49:7-27 ... 62
56:7 ... 233	15:19-20 ... 114, 129	50:15, 27-28 ... 73
58:1-8 ... 157, 165, 169	16 ... 122	50:45 ... 61
60:5-7, 14 ... 67	16:1, 8-9 ... 123	51:20-23 ... 61
60:6-14 ... 63	17 ... 114, 126	51:35-40 ... 73
60:7 ... 71	17:7 ... 18	
60-61 ... 75	17:9 ... 228	Lam.
61:1-2 ... 155	17:12-18 ... 120	4:6 ... 61
63:1-6 ... 158	17:14-18 ... 129	5:7 ... 90
65:20 ... 80	17:15 ... 119	
65:23 ... 158	17:18 ... 117	Ezk.
66:15-16 ... 158	18 ... 114, 126, 130	1-24 ... 62
	18:11 ... 233	4:4-6, 8 ... 130
Jer.	18:18 ... 115, 119, 129	5:1-5 ... 124
1 ... 116	18:18-23 ... 129	5:5 ... 124
1:1-25:14 ... 62	18:19-23 ... 115	6:14 ... 70
1:6-7 ... 88	18:20 ... 119-120	7:2, 23, 27 ... 70
1:7, 9 ... 122	18:21-23 ... 117	8:17 ... 70
1-20 ... 123	19 ... 130	9:9 ... 70
2:5 ... 90	20 ... 114, 126, 130	11:15, 17 ... 70
2:27 ... 51	20:1 ... 119	12:1-14 ... 124
3:25 ... 90	20:7-11 ... 129	12:2, 11 ... 124
5:7 ... 91	20:7b-10 ... 129	12:3-7 ... 130
6:16 ... 233	20:8 ... 119	12:13, 19, 22 ... 70
7:1-15 ... 144, 149, 169	20:9 ... 119, 122	18:2, 4 ... 90
7:6 ... 93	20:10, 11 ... 114	18:5-9 ... 9, 165
7:11 ... 155, 234	20:16 ... 61	18:20 ... 91
7:13-14 ... 160	21:2 ... 120, 129	20:15 ... 90
7:16 ... 120	22:1-5 ... 163	20:21 ... 91
7:22-23 ... 234	22:15-17 ... 66	21:5(20:49) ... 130
11:10 ... 90	23:9-40 ... 144	22:7 ... 93
11:18 ... 129	25:13a ... 62	24 ... 124
11:18-20, 21-23 ... 120, 129	25:13b ... 73	24:15-24 ... 124
11:20 ... 114, 236	25:15-29, 30-31, 32-33 ... 73	25:1-32 ... 61
11:21, 22 ... 114		25:31 ... 62

25-32 ... 62	14 ... 133, 135, 142	2:1-15 ... 61
29:1-32 ... 62	14:2-4(1-3) ... 141	2:9-11 ... 62
29:32 ... 62	14:2-9(1-8) ... 139	2:10-11 ... 73
33:13-14 ... 165	14:2-10(1-9) ... 133	2:11 ... 72
33-38 ... 62	14:5(4) ... 141	2:13-15 ... 61
34:13, 27 ... 70		3:8-10 ... 62, 73
36:17 ... 70	Joel	3:10 ... 73
37:12, 14 ... 75	2:12-14 ... 237	
37:24, 25 ... 66	4:16(3:16) ... 73	Hag.
39:26, 28 ... 75	4:19-20(3:19-21) ... 66	2:11-13 ... 149
41:21 ... 158		
43:1-5 ... 158	Am.	Zech.
43:15 ... 158	1:2 ... 61, 73	1:2-6 ... 233
44:6 ... 158	1:3-2:16 ... 73	7:2-3 ... 149
	4:4 ... 157	7:10 ... 92
Dan.	4:13 ... 32	8:4, 5 ... 83
3:33; 4:3, 34 ... 231	5:4-6 ... 157	9:10 ... 67
6:27(26) ... 231	5:5 ... 151	14:16-19 ... 73
7 ... 73	5:8-9 ... 32	14:17 ... 230
12:2 ... 73, 138	5:14-15 ... 13, 157	
	5:21-24 ... 157, 234	Mal.
Hos.	7:1-3 ... 120	2:7-9 ... 149
1 ... 133, 135, 142	7:1-6 ... 116	3:7 ... 233
1:10-2:1	7:4-6 ... 120	3:24(4:6) ... 91
(2:1-3) ... 134-136, 138	9:5-6 ... 32	
2 ... 133, 135, 142	9:8 ... 120	Mt.
2:3(1) ... 139	11:13 ... 120	3:9 ... 51
2:4-5(2-3) ... 90		4:17 ... 233
2:16-17(14-15) ... 134	Ob.	4:20 ... 241
2:16-25(14-23) ... 135, 139	1:15-21 ... 231	5:3-12 ... 230
2:18-25(16-23) ... 134, 138		5:3, 10 ... 237
3 ... 134-135	Jonah	5:8 ... 228
3:1 ... 123	4:4, 9 ... 128	5:17 ... 233
3:1-4 ... 139	4:11 ... 61	5:17-19 ... 231
3:5 ... 138, 140, 142		5:21-48 ... 232
4:1-3 ... 165	Mic.	5:23-24 ... 235
4:5 ... 144	2:6-11 ... 144	5:28 ... 14
4:13 ... 138	3:5-7 ... 144	5:32 ... 232
5:15 ... 151	6:6-7 ... 149	5:38-44 ... 236
6:4-6 ... 157	6:6-8 ... 147, 149, 156, 234	5:43-48 ... 14
6:6 ... 234	6:8 ... 147, 149, 231, 235	5:47 ... 241
9:7-8 ... 144	7:6 ... 94	5:48 ... 240
11 ... 133, 135, 142		6:7, 32 ... 241
11:1 ... 141, 231	Nah.	6:9-10 ... 231
11:8-9 ... 134, 137-138,	2:12(13) ... 61	6:19-20 ... 240
140-141	3:4, 10, 19b ... 61	6:31-33 ... 229
11:8-11 ... 135		6:33 ... 231
11:9a, b, d ... 144	Hab.	7:28 ... 231
11:9b ... 134	3:8 ... 68	8:3 ... 242
11:9c ... 139		8:4 ... 233
11:10 ... 141	Zeph.	8:20 ... 240-241
12:7(6) ... 233	1 ... 261, 270	9:13 ... 233

INDEX

10:37-38	240	
11:18, 19, 20-24	229	
12:2	231	
12:7	233	
12:38-45	229	
13:44-46	230	
15:1-20	231	
15:18-19	228	
16:4	229	
17:17	229	
18:3	231	
18:15-17	232	
18:22	236	
19:9	232	
19:14	237	
19:16	230	
19:16-22	162	
19:18-19	233	
19:21, 23	240	
20:25	241	
21:13	233	
22	267, 270	
22:34-40	235, 236	
23:16-22	233	
23:23	233	
24:45 ff.	239	
25:31-46	239	
26:24	241	
26:28	232	

Mk.

1:15	233
7:1-23	232
7:21-22	228
9:43, 45, 47	230
10:11-12	232
10:15	231
10:21	240
10:30	229-230
12:40-44	237
15:41	237

Lk.

2:14	270
3:23	95
4:19, 24	270
6:20	237
6:20-22, 24-26	230
6:27-36	15, 233
6:28-30	236
6:36	240
7:16	269

7:33, 34	229
8:2	240
9:8	269
9:51	254
9:51-18:43	254
9:58	240-241
9-18	270
10:13-15	229
10:29-37	236
10:36-37	237
11:2	231
11:42	233
12:14	237
12:29-31	229
12:31	231
12:33	240
12:42 ff.	239
12:57	238
14	254, 256, 258, 262, 267
14:7	259
14:7-8	259
14:7-14	257, 259
14:8-14	259
14:9-18	270
14:13	259, 261
14:13-14	238
14:14	259
14:14-15	257, 260
14:15	257
14:15-35	254
14:16-17	260
14:16-24	259
14:18-20	257, 260
14:21	247, 259, 260, 261
14:21-24	260
14:23	260
14:24	259, 264
14:26-27	240
14:28 ff.	241
14:33	240
14-16	258
15	258
16:18	232
16:19-31	237
16:25, 26	258
17:4	236
17:14	165, 233
18	254
18:17	231
18:22	240
18:30	229

19:8-9	240
20:47	237
21:1-4	237
21:34	239
22:15	233
23:3	95

Jn.

1:13	258
3:8	31

Acts

3:22	155

Col.

3:20-21	92

Bar.

3:32	38

2 Esd.

4	32

Sir.

1:4, 9	32
4:6	32
5:1, 3, 8	18
5:3	26
5:3-6	37
7:9	37
7:15, 30	32
8:7	47
9:5, 8	17
9:8-9	18
10:12	32
11:4	32
11:24-25	18
14:3	18
14:9	17
14:17	47
15:11-12	38
15:14	32
15:18	38
16:17, 21-22	38
16:26-30	32
17:1-20	32
17:15	17
18:1-7	32
18:6	48
23:16, 23, 27	18
23:18-27	18
23:19	17

24:9 32	39:14b, 16-17 30	IQM
26:9 17	39:16-35 31	ii 5-22 261-262
27:22 17	39:21-35 32	iii 2, iv 10 263
27:30-28:7 19	39:21, 34 38	x 5-6 257
31:5-8 18	39:24, 32-33, 35 31	
32:13 32	40:25-26 18	IQSa
33:13, 15 32	42:15-43:33 32	i 27-ii 3 263
36:1-17 37		1QPs^a, CD, IQH 155
36:6 37	Tob.	Thomas 64 .... 267, 270
38:4, 15 32	3:2 39	Midrash Lam. 4:2 270
38:22 47		1 Macc. 2:49-70 206
38:24-39:11 183	Wisd.	2 Macc. 6-7 206
39:5 32	11:23-12:2 39	Test. Moses 2-10,
		11-12 207

C. INDEX OF HEBREW WORDS

'abh 95
'abhanîm 51
'adhamah 70
'aelohîm 45, 262
'ahar 109
'aph 100, 108
'amar 114, 185
'anî 50, 124
'arûr 9
'asher 43
'el 30
'elai 123
'er'eh 114
'erets 70
'eth 29, 39, 43, 48, 100
'îsh 61
'ohel 160
'ôthî 114
'ulai 114
bacal 64
banîm 51
bara' 30
be 50, 100
belibbam 39, 41
ben 270
benî 174
berakhah 158
berîth 8, 11, 108
bêth 124
bhecittô 34
bighebhûroth 80
biqqesh 151, 157
bn 207
bore'ekha 30
galut 195
gam 26, 39, 45, 47, 50

ger 270
gibhôr 152
gûr 155, 159, 160
dabhar 185
darash 151, 157
dhebhar 123
habba' 40
ha'adham 41, 43
ha'aelohim 43
habhalîm 44
habhel 44
hahêtebh 128
haggadah 233
hazzeh 40
hacinyan 28
hakkol 29-31, 45, 47
hammacaseh 43
hacolam 28, 39, 40, 41, 42, 53
har 150
harabbim 260
haster 42
lehavdil 197
hikhcîs 100, 108
hinenî 114
hith'annaph 100, 108-109
hpk 61
ûbhekhen 50
ûphantithi 50
va'er'eh 50
velacasôth 30
vayehî 123
vayhvh 114
vayyo'mer 123
vegam 50
veha'aelohim 48

velo' 114
venasa'tha 124
venifqadta 193
venukhelah 114
vecadh 45
veshabhti 50
vihyithem 109
zeh 50
zeman 26, 34
zo'th 124
hamah 109
hamas 72
harah 100, 108, 128
heleq 29-30
hôzeh 38
hokhmah 32
tobh 28
tôbhîm 30
yadhactî 49-50
yapheh 29
yebhaggesh 48
yeladhîm 84
yephutteh 114
yerûshalaim 124
yeshûcah 68
yhvh 100, 109, 114-115, 123, 150-152, 174, 185
yikkashelû 114
yimtsa' 43
yippaqed 193
yir'ath 45, 174
yisra'el 124, 195
yôdheac 50
ycqb 207
yukhalû 114
yûmath 9

285

INDEX

kabhôdh ...151	mibbelî ...26, 43, 45	cetsah ...185
ken ...114	milḥamah ...152	colam ...40-41
kephî ...129	miqreh ...35	côlam ...152
kethubhim ...227	mocedh ...263	parar ...108
khol ...38	môpheth ...124	phoqedh ...114
kî ...50, 193	môphethekhem ...124	pithhê ...152
koh ...114, 185	môphethîm ...130	tsaddiq ...28
kolam ...30	moshavekha ...193	tsebha'oth ...151
lakhen ...114	môth ...9	tsedhaqah ...28, 51, 158
leḥem ...262	nathan ...39	tselem ...40
lemôpheth ...124	nekar ...270	tsibbûr ...120
lecênêhem ...130	niqmathekha ...114	qara' ...269
libhkoth ...34	niqra'im ...263	qeri'ê ...263
libhnê ...41	niqro'im ...263	qodshekha ...150
libhnôth ...34	nirdaph ...48	qodhshô ...150
lire'ôth ...50	nptly ...207	qûm ...160
lo' ...43, 114	ntn ...51	qru'ıṇ ...263
lcôlam ...48	savva'ah ...207	r'vbn ...207
ma'as ...108	sephôdh ...34	ra'îthî ...50
mayim ...74	sôph ...26, 45	rabbim ...74
mal'akhê ...265	svv't ...207	rac ...29-30
malakh ...152	cavon ...124	racah ...72
malkhûth ...230	cazabh ...108	reqôdh ...34
mamzer ...270	cal ...114	rodhephai ...114
macasê ...30	calah ...150	rucaḥ ...199
mdb ...64	calêhem ...114	shaliaḥ ...120
mehem ...114	cam ...195	shakhan ...159
memashshel ...130	casah ...29, 43	thihyeh ...129
meqôm ...150	cebhedh ...84, 127	torah ...126
mero'sh ...45	cervah ...9	toroth ...148
meshalîm ...130	ceth ...34, 35, 50	

D. INDEX OF GREEK WORDS

aesthetikos	218	
aiona	40	
basileia	230	
cosmos	218	
deipnon	261	
dektos	270	
diatheke	207	
ecstasis	217	
edoken	40	
eidos	38	
ekalesen	260	
eudokia	270	
eugenia	220	
gamos	261	
ge	40	
ho	38	
kai	40, 260	
kaleo	258, 259, 261	
keklemenoi	256, 259-261, 264	
logoi	217	
logos	223	
mias	151	
noetos	218	
orthos	223	
panta	38	
paradosis	232	
parakaleo	258	
parateisthai	260	
philanthropia	220	
pneuma	199	
pollous	260	
ptochoi	264	
sabbaton	151	
sun	40	
ta	38	
tes	151	
ton	40